Britain and America since Independence

British Studies Series

General Editor JEREMY BLACK

Published

Alan Booth **The British Economy in the Twentieth Century**
John Charmley **A History of Conservative Politics, 1900–1996**
David Childs **Britain since 1939 (2nd edn)**
John Davis **A History of Britain, 1885–1939**
David Eastwood **Government and Community in the English Provinces, 1700–1870**
Philip Edwards **The Making of the Modern English State, 1460–1660**
W. H. Fraser **A History of British Trade Unionism, 1700–1998**
John Garrard **Democratisation in Britain: Elites, Civil Society and Reform since 1800**
Brian Hill **The Early Parties and Politics in Britain, 1688–1832**
Katrina Honeyman **Women, Gender and Industrialisation in England, 1700–1870**
Kevin Jefferys **Retreat from New Jerusalem: British Politics, 1951–1964**
T. A. Jenkins **The Liberal Ascendancy, 1830–1886**
David Loades **Power in Tudor England**
Ian Machin **The Rise of Democracy in Britain, 1830–1918**
Alexander Murdoch **British History, 1660–1832: National Identity and Local Culture**
Anthony Musson and W. M. Ormrod **The Evolution of English Justice: Law, Politics and Society in the Fourteenth Century**
Murray G. H. Pittock **Inventing and Resisting Britain: Cultural Identities in Britain and Ireland, 1685–1789**
Nick Smart **The National Government, 1931–40**
Howard Temperley **Britain and America since Independence**
Andrew Thorpe **A History of the British Labour Party (2nd edn)**

British Studies Series
Series Standing Order
ISBN 0–333–71691–4 hardcover
ISBN 0–333–69332–9 paperback
(outside North America only)

You can receive future titles in this series as they are published by placing a standing order. Please contact your bookseller or, in case of difficulty, write to us at the address below with your name and address, the title of the series and the ISBN quoted above.

Customer Services Department, Macmillan Distribution Ltd
Houndmills, Basingstoke, Hampshire RG21 6XS, England

Britain and America since Independence

Howard Temperley

palgrave

First published 2002 by
PALGRAVE
Houndmills, Basingstoke, Hampshire RG21 6XS and
175 Fifth Avenue, New York, N. Y. 10010
Companies and representatives throughout the world

PALGRAVE is the new global academic imprint of St. Martin's Press LLC
Scholarly and Reference Division and Palgrave Publishers Ltd (formerly
Macmillan Press Ltd).

ISBN 0–333–67235–6 hardcover
ISBN 0–333–67236–4 paperback

This book is printed on paper suitable for recycling and
made from fully managed and sustained forest sources.

A catalogue record for this book is available
from the British Library.

Library of Congress Cataloging-in-Publication Data

Temperley, Howard.
    Britain and America since independence / Howard Temperley.
        p. cm.
    Includes bibliographical references and index.
    ISBN 0–333–67235–6 (cloth)—ISBN 0–333–67236–4 (pbk.)
        1. United States—Relations—Great Britain. 2. Great Britain—
    Relations—United States. 3. National characteristics, American.
    4. National characteristics, British. I. Title.

E183.8.G7 T34 2002
303..48'2973041—dc21   2001059005

10 9 8 7 6 5 4 3 2 1
11 10 09 08 07 06 05 04 03 02

Printed in China

Contents

To Kitty

Introduction

In any conversation between two people, Oliver Wendell Holmes tells us, *six* people are involved: the two people as they actually are, the two as they see themselves and the two as they see one another. 'Of these,' adds Holmes, 'the least important, philosophically speaking, is the one we have called the real person. No wonder two disputants get angry when there are six of them talking and listening all at the same time.'[1]

Whatever its philosophical merits, Holmes's proposition accurately describes a phenomenon familiar to students of Anglo-American relations. In observing one another, Americans and the British have frequently failed to pay adequate attention to what they saw. Often, indeed, the details have interested them very little. Usually that was because what primarily concerned them were non-visible concepts – ideas about their own relative positions in the world, about what were or were not acceptable codes of conduct, or simply evidence to support preconceived notions derived from the folklore which each nation has built up about the other. Whatever the 'real' United States and the 'real' Britain – both complex societies in process of rapid change – what observers have tended to see when they looked across the Atlantic have mostly been simplified models illustrating particular vices or virtues – the errors of kingship, the perils of democracy, the dangers of creeping socialism, or the iniquities of unrestrained capitalism.

To be sure, many have had the opportunity, particularly in recent years, to put their ideas to the test by actually crossing the Atlantic and observing life on the other side. Latterly, also, the influences of the cinema and television have helped to dispel many of the cruder misconceptions that flourished when most people were compelled to rely simply on what they gleaned from books and newspapers. 'Have you ever been to England?' asks Martin Chuzzlewit, in Dickens's novel, of one of his American interlocutors who insists that Queen Victoria lives in the Tower of London; 'In print I have, sir,' his interlocutor replies, 'but not otherwise.'[2] Fewer Britons than formerly, one imagines, labour under the illusion that Washington DC and Washington State are one and the same.

Misunderstandings such as these are, of course, easily corrected. Much harder to deal with are erroneous notions of a more general kind, that is to say ideas about innocence and experience, vice and virtue, freedom and equality, tradition and innovation, which over the years have featured in the Anglo-American dialogue. To a degree, it is true, such notions can be 'disproved' in that they can be shown to conceal the true complexities of a situation. Despite all that has been said and written, real life on the two sides of the Atlantic does not readily lend itself to treatment in terms of such simple dichotomies. Correcting such misapprehensions is a legitimate and necessary task.

But to achieve full understanding, as Oliver Wendell Holmes suggests, another type of approach is needed. This involves treating such beliefs not as reflections of some external reality but as expressions of the aspirations and values of those holding them. Viewed in this way, what is interesting about the Anglo-American dialogue is not so much whether the assumptions on which it was based are true or false, but what they reveal about the notions that, over the years, Britons and Americans have cherished about themselves. In other words, what Americans have believed about the British and vice versa has often had less to do with what their eyes and ears told them than with the need to establish their own sense of identity. If Americans were one thing, say, innovative, then it followed that the British must necessarily be the opposite, namely traditional. If England was the home of the aristocratic gentleman, then America was the home of the common man.

One consequence of such antithetical thinking has often been to exaggerate the differences between the two nations, masking many of the features they have in common. Another is the way in which they have given rise to beliefs that have enjoyed remarkable longevity, far outlasting the particular circumstances that gave them birth. What we are dealing with, in a sense, is a kind of international folklore, sometimes, as in the hands of caricaturists, merely a source of amusement, at other times capable of generating political action. Calling it folklore does not, of course, mean that it has been static. Rather, it has been part of an ongoing dialogue that, beginning with the foundation of the earliest colonies, has been carried in to the present and shows every sign of continuing into the future.

Nevertheless, revealing though the Anglo-American dialogue has been, it is as well to remind ourselves at the outset that it has been far from exclusive. Nations like to think well of themselves, as do people. Thus, when Americans and Britons have asked 'Who exactly are we?' or 'What is our identity as a nation?', in part what they have been asking is 'What is our standing in the world?', or 'What is our worth in relation to other peoples?' Mixed up with the notions Britons and Americans have held about one another have been beliefs about other nations. Defining one's own nation's identity by creating collective images of foreign peoples is thus a universal practice. If Americans and Britons have mythologised one another, so too have French and Germans, Russians and Poles and Chinese and Japanese. Viewed in this broader context it is plain that the Anglo-American relationship has much in common with other relationships that have existed throughout history. Long ago Aristotle attributed the peculiar virtues of the Greeks to the geographic chance that placed them between the 'energetic but anarchic peoples' of Europe and the 'ingenious but servile' peoples of Asia – which looks uncommonly like the Jeffersonian view that placed the United States between the 'artificial' Europeans and the 'primitive' Indians of the North American interior.[3]

It has been argued that, for historical reasons, Americans have felt a compelling need to engage in such acts of cultural triangulation more frequently than other peoples. As a nation of immigrants, founded in historical daylight and ideologically committed to certain supposedly universal values, Americans have been peculiarly concerned with national self-definition. The English, whether because of their earlier achievement of world-power status, deeper historical roots, a more pragmatic approach to government, longer involvement in world affairs, or greater preoccupation with class distinctions have until lately been more inclined to take such matters for granted. There are no British counterparts to the Declaration of Independence or the American Constitution, nor has there ever been a Parliamentary Committee on Un-British Activities. Apart from treason, it is hard to imagine what an un-British activity would be. Problems of national identity, however, are by no means unfamiliar to the British. Traditionally they have more often been associated with the Scots and Welsh than with the English, although with creation of Scottish and Welsh assemblies and the increasing transfer of power to the European Union they have latterly become a problem for the English too.

Granting, however, that the Anglo-American relationship needs to be looked at in the broad context of international relations generally, the fact remains that it has been commonly perceived as qualitatively different from other relationships. Here are two peoples, one originally an outgrowth of the other, sharing a common language and legal tradition, and retaining, in spite of two centuries of political separation, many other striking affinities. One consequence of this has been that neither has fully

adjusted its mind to thinking of the members of the other as 'foreigners'.
Writing from London in 1863, Henry Adams noted:

> In fact we are now one of the known and acknowledged units of the
> London and English world, and . . . the majority of people receive us
> much as they would Englishmen, and seem to consider us as such. I
> have been much struck by the way in which they affect to distinguish
> here between us and 'foreigners'; that is persons who don't speak
> English.[4]

British visitors to the United States express similar views. Looking back
on her arrival in America in 1832, the actress Frances Kemble recalls:
'The whole country was like some remote part of England that I had
never seen before, the people were like *queer* English people.'[5]

That the United States *was* a foreign nation was, of course, a point that
Americans themselves, particularly during the Republic's early years,
were anxious to establish. The right of British subjects to assume
American nationality and for United States vessels to freely navigate the
high seas were among the precipitating causes of the War of 1812. Yet, in
spite of this and the fact that over the years Americans of British descent
have come to represent only a minority of the US population, there has
remained on the American side a lively sense of cultural debt to Britain.
'Our civility,' declared Emerson in 1844, 'England determines the style
of, inasmuch as England is the strongest of the family of existing nations
and as we are an extension of that people.'[6] Given that the United States
has become the strongest nation – not merely militarily, but economically, politically, and culturally as well – the same might equally well be said
today by the British.

Such expressions of affinity do not, of course, adequately sum up a
relationship that has, historically speaking, been characterised as often by
expressions of enmity as of friendship. Until well into the nineteenth century Britain was America's traditional enemy, while the United States'
imperial ambitions in North America made her a potent danger to British
interests there. Yet, at the time when relations were at their very worst
(and on more than one occasion in the mid-nineteenth century the two
nations came close to war), Shakespeare remained Americans' favourite
playwright and Dickens and Scott among their favourite novelists.

The ambiguities of this relationship have long teased the imaginations
of statesmen, writers and scholars. How, within the limited scope of this
book, is the Anglo-American relationship to be characterised? Plainly it is

not like the Anglo-French relationship, which involves differences of language, not to mention distinct institutional and cultural traditions. And, again, it is not quite like the Anglo-Canadian connection, where links of a political nature endured for much longer and which lacks those elements of international rivalry which have so frequently characterised relations between Britain and the United States. Are Americans to be regarded as deracinated Britons whose culture has been progressively diluted by immigration from elsewhere and the vicissitudes of life on a faraway land? Or are they, as Americans themselves have sometimes claimed, the true heirs of British culture, having realised on a broad continent aspirations which the British, struggling with the detritus of history on their cramped and cluttered little island, were incapable of achieving?

Plainly these are questions to which no definitive answer can be given. What is clear, as the following pages will endeavour to show, is that the Anglo-American connection since 1783 has involved much more than the diplomatic exchanges between their respective governments, although these will also be touched on. Even when governmental relations were at their most fraught, other relationships flourished. Culturally, the two nations have never ceased to look to one another for guidance and inspiration. The same two-way process is evident in the fields of science and technology. Economically, the two countries' affairs have been so closely intertwined that for much of the last two hundred years it has been more accurate to think of them as constituent parts of a single transatlantic enterprise than as two separate economies. Thus, thanks to their common language and heritage, political separation has in no way diminished the eagerness with which each has actively sought to learn and profit from the achievements and failures of the other.

1 The Colonial Legacy

The Treaty of Versailles in 1783 ended a war that began as a domestic quarrel over taxes and developed into an international struggle involving France, Spain and Holland. Not surprisingly, the major powers of the day saw Britain's troubles as an opportunity to be exploited. Only a short time before, in the Seven Years' War (1756–63), after a century and a half of rivalry, Britain had succeeded in driving the French from North America. It was, however, a costly victory, for it was the attempt to have the colonists contribute financially to their own defence that led to disagreements over Parliament's right to levy taxes, the summoning of the Continental Congress, armed rebellion, the Declaration of Independence, seven years of armed struggle, and finally, recognition of American independence. A more ignominious end to Britain's aim to establish mastery over the whole of the North American continent could scarcely be imagined.

Beginning in 1607 with the settlement of Jamestown, British rule had lasted for 176 years, which is to say for a period roughly as long as from Queen Victoria's accession to our own day. During that time it set its stamp on American culture in ways that have continued to shape Anglo-American relations up to the present. To say, as the British have latterly been given to doing, that they have enjoyed a 'special relationship' with the United States, implying that the two nations have generally seen eye to eye on issues, is patently false – frequently the opposite has been the case. Yet, however fraught the political relationship, there has always been a sense of kinship based partly on a shared history and culture but above all on a common language. Only a small proportion of today's Americans are of British stock, but by virtue of being the first to arrive it was the British who set the agenda, making English the standard means of communication. The English they brought with them was Jacobean English, which is to say a language that was diverse, adaptable and rapidly changing. It was the English of Shakespeare and the King James Bible, a fluid medium, unconstrained by dictionaries, and open to the incorporation of new words and expressions. There being no fixed rules regarding spelling and pronunciation, American English soon began to acquire characteristics of its own. From the start, there was a need for new words. *Racoon, skunk, pecan* and *squash* were Anglicised versions of Indian words, as were *Mississippi* and *Susquehanna*. *Maize* and *barbecue* came from Spanish, *swamp* from German, *ravine* from French, and *bluff* (meaning a high, steep bank) from Dutch. There were dialect words not commonly used in Britain (although subsequently reimported from America), like *skedaddle, gumption* and *skulduggery*. Others, like *glow-worm, copperhead* and *whippoorwill*, were simply made up. Gradually, in spite of continuing cross-fertilisation, the two languages diverged as some words disappeared and new ones were introduced.[1]

Similar evolutionary processes are evident in the colonists' approach to institutional matters. The Puritans of New England and the Quakers of Pennsylvania had migrated with the specific intention of freeing themselves from practices of which they disapproved. The institutions they set up, therefore, diverged from England's for reasons that were conscious and deliberate. But even when that was not the case, what emerged were ways of doing things that differed from those of the mother country. All the same, when allowance is made for the special circumstances of life on a strange continent, the influence of English precedents and modes of thought are clearly evident. Had the first arrivals come from elsewhere, or simply arrived at a different time, the institutions – and language – of America would have been different.

Even in the seventeenth century North America was something of a melting pot. New York was originally settled by the Dutch and Delaware by Swedes. Apart from the French in Canada and Louisiana and the Spanish in Florida, however, it was the English who, by the 1670s, were in overall charge. They were also the most numerous, although by the end of the seventeenth century, with the arrival of increasing numbers of Germans, Scots, Scots-Irish (which is to say Ulstermen), Swiss and, of course, Africans, that too began to change. By the time of the Revolution, well over half of the population south of New England was of non-English stock. Like many later settlers, these new arrivals attempted to preserve the languages and follow the customs of their native countries. Colonial travellers were struck by the diversities of language and custom they encountered – the contrast, for example, between the prosperous German farmers of Pennsylvania and the indigent Scots-Irish of the southern back country.[2]

Up to the middle of the eighteenth century, the British had taken little interest in the internal affairs of their American colonies. They viewed the colonies as evidence of the swelling might of the British nation and valued them for the contribution they made to the Atlantic commerce on which Britain's prosperity depended. Interference in the colonies' internal affairs, however, scarcely seemed worthwhile. Unlike, for example, Spain's colonies, or even the tiny sugar-producing island of Barbados – in the seventeenth century by far Britain's most profitable New World colony – Britain's mainland settlements had signally failed to live up to expectations. Early exponents of colonisation had looked forward to the day when Britain's overseas possessions, like Spain's, would be supplying the mother country with cargoes of gold, silver and other riches. That did not happen. North America kept Britain supplied with tobacco, rice and indigo, and provided a market for British manufactures, but when compared with Jamaica and other Caribbean colonies, its wealth-producing capabilities were relatively meagre. It did, of course, contribute to the overall success of the nation's Atlantic trading system, as by supplying the West Indies with timber and foodstuffs. Still, the cost of its development – admittedly largely borne by private investors and the settlers themselves – was high. So, too, was that of defence. Why interfere in the colonies' internal affairs knowing that it would only stir up trouble? Not until the 1760s, triumphant at having driven the French out of North America but appalled at the cost, did the British wake up to the fact that their North American colonists had grown prosperous. Unlike the starveling settlers of a century before, they were at least as well off as the British themselves.

A Transoceanic Nation?

By that time the British had begun to regard the American colonies as a sort of Greater Britain, a natural extension of their own body politic, not unlike Ireland but situated further out across the ocean. They also took pride in the degree to which the colonists ran their own affairs. Political liberty and representative government were what distinguished their Empire from its rivals. They were also what distinguished Britain itself from the absolutist powers across the channel. Freedom encouraged initiative, enterprise, self-help; it liberated the British from the dead hand of government; it allowed them to become rich; it explained why they, rather than the French or the Spanish, had emerged victorious from the late struggles.

This was a view largely shared by the colonists themselves. Up to the 1760s it was no more difficult to be American and British than to be Welsh, or Scots, and British. And being British had many advantages, not least that of belonging to the nation that in the course of the previous century had established itself as the world's leading maritime power. It also allowed one to get on with one's own affairs without the government breathing down one's neck. Scattered as they were across the face of the land, most colonists had probably never set eyes on a British official. Insofar as they encountered government at all it was most likely to be at the township or county level, in which case it would be with a body of their own choosing. Colonial government was apt to appear as remote to most colonists as the government in Westminster was to most English people. In theory, they were governed by a combination of British-appointed officials and locally-elected gentry under a constitutional system approved by the Privy Council. Their assumption was that this mirrored Britain's own system of government, the colonial governors representing the monarch and the colonial assemblies substituting for Parliament. British liberties were famous the world over. As British subjects they saw themselves as entitled to the same privileges as the inhabitants of Britain itself. In practice they enjoyed many more. Nowhere else within Europe's expanding sphere of influence did people exercise as much control over their own affairs as in Britain's North American colonies.

This arose naturally out of the need to adapt to the exigencies of life in a frontier society. Only after 1763, in response to Britain's persistent attempts to raise taxes, did it dawn on the colonists that Whitehall regarded the matter quite differently. In the British view, they were under an obligation to pay their way. Preferably the colonies should be a source of profit – which, after all, was why they had been established in the first place – but at the very least they should not be a drain on the national exchequer. Yet that was precisely what – or so it seemed – they had become. It was only fair that as British subjects the colonists should make a contribution to the maintenance of the empire of which they were part, if only to the extent of meeting a proportion of their own defence costs. But leaving the question of fairness aside, how could an empire *be* an empire if its constituent parts were free to run their affairs as they chose? There had to be a sovereign authority, in this case the Crown in Parliament, if there was to be any sort of unity.[3]

It thus transpired that Americans did not have the same rights as the British themselves, at least not in terms of the right to levy their own taxes. What they had cherished as natural and time-honoured privileges were in the British view nothing of the sort, but merely practices that had developed as a result of imperial inertia. So, by gradual stages, it dawned on both parties that not only were they at cross purposes over taxation but over the origins and nature of political authority as well. Either the colonies' representative institutions were subordinate to Britain's and could be ignored or overridden by Parliament at will, or they were of equal standing, in which case the colonies were effectively sovereign entities, independent in all but name.

As relations worsened, it was increasingly the latter that impressed the colonists as the more plausible interpretation. In their view it was not they who had broken the compact but the British. If the idea of all men being created equal meant anything it meant that citizens of the colonies had as much right to institutions elected by them and responsive to their needs as did the inhabitants of Britain. 'No taxation without representation' had been the rallying cry of the British parliamentarians in the days of Charles I. It was, as the Declaration of Independence said, the British who, by their 'long train of abuses and usurpations', had caused the problem. Once the principle of Parliament's right to impose taxes had been conceded, who could say where it would all end? In refusing to be taxed, Americans believed that they were reaffirming their traditional rights as British subjects.

Revolutionary Ideology

In time, of course, the colonists' ideas advanced a good deal further. What, in fact, made the achievement of American independence historically important was not so much the demonstration that a colonial people could throw off imperial rule as the political principles invoked. In framing their case in terms of universal human rights Americans endowed it with a significance quite out of proportion to their position in the world and the wrongs they had endured. Compared to the sufferings of other colonial peoples, those inflicted on the Americans were relatively trifling. Asians and Africans who later came under British rule would have welcomed the kind of treatment Americans received. What makes the Declaration of Independence a pivotal document in modern history is not its rambling account of American grumbles over British wrongdoing, but the assumptions regarding the origin and purpose of governmental authority on which it is based. The assertion that 'Governments are instituted among Men, deriving their just Powers from the consent of the governed' effectively demystifies the whole question. For too long people had been blinded by claims about authority deriving from God, History or some other superior power. In the final analysis it was not kings and their ministers who were sovereign, but the people.[4]

Britain's colonists thus invoked principles that turned prevailing notions about government upside down. Their immediate intention was to challenge the authority of the King and Parliament; the effect, however, was to raise doubts not only about the legitimacy of Britain's right to rule the colonies but about the legitimacy of governmental authority as traditionally conceived. Americans had not, of course, invented the principles in question. They had simply seized on what they thought was the best way of justifying their response to British high-handedness. The arguments they used were the product of eighteenth-century Enlightenment thinking and, to that extent, essentially a European creation. Philosophers had bandied them about for years. The basic framework had been outlined almost a century earlier by John Locke in his *Two Treatises on Civil Government*, written in defence of another rebellion, the so-called Glorious Revolution of 1688. Nevertheless, Americans were the first to put Locke's ideas into practice by using them as a basis on which to erect an entire governmental system. In a sense they had little choice. Having once embarked on the perilous task of ending British rule they needed to invoke *some* alternative source of authority in justification of their actions. Appeals to force or historical tradition would hardly have done. Americans were too legal-minded for justifications based on the notion of might making right, and their colonies were not long enough established to warrant invocations of immemorial practice. On the other hand, the Lockean notion of there being a social contract – the belief that citizens voluntarily sacrificed a proportion of their liberty in order to enjoy the benefits of government – was ideally suited to their needs. By basing their claim to self-government on universal abstract rights they made the War of Independence not simply a struggle to separate themselves from Britain but, by implication, a crusade for the rights of all men everywhere.

Still, Americans would hardly have taken the path they did had not the new ideas accorded, as least to some degree, with their own historical experience. Colonial towns might look like English towns and colonists dress and speak much like English men and women, but the dynamics of colonial life were quite different from those of England. For one thing, the institutions governing colonial life were of recent origin and generally of the colonists' own devising. Those of England had mostly originated in the far distant past. Much of British history involved struggles between kings and barons, neither of whom showed much concern for the well-being of society's lower orders. In such a context the notion of a social compact appeared an abstract and possibly subversive concept. In the case of the colonies, however, it bore a remarkably close resemblance to the way their own governments had actually come into being. The practice went back to the Virginia Company charters and the Mayflower Compact and had been repeated time and again as new settlements were established. Apart from Magna Carta, the British were not much familiar with charters or compacts. Monarchs had come and gone, but starting out *de novo* was not something the British had had much occasion to do. Like British society itself, the British system of government had simply evolved. From a strictly rationalist viewpoint, as Thomas Paine in *Common Sense* (1776) pointed out, neither bore close scrutiny. No rational principle governed the way wealth and property were distributed, nor could anyone have *invented* anything as bizarre as the pre-1832 allocation of parliamentary seats. That, of course, is to overlook the way human institutions change over time. As a last resort, British institutions could always be defended on the grounds of custom and the fact that they worked. The same considerations, however, did not apply to the same extent to colonial institutions, most of which were of more recent creation and had been set up with very specific objects in view.

Thus, from the very beginning, colonial experience diverged from that of the mother country. In Britain the exercise of power was not constrained by written charters or constitutions. No clear line of distinction existed between the government's executive and legislative functions, the executive being the cabinet, whose members were drawn from one or other of the houses of Parliament. In the colonies, by way of contrast, these functions were kept strictly separate. There the form of government, as prescribed by royal charters, consisted of an executive arm made up of the royally-appointed governors and their councils and a legislative arm made up of the assemblies elected by, and answerable to, the colonists. During and after the Revolution, when Americans set about creating new systems of government, first at the state and later at the federal level, they naturally opted for versions of those with which they were already familiar, namely ones based on written constitutions and a separation of powers.

The Formative Influence of Free Land

There were other differences too. What more than anything distinguished the colonies from the mother country was the ready availability of land. Nowhere in Britain, or in Europe for that matter, was land open for settlement in the way it was in America. It affected every aspect of life, from farming practices and the way towns were laid out to the relationship between servants and employers and the way wealth was distributed.

It was largely the prospect of acquiring land that drew successive waves of settlers across the Atlantic. Most migrants entertained hopes of bettering their conditions and, in the process, of re-creating something not unlike the kind of society they had left behind. But what they almost invariably ended up with was something markedly different. Among the most quickly disabused were those who had received large land grants and arrived in America under the impression that they would be able to set themselves up as country gentlemen. Some even dreamed of establishing feudal estates, only to discover that, without the labour required for its cultivation, land was valueless. For Europeans this was a hard concept to grasp. In Britain, where land was scarce and labour plentiful, no problem arose. The ownership of land was enough to ensure wealth, respect and position. Labour was a secondary consideration. There were always enough landless people to perform the tasks required. In Britain, as in Europe generally, the pre-industrial social order was based almost entirely on distinctions arising out of the ownership, or non-ownership, of land.

In the colonies the situation was different. Although land was not quite free for the taking, and capital was necessary for its development, there was more than enough to render attempts to reproduce European notions of hierarchy impractical. Given the option, most chose to become landholders in their own right. Cultivating a smallholding might not make them rich, but even in America landholding conferred status, and in time, with the ground cleared and fields under cultivation, it offered a reasonable competency. To become rich, on the other hand, it was necessary to have a labour force. That meant employing either slaves or indentured servants, which is to say Africans or newly arrived immigrants who had mortgaged their labour in return for their passage. Both, however, were beyond the means of most settlers, the great majority of whom remained small farmers, dependent either on selling produce to local markets or growing crops for their own consumption.

As a consequence there was much less variation in wealth than in Britain, most colonists being as rich or as poor as their family farms made them. According to Hector St John de Crèvecoeur, a former French officer who had gone to live in New York following the fall of Quebec, pre-Revolutionary America was the most egalitarian society existing anywhere in the world:

Some few towns excepted, we are all tillers of the earth, from Nova Scotia to West Florida. We are a people of cultivators scattered over an immense territory, communicating with one another by means of good roads and navigable rivers, united by the silken bands of mild government, all respecting the laws without dreading their power because they are equitable. We are all animated by the spirit of industry, which is unfettered and unrestrained because each person works for himself. If he travels through our country districts the traveller views not the hostile castle and the haughty mansion contrasted with the clay hut and miserable cabin. . . . A pleasing uniformity of decent competence appears throughout our habitations. Lawyer and merchant are the fairest titles our towns afford: that of farmer the only appellation of the rural inhabitants of our country.[5]

There were, of course, exceptions, most notably the slaveholding planters of the southern tidewater, whose control of African labour and exports of tobacco allowed them a lifestyle distinctly superior to that of their small-farming neighbours. Some built large houses and even acquired aristocratic pretensions. In addition, as Crèvecoeur mentions, throughout the colonies there were merchants and lawyers, looked up to because of their wealth and education. These were the colonial elite, the local arbiters of taste and style, the American counterparts of the lawyers and tradesmen of British provincial towns like Norwich or Coventry.

None of this, however, came near to representing a class ascendancy of the English kind. Eighteenth-century England was controlled by some four hundred families whose fabulous scale of landed wealth, political influence and aristocratic grandeur was unmatched elsewhere under the Crown. In North America there was no titled pyramid with dukes at the top and marquises, earls, viscounts and barons arranged in descending order below. American society was made up of families that had been obliged to make their own way in the world. Even those at the very pinnacle of colonial society, men like George Washington and Thomas Jefferson, lived in modest circumstances as compared with the English peerage with its enormous estates, vast houses and retinues of servants. In this respect the American colonies were more like Scotland, another outlying province of the greater British world with its own traditions, pride and local elite. Absent, too, was the Church of England hierarchy with its princely archbishops and bishops. In its place was a huge variety of what in England would have been termed dissenting sects – Baptists and Presbyterians, Congregationalists and Unitarians – who, along with

Catholics and Jews, had been attracted to the colonies not only by the economic opportunities they offered but also by the prospect of religious toleration.

The ready availability of land had other consequences. In the colonies, as in England, the right to vote was limited to property holders. In the case of the English shires that meant forty-shilling freeholders, which is to say owners of land that could be rented for a notional forty shillings a year. When the same rule was adopted in the colonies, however, the effect was to enfranchise a majority of the adult male population, a situation that would not obtain in Britain until the latter part of the nineteenth century.[6] Thus, even before the War of Independence, Americans were accustomed not only to electing candidates to political office but to holding elective office themselves.

The political awareness this engendered was enhanced by the War of Independence itself. With the colonial governors gone and the machinery of government at a standstill Americans had to consider how they were to fight the war and how they were to be governed in future. That meant drafting new constitutions, first at the state and later at the national level. It also involved delegating power to local representatives and debating broad issues. Because what had hitherto bound the colonies together had been their links with Britain, there never had been a single body capable of representing the colonies as a whole. How much power, therefore, was it appropriate to allocate to such a national body? What safeguards were necessary to ensure that it did not assume authority over matters beyond its remit? Having lived through turbulent times Americans were familiar with the temptations of power. Thus perfectly ordinary Americans – farmers, merchants, small-town lawyers – found themselves occupying positions of authority and making decisions that at other times, even in America, would never have fallen to their lot.

In Britain, of course, dealing with such matters was the prerogative of a privileged social class. Americans had met members of that class and learned to resent its haughty ways. Colonial governors had not always been tactful. The same applied to the military. Nothing grated on American sensibilities more than being condescended to or ordered about by those who assumed they were by right entitled to the same sort of deference in America that they were used to in Britain. Having, by their own efforts, carved a civilisation out of the forest, Americans rejected the notion that birth rendered some people superior to others. In breaking with Britain, they determined to do away with honours, titles, and everything else associated with hereditary principles.

But with the ratification of the Treaty of Versailles all that was at an end. Henceforward they could run their affairs in whatever way they saw fit, while the British, in turn, were disencumbered of their rude and rebellious colonists. Yet it was far from being a clean break. There remained important issues to be decided. One was the effect the loss of the colonies would have on Britain's economy and international standing. Another was whether such a disputatious group of people as Britain's former colonists were capable of working together now the struggle was over and they were responsible for shaping their own destiny.

2 Troubled Times: 1783–1815

The Post-War Settlement

Under the terms of peace the United States was granted the entire territory east of the Mississippi, south of the Great Lakes, and north of
Spanish Florida. They would have liked to get Canada too, but their
claims were rejected out of hand. Nevertheless it was, by any reckoning, a
generous settlement. Remarkably, Britain agreed to give up what subsequently became known as the 'Old Northwest', a vast wilderness stretching northward from the Ohio River to the Great Lakes, still largely
unexplored and virtually uninhabited except by Native Americans, to
which the United States had only a tenuous claim. But although
Americans might have been browbeaten into agreeing to a boundary
along the crest of the Appalachians, it was plain to Britain's negotiators
that settlers would soon begin pressing westward. Having fought one war,
they saw it as imprudent to create a situation destined sooner or later to
lead to another.[1]

In terms of size the new republic was, of course, vastly larger than the
British Isles, although the area actually settled was not greatly different. It
extended some 2000 miles from Massachusetts in the north to Georgia in
the south. In the west, it was still largely bounded by the Allegheny
Mountains, which prevented easy access into the interior and made the
transportation of goods impossible except by mule. In fact, travelling by
land in any direction was so difficult that most long-distance travel, and
virtually all transportation of heavy goods, was by water.

The population of the United States in 1790 stood at just under four
million, approximately a third of Great Britain's. Along the Atlantic coast
there were numerous seaport towns, the largest being the nation's temporary capital, Philadelphia, with some 50 000 inhabitants. Philadelphia
was also the nation's principal scientific and intellectual centre and its
main financial market. New York and Boston, with populations of 35 000
and 25 000 respectively, were likewise commercial rather than industrial
centres and as such much smaller than the newly-emerging industrial
cities of Britain like Manchester, Glasgow, Liverpool and Birmingham,

all of which had populations in excess of 70 000. London, with its 864 000 inhabitants, was in a class all of its own, the largest city not only in Europe but in the world.[2] The United States did not have, and would never acquire, a single dominant metropolitan city, like London, Paris or Rome, capable of serving at once the centre of government, commerce and culture. Instead, being a continent-wide nation, it developed regional capitals, some of which would in due course acquire particular specialities, New York becoming the nation's financial capital and Boston, at least for a time, its cultural centre. Washington, which eventually became the nation's new capital, was the centre of government but little else, being scarcely more than a provincial town in terms of its general facilities until well into the twentieth century.

Among the concessions made to Americans by the Treaty of Versailles was the right to continue fishing in their accustomed grounds off Newfoundland and to land and dry their catches on the unsettled shores of Nova Scotia and Labrador. In return, the Continental Congress agreed to pay off pre-Revolutionary debts owed to British creditors and to use their best offices to persuade individual states either to restore or pay compensation for the properties of Loyalists seized during the hostilities. This last was a tricky issue in that under the Articles of Confederation the US amounted to little more than an assembly of what the Treaty itself referred to 'free, sovereign and Independent States'. What power Congress had to get the states to pay compensation was unclear, as it had no power to impose or collect taxes or compel compliance to its laws. It did not even have a properly designated executive body empowered to carry out its decrees. Was the United States a nation or a collection of sovereign states? The Articles themselves described it as a 'league of friendship' between states, each of which retained its 'sovereignty, independence and freedom'.[3]

But, whatever it was, the United States in the immediate post-war years was plainly not a national government of the kind with which European states were used to dealing. Nor, for that matter, did it appear to be one well adapted to fulfilling its international obligations. For this reason, and in defiance of the Treaty of Versailles, the British continued to maintain forts and garrisons in the territories south of the Great Lakes on what was now indubitably American soil. If nothing else, they could be used to exert leverage should the United States fail to live up to its promises. Prompt withdrawal would also have meant abandoning Britain's Native American allies, not mentioned in the peace treaty, for whom it hoped some provision could eventually be made. In addition, it would have meant foregoing the substantial profits still to be derived from the local fur trade. Most important of all, however, were continuing doubts in Whitehall as to the future viability of the United States as a political entity. If, as seemed more than likely, it were to fall apart, there was much to be said for having a military force already in place.

A collapse of the American Union was something that many would have welcomed, not least the 40 000 Loyalist refugees wintering in temporary camps north of the Canadian border. Apart from the former French colony of Quebec, and a thin scattering of French-speaking Acadian settlers elsewhere, Canada had been virtually unsettled prior to the Loyalists' arrival. For these exiles, severed from relations and friends, deprived of possessions, the British defeat had been a bitter experience. Winters were longer and colder than those to which they were accustomed and the territories in which they found themselves were uncultivated, unmapped and in many cases virtually unexplored. Whether the lands on which they found themselves were even suited to settlement was initially unclear. The journalist William Cobbett, who visited the Canadian Maritimes shortly after the Loyalists' arrival, observed that 'Nova Scotia, New Brunswick and Canada are the horns, the head, the neck, the shins and the hoof of the ox, and the United States are the ribs, the sirloin, the kidneys, and the rest of the body.'[4] This was not entirely true. Ontario was eventually found to be one of the most fertile parts of North America. All the same, such thoughts must have crossed the minds of many that first winter as they huddled around their fires in their snowbound wilderness.

Britain did what it could to alleviate their plight, providing temporary relief, surveying lands, allocating farms and establishing townships. Former officers who had fought on the British side continued to draw half-pay and a number of leading Loyalists found employment on the colonial payroll as judges or administrators. Eventually, too, thanks to Britain's continuing pressure on the American government, those who had lost property as a consequence of their support of the British cause received a measure of compensation for their losses. In all, upwards of £1.3 million in the form of payments to Loyalists was injected into the British North American economy in the decades following the defeat. Because these payments went principally to leading Loyalists, the new order that arose showed a striking degree of continuity with the social stratification that had existed south of the border, in that those who had held positions of rank and distinction in the old colonies by and large came to occupy similar positions in the new.

In time conditions for the exiles improved. Sarah Frost, a refugee from Connecticut who had arrived at St John, New Brunswick, in 1783, noted in her diary that 'It is, I think, the roughest land I ever saw . . . . But this is to be the *city* they say.' Yet only eight years later a British traveller, Patrick Campbell, found the town 'well planned; the streets cut at right angles . . . . It consists of about five hundred houses, all of timber, well painted. They have a neat appearance, and some of them even elegant.' Some Canadian exiles decamped to Britain or the West Indies, others drifted back to the United States, but the great majority clung staunchly to their Tory principles, scornful of the levelling notions now prevailing south of the border and determined to create a society that would outshine that from which they had been expelled.[5]

For a nation that had lost a war to provide compensation on this scale was unprecedented. It may be doubted if Britain would have behaved as generously if it had not seen that there were advantages to be gained, most notably the need to create a bulwark against future encroachment by the United States into what remained of British North America. In the aftermath of the Revolution, however, this hardly constituted an immediate threat. With their army demobilised, their government in debt, no taxes coming in, their Congress often too ill-attended to pass legislation, and lacking even a proper national currency, Americans, at least for the time being, represented no threat to anyone, except possibly themselves.

Post-War Bargaining

Among the issues left over for further discussion at the peace negotiations was the question of future trading relations. During their struggle with Britain, Americans had looked forward eagerly to being free of restrictions on their commerce. At last they would be at liberty to trade with whom they liked. What they had not calculated on was that, no longer being British subjects, they would find themselves shut out of many of their most lucrative markets. As a maritime nation still heavily dependent on overseas trade for their prosperity, this was a severe disadvantage.

The British saw little need to make concessions. Nothing the Americans said could be taken at face value. The weakness of the their central government under the Articles meant that individual states were free to flout any agreements that it made. Some had lost no time in passing laws impeding the collection of British debts. In any case it was now to Britain's advantage to divert trade so as to benefit British carriers and those of Britain's colonies that had remained loyal. There was also a feeling, especially in Tory circles, that Americans should be made to pay for the trouble they had caused. An Order in Council of December 1783 accordingly banned American ships from trading with any of Britain's overseas possessions, including Canada and the British Caribbean. Americans thus found themselves prevented from carrying timber, livestock and foodstuffs to the West Indies, a lucrative traffic which in pre-Revolutionary times had absorbed almost 60 per cent of New England's exports. This, in turn, affected imports of molasses on which New England's rum trade depended. American vessels were still allowed into British ports but were subjected to high docking charges. Because over half of America's exports went either to the United Kingdom or to British possessions overseas, this naturally cut into America's share of the carrying trade.

Yet in spite of these changes the commercial arrangements built up over the previous century remained largely in place. Britain was still the United States' principal source of hardware, woollens and other manufactured goods. Americans also remained dependent on British merchants who alone were capable of supplying them with the long-term credits they required. Britain meanwhile continued to consume a high proportion of America's exports of tobacco and rice. Thus the trading relations built up before the war continued to function much as they had done previously, with Britain being still very much the dominant partner.[6]

Although John Adams had arrived in London in 1785 as America's first diplomatic representative, it was not until 1791, largely on account of the uncertain nature of America's internal arrangements, that Britain deigned to send a Minister to the United States. There was also growing exasperation in Britain over what was seen as American foot-dragging over the payment of debts. Many doubted that anything useful could be achieved by even attempting to negotiate with such a country.

The adoption of the new Constitution in 1788 and Washington's inauguration as President transformed the situation. Now the United States had an active central government with the authority to speak for Americans as a whole. No longer did it have to go cap in hand to the states to beg for funds, or stand by impotently while its rulings were ignored. Thanks to the efforts of Alexander Hamilton, it also acquired a national currency of assured value: the US dollar. Congress's new tax-raising powers provided further assurance that henceforth the country would be better placed to meet its international obligations. With a strong executive now in power there was even a possibility that, as urged by

Secretary of State Thomas Jefferson, the United States would take retaliatory measures against British imports.

In the hope of settling outstanding differences, the United States in 1794 despatched a special commission to Britain, led by the Chief Justice John Jay. High on the Americans' list of grievances was Britain's continued refusal to remove its garrisons from United States soil. Not only was their presence an infringement of US sovereignty but there was a growing belief that Britain was aiming to create a permanent Indian buffer state, thereby cutting off access to the rich lands of the West. Americans attempting to enter the area had thrice been repelled by Indian forces using arms supplied by the British. As regards Britain's intent, American suppositions were not entirely correct. It was nevertheless the case that earnings from the fur trade had been used to acquire weapons which, on occasion, Indians had used to repel American intruders. It was also true that in 1794, shortly before Jay's departure, the royal governor of Canada delivered a fiery speech to an Indian audience calling on them to burn American settlements. If events were allowed to pursue their course it seemed more than likely that the two countries would soon find themselves once again at war.

Britain's agreement to withdraw her troops by June 1796 removed that particular danger. In return, the United States undertook to refer the questions of loyalist reparations and the outstanding debts owed to British merchants to joint commissions. (These claims were eventually settled by an American payment of some two-and-a-half million of Hamilton's new US dollars.) Britain also agreed to allow US vessels access to both East and West Indian ports on condition the US gave up its carrying trade in such staples as molasses, sugar and cotton. The US Senate, which under the new Constitution was required to ratify all treaties, refused to accept this latter provision, the effect of which would have been to give British shippers almost a monopoly of the inter-oceanic carrying trade. Plainly the British were intent on driving a hard bargain. The American press was furious. Yet, in spite of popular opposition, the rest of the treaty was approved by the necessary two-thirds majority, albeit by the narrowest of margins.[7]

Given the United States' weak bargaining position, Jay's Treaty was not the abject capitulation Americans supposed. In conjunction with the Treaty of San Lorenzo, negotiated with Spain the following year, it prepared the way for opening up the Mississippi basin to commerce. Now that, with Spain's agreement, Americans enjoyed free navigation of the river, the only major problem remaining was the need to come to terms with the Indians. Nothing was said about them in Jay's Treaty, the British taking the view that they had no choice but to leave the question to be decided by the parties concerned. In the event it had been virtually settled by the time of Jay's return as a consequence of General Anthony Wayne's victory at the Battle of Fallen Timbers. By the subsequent Treaty of Greenville, signed by the 12 leading tribes north of the Ohio in August 1795, the United States gained effective control of the entire area ceded to them under the Versailles Treaty.[8]

Britain, America and the French Wars

These developments occurred against a background of growing international tension arising out of the French Revolution. British and American responses to that event were initially mixed. Some saw it as heralding the arrival of a new age of freedom. The British Whig leader Charles James Fox went so far as to call the fall of the Bastille the greatest event in the history of the world. His fellow Whig, Edmund Burke, took a contrary view, foreseeing the revolution's subsequent descent into tyranny, civil strife and war. As he correctly perceived, there was a world of difference between the American Revolution, an event broadly in tune with the prevailing character and traditions of the American people, and the wholesale destruction of an existing society, which he took to be the aim of France's new leaders.[9] Americans, not surprisingly, proved less perceptive in this regard, seeing the French Revolution as a continuation of their own struggle.

In certain respects this was justified. Both the American and French revolutions reflected the spirit of the Enlightenment. Each was predicated on a belief in the need to sweep aside old habits of deference and reorganise society on more rational lines. There were also more specific connections. It was the debts accumulated in support of the American war that forced the French king to take the fateful step of summoning the Estates General, a body that had been in abeyance for the preceding 174 years, thereby setting in motion the train of events leading to the collapse of the whole authoritarian system under which the French had latterly been governed. Troops who had served in America were among the first to join the revolutionary cause. Among the more prominent supporters of the revolution were the Marquis de Lafayette and Thomas Paine, veterans of America's own struggles. It looked as if the spark Americans had lit at Lexington and Concord had grown into a mighty conflagration that had leaped the Atlantic and was now about to sweep Europe. Caught up in the excitement of the moment some Americans took to addressing one another as 'citizen' and 'citizeness'. Not until the news arrived of the execution of the king, France's declaration of war on Britain and the onset of the Terror did Americans begin to grasp the difference between their bid for independence and what was now transpiring on the streets of Paris.

Contrasting responses to these events reinforced the already emerging division between the pro-British and the pro-French factions in Washington's cabinet. As the first US representative to France, Jefferson had acquired a warm sympathy for the French people and a correspondingly strong disdain for the absolutist system under which they laboured. While not exactly condoning the excesses of the Jacobins, he regarded them as the natural response of a people suddenly freed from the yoke of an unjust and repressive regime. As Washington's Secretary of State he therefore viewed events with a more tolerant eye than most of his cabinet colleagues. By contrast, Alexander Hamilton, Washington's Secretary of the Treasury, saw events in France as the work of a rabble bent on destroying the very foundations of civilised society. Americans had fought to *preserve* their liberties, not to replace the organs of government with some sanguinary scheme aimed at achieving social equality through the exercise of state power. Hamilton had always admired the British economic and social system, which he regarded as providing a model for America's own future development. In any case, given a choice between Britain and France, he believed it would be safer to side with Britain, the United States having more to fear from the British Navy than from the French Army. Washington's own view was that Americans should remain strictly neutral. This was all very well in theory; in practice it became increasingly difficult.

The problem was brought home by the arrival of Edmond Genêt as France's Minister to the United States. Genêt had been dispatched with instructions to enlist support for France's military efforts in the hope that Americans would regard themselves as still bound to come to France's defence by the treaty of alliance of 1778. Arriving in Charleston on 8 April 1793, Citizen Genêt, as he became known, promptly set about recruiting volunteers to attack Spanish garrisons in Florida and Louisiana. Although he found no lack of recruits, the attempt eventually fizzled out for lack of money. He had more success in commissioning American privateers to prey on British shipping in the Caribbean and along the American coast, and in arranging for French consuls to sell the vessels they captured. This required few funds as the sailors concerned could reward themselves from the sale of whatever they seized. Within months a dozen American-manned vessels were at sea flying the French flag. On his arrival in Philadelphia, however, having travelled north in what amounted almost to a triumphal progress, Genêt received a cold reception from Washington and his cabinet, who were afraid that his activities would draw them into renewed conflict with Britain. Genêt was accordingly informed that his privateers could not send their prizes to American ports and should leave American waters forthwith. When, in spite of this warning, he persisted, Washington demanded his recall. A full account of the affair went to Congress, explaining that Genêt's conduct had threatened to involve the US 'in war abroad, and discord and anarchy at home'.[10]

Meanwhile, the British had also incurred American wrath by seizing US vessels trading with the French Caribbean on the grounds that they were trading with the enemy. As the goods involved were not war materials and the United States was a neutral, Americans argued that their vessels had every right to trade with France's colonies. In fact, American vessels were taking advantage of French wartime measures designed to keep their colonial trade going in spite of Britain's maritime preponderance. Britain's arguments, however, failed to convince the United States, which took the view that as a neutral its vessels were free to trade with whom they liked except when ports were blockaded or war matériel was involved, which in the present instance was not the case.

Thus began a wrangle over maritime rights that was to bedevil Anglo-American relations throughout the nineteenth century and beyond. As the world's leading neutral shipper, it was plainly to the United States' advantage to continue trading with belligerents, expanding its opportunities as and when circumstances allowed. By contrast, it was to the advantage of belligerents to divert US commerce so as to benefit themselves while denying its benefits to their enemies. This was the sort of situation that maritime law was supposedly designed to cover. The trouble was that by the late eighteenth century maritime law was in a state of some confusion. In any case, locked as they were in a life-and-death struggle, neither Britain nor France was much inclined to pay attention to the niceties of legal precedent. It thus seemed to Americans that both powers – but the British in particular, since they dominated the world's sea lanes – were failing to give due recognition to the United States' new-found sovereign status. The British, in turn, were furious at the sight of their erstwhile colonists profiting at Britain's expense by trading with her enemies.[11]

It was the French, however, who initially came closest to embroiling the United States in the conflict. They were disappointed by American's apparent forgetfulness of their contribution to the United States' independence and what they interpreted as the pro-British tenor of Washington's administration. Jay's Treaty, in their eyes, constituted an abject American surrender to British interests. Their hope that Washington's retirement would bring about a change in attitude was dashed when, instead of the Francophile Jefferson, John Adams was elected. They therefore refused to accept Adams' nominee as American Minister, and announced that they would treat American shipping in precisely the same way the British were doing by intercepting vessels on the high seas and diverting them to their own ports for thorough searching. In one respect they went a good deal further, issuing instructions that Americans found serving on British vessels be hanged. Within a year they had seized over 300 vessels, thereby provoking vociferous American demands for war.

In the hope of finding a solution to these problems, Adams despatched a peace commission to Paris. Instead of being received with the deference normally accorded representatives of a sovereign nation, however, the delegates were kept hanging about while hints were dropped that they might expedite matters by agreeing to provide a loan of $12 million (together with a $250 000 sweetener for the officials concerned). News of these events added fuel to the rising tide of American indignation. Congress repudiated the 1778 treaty of amity, increased military spending, recalled Washington and Hamilton to duty, and authorised American ships to seize French vessels as and when the opportunity arose. For the next two years the United States and France fought what was effectively a war on the high seas.

These developments naturally delighted the British, who went so far as to offer American vessels convoy protection. It even looked for a moment as if the two countries might become allies. Alarmed at this prospect, the French became more conciliatory. An American envoy, they announced, would be welcome and would be treated with respect. When the newly appointed Minister, William Vans Murray, arrived in Paris he found Napoleon in control and anxious for better relations. Although Murray failed to obtain compensation for American losses he was able to report that France now sought America's friendship and that the two countries saw eye to eye on maritime questions.

The presidential election of 1800 dealt a further blow to the prospects of Anglo-American agreement by putting Thomas Jefferson in the White House. Misled by the Republicans' rhetorical excesses, many on both sides of the Atlantic took them to be dyed-in-the-wool Jacobins. This was far from the case. In fact, so far as foreign policy was concerned, little changed. His First Inaugural echoed Washington's Farewell Address, warning against 'entangling alliances' and stressing the United States' need to avoid being drawn into Europe's struggles. Nevertheless, it was plain that the new administration was distinctly less Anglophile than its predecessor.

Following Nelson's defeat of the French fleet at the Battle of Trafalgar in 1805, relations worsened. With virtually complete control of the seas, the British displayed increasing arrogance, interpreting maritime law and convention to suit their interests. Despite Americans' protests they expanded the list of items listed as contraband, redefined the restrictions governing their right to re-export goods imported from abroad, and imposed new impediments on the carrying of cargoes picked up from foreign ports. In retaliation, the French adopted similar measures. But it was Britain with whom Americans were most frequently in dispute. This tit-for-tat competition reached new levels in 1807 when the British issued Orders in Council barring neutral shipping from virtually the entire European coastline. Napoleon responded by declaring a blockade of the British Isles and proclaiming that vessels breaking the blockade would be subject to French seizure. Thereafter, any American merchant vessel approaching European waters was liable to capture by one or other of the powers. In all, some 1500 ships were taken, two-thirds by the British, the remainder by the French.

In one respect, however, Britain's offences were much graver than France's. This was because, unlike the French whose concern was simply with cargoes, the British were in the habit of seizing American seamen as well. Ostensibly these were British deserters. Given the conditions of life in the Royal Navy it is hardly a wonder that sailors deserted. Nor was it surprising that, as many of these desertions occurred in foreign ports, deserters joined American ships, life there being safer, the language the same, and the pay better. Just how bad conditions were in the Royal Navy was brought to public attention in 1797 when the Channel and North Sea fleets mutinied. Often sailors were tricked or press-ganged into serving. In a day before police forces and national registers of population such rough-and-ready methods were often necessary to bring the navy up to full complement. Sailors, therefore, had little compunction about deserting when the opportunity offered. According to one American observer the British by 1807 were losing some 2500 sailors a year to American vessels. So desperate was the shortage of hands that officers employed in searching British merchantmen routinely made up for missing crew members. Those inducted into His Majesty's service would then be required to serve for the duration of the war. But by no means all of those taken from American vessels were British deserters. Unlike the United States, Britain did not concede a right of expatriation. Anyone born a British subject remained a British subject. Some of those seized were British-born emigrants to the United States to whose services the Crown could be said to have a valid claim, but many others – how many it is impossible to say, but they numbered in the thousands – were bona fide American-born nationals. When crewmen were needed, officers were not choosy about whom they took.[12]

Such high-handed behaviour, not surprisingly, aroused deep resentment. A crisis was reached in June 1807 when a British frigate, the *Leopard*, patrolling off the coast of Virginia, encountered a US naval frigate, the *Chesapeake*, and, supposing that she contained British deserters, ordered her to haul to in readiness for boarding. When the American captain refused, the *Leopard* fired successive broadsides into her, killing three Americans and wounding a further eighteen. The *Chesapeake*, having just begun a long voyage to the Mediterranean, was unprepared for battle and had no option but to surrender. Its captain offered up his sword to the British boarding party, which took away four seamen, leaving the damaged vessel to limp back into harbour. Only one of the seamen seized, it later turned out, was a genuine deserter. Whether this happened in American coastal waters was a matter of dispute, but to attack a United States government ship even on the high seas represented an escalation of British maritime policy and a new affront to US national pride.

Americans responded with outrage. To judge from the tone of newspaper comment the country was eager for war. 'Never since the battle of Lexington', Jefferson declared, 'have I seen the country in such a state of exasperation as at present, and even that did not produce such unanimity.'[13] But, rather than embark on war, Jefferson resorted to economic sanctions, believing that Britain's dependence on American trade would soon bring her to the negotiating table. He persuaded Congress to pass an Embargo Act providing that American vessels, apart from those engaged in coastal trade, be confined to port. The Act also banned British warships from entering American waters and imposed restrictions on the importation of British goods.

Unfortunately, these measures placed a heavier burden on the US than on Britain. Exports fell by over 75 per cent and imports by more than half. Producers of tobacco, hemp and other staples, cut off from their European markets, saw prices plummet and surpluses pile up at the docksides. In mercantile cities such as Boston and New York bankruptcies multiplied. Unemployed sailors thronged the streets while ships stood idle. British shipping houses were only too delighted to be relieved of American competition. New England, from which the bulk of American shipping came, was one of the areas hardest hit. In 1808 the Republicans succeeded once again in capturing both Congress and the presidency, but with reduced majorities. Jefferson's successor, James Madison, lost no time in repealing the Embargo Act, substituting a so-called Non-Intercourse Act that formally re-established trade with all nations except Britain and France.

The War of 1812

There followed three years of misunderstanding, ineptitude and blunder. The fault was by no means entirely Madison's. Anxious as he was to defend American interests, there was little that he could do when the great nations of Europe were bent on fighting a global war. Although a significant mercantile power, the United States was still a relatively puny one in military terms. From the point of view of the British, fighting for their very survival as a nation, what the United States did or did not do was of little concern as compared with the need to defeat France. If that meant riding roughshod over American interests and sensibilities, so be it. Preferably it could be done without actually provoking the United States into declaring war, although even that was a risk worth taking.

That war was a distinct possibility had become clear at the time of the *Chesapeake* incident. Britain's principal point of vulnerability was Canada. Unwilling to spare troops from Europe, it did what it could to prepare for Canada's defence by organising militia companies among the Loyalists and French Canadians. Given that the United States' population outnumbered that of Canada by some 25 to 1, this hardly seemed an adequate provision. Nevertheless, Britain adamantly refused to back down over the issues of impressment and maritime rights. France, more cunningly, promised to lift its restrictions while continuing to enforce them much as before.

What the British had not counted on was the mounting exasperation of Americans. This was reflected in the mid-term elections of 1810 by the appearance of a group of belligerent young Republicans known as the 'War Hawks'. Most were Midwesterners who took at face value plausible, albeit inaccurate, stories attributing recent Indian troubles in the Lake

Michigan region to the machinations of British agents. The problem actually arose out of the westward advance of American pioneers, compounded by the fact that efforts to resolve it by military means had had the unintended effect of making the Indians look to Britain for support. Whatever the rights and wrongs of the matter, Americans took note that, with Britain and Spain embroiled in Europe, no more favourable occasion was likely to arise for acquiring Canada and Florida, so opening the way for what many regarded as their preordained right to occupy the whole of North America.[14]

In his message to Congress on 1 June 1812, President Madison listed four major grounds for war: the impressment of American seamen, violation of US neutral rights, the blockading of American ports, and Britain's refusal to revoke the Orders in Council restricting US commerce with Europe. Unbeknown to the President, Britain had two days earlier undertaken to rescind the hated Orders. Whether Congress would have voted for war had this been known is a matter for speculation. What is clear is that the country was deeply divided. Support for the President was firmest in the South and West, where expansionist sentiments were strongest. In New England, New York, New Jersey and Delaware, the leading commercial and maritime states, there was strong opposition. The fact that these were the areas most directly affected by Britain's policies raises questions about the government's true motives. Not for the last time in its history, the United States appeared to be declaring war for one reason but fighting for quite another.

Given the United States' numerical preponderance, there were strong grounds for supposing that the war on land would be short and decisive. Half a million Canadians, the majority French and a good proportion of the remainder recently arrived refugees from south of the border, looked ill-equipped to resist a determined assault by a nation whose population was now approaching seven million. All that was needed, it seemed, was one determined push and the issue would be settled. What was overlooked was the United States' poor state of military preparedness and the determination of the Loyalists and the French to resist. The combination of Jeffersonian frugality and depleted revenues resulting from the embargo had reduced the United States regular army to a force of less than 7000 poorly trained troops. There were, of course, the state militias, but they were mostly unprepared for combat and in any case saw themselves as having an essentially defensive role. Opposing them were 12 000 Canadians, mostly militia, anxious to defend their territory, and willing to fight.

The result was a series of inconclusive battles as successive American armies marched to the Canadian border and were driven back in disarray. Towards the end of the war, with the arrival of seasoned troops from Europe, the British carried the struggle on to American soil and occupied a large swathe of northern Maine. The one major United States success in this northern sphere of operations was that of Captain Oliver Hazard Perry's fir-built frigates on Lake Erie, which caused the British to abandon the area they had captured around Detroit and fall back on a defensive line along the Niagara frontier. In the South, American forces fared scarcely better, failing to conquer Spanish Florida. Nevertheless, it was in the South that they won their greatest victory when an army under General Andrew Jackson routed the British in front of New Orleans. This triumph, however, was somewhat marred by the fact that it occurred some two weeks after the signing of the peace treaty.

As the British had no wish to re-enact the War of Independence, the only serious threat to the integrity of the United States arose out of internal opposition to the war. Militarily it was largely a peripheral affair. On the high seas the US Navy gave a good account of itself, inflicting significant damage on the British mercantile marine. Ship for ship, US frigates proved more than equal to those of the Royal Navy, but were eventually driven from the seas on account of Britain's sheer numerical superiority. That left the US coastline vulnerable to seaborne attack. In August 1814 a force of 4000 British troops entered the Chesapeake and captured Washington. President Madison fled the White House in such haste that a meal was left on the table, to which the British commanders helped themselves before setting light to the building. Having retreated to Georgetown, Madison and his cabinet looked on helplessly as the nation's new capital and naval yards went up in flames. The British, however, did not have it all their own way. Their subsequent attack on Baltimore was successfully repulsed, thereby providing inspiration for what eventually became the country's national anthem, Francis Scott Key's 'The Star-Spangled Banner'.[15]

The Treaty of Ghent, signed on Christmas Eve 1814, resolved none of the issues that had given rise to the conflict. The British had not sought the war and had no reason to regret its outcome, which simply restored the status quo ante bellum. Their concerns were in Europe. The Americans, on the other hand, had harboured greater ambitions and had cause for disappointment. Despite their numerical superiority they had failed to drive the British out of Canada. There had even been a moment late in the war when it looked as if their plans had miscarried to such an extent that the United States itself might be in danger of breaking up. This was in late 1814 when New England Federalists, meeting in Hartford, Connecticut, adopted a series of resolutions expressing New England's hostility to the war. Some extremists even spoke of secession. But by the time the Hartford delegates got to Washington news had arrived of the signing of the peace treaty and of Jackson's victory, so bringing these proceedings to an abrupt end.

Nothing was said in the Ghent Treaty about neutral rights or impressment, but as the Anglo-French struggles were now over these were no longer questions of immediate moment. Nor was anything done to resolve outstanding disagreements over fisheries and boundaries, although several such issues were referred to joint commissions for future settlement. As a follow-up to the Treaty of Ghent, the Convention of 1818 gave US citizens certain limited fishing rights off the Canadian coast, established the north-west boundary between Lake Superior and the Rocky Mountains at the 49th parallel, and stipulated that for the time being the virtually unoccupied territory west of the Rockies be left open to settlers of both nations.

The United States meanwhile held on to West Florida, the area between New Orleans and Pensacola, which it had occupied in 1813. This meagre acquisition was little consolation to those who had dreamed of vast new accessions. Nevertheless, as they recalled the doughty exploits of their naval officers on the Great Lakes and high seas and Jackson's resounding victory before New Orleans, they found cause for satisfaction. They had fought the world's leading military power, the one that had defeated Napoleon's forces at Trafalgar and Waterloo, and emerged, if not exactly triumphant, at least in a position no weaker than the one from which they started out. It was not all that had been hoped, but more than enough to give an additional fillip to their growing sense of national pride.

3 Political Rivalries and Cultural Affinities: 1815–1865

Economic Relations

Britain emerged from its long-drawn-out struggles with France reassured in its view of itself as the world's leading nation. Fears that the loss of her American colonies presaged the ending of its status as a great power had by 1815 long since evaporated. Unexpected and humiliating though that event had been, its effects were soon offset by the acquisition of a vast new empire in India. The population of the rebellious colonies at the time of the War of Independence had been a mere 4 million, whereas that of India was not much short of 150 million. The United States might be large in a geographical sense but its towns, cities and other human constructs were diminutive by comparison with those of India. Almost everything about the United States had a provisional, impermanent look about it, as if it was either in the process of construction or about to be pulled down. Early nineteenth-century drawings of New York, Philadelphia and other cities show a scattering of dockyards, warehouses, shops, churches and dwellings, built mostly of wood. Beyond the narrow coastal strip of settlement, seldom more than 150 miles wide, stretched thousands of miles of wilderness. America was raw and new, a land of wide-open spaces, its potential yet to be realised. India, by contrast, was an old civilisation, a continent swarming with people, made up of peasant farms, marble temples and busy cities. Nowhere in North America was there anything to compare with the gigantic fortresses of the Mogul Emperors, or, in terms of wealth, with its princely rulers and their retinues. The contemplation of the sheer grandeur of it all was enough to stir the national imagination. More important, India possessed precisely those attributes Britain's American colonies had lacked: a ready acceptance of distinctions of class and caste, a tradition of deference to authority, well-developed machinery for collecting taxes, professional standing armies, and a ruling class generally willing to accept British domination in return for protection. Here was a hierarchical society with layered gradations not unlike Britain's own, and as yet unfamiliar with troublesome notions about social contracts and natural rights.[1]

Meanwhile, in Britain itself, as one technical innovation led to another, the economy had begun to grow at an unprecedented rate. Britain was rich in coal and iron, the basic requirements of the emerging Steam Age. The result was a self-sustaining increase in productivity of a kind never previously experienced anywhere. A steam-driven loom had several hundred times the capacity of a hand-loom. Through improved methods of organising labour and by substituting mechanical power for muscle power, Britain succeeded in raising per capita output far above that of any other country. Horrendous though the working and living conditions of many workers were in the new factories and industrial towns that were springing up across the face of the land, this increase in productivity brought material benefits to the working population. Between 1815 and 1850 average real wages rose by 15 to 25 per cent.[2]

These technological advances strengthened Britain's already dominant position as a trading nation. Its mercantile marine, protected by the Royal Navy, freely navigated the oceans of the world, selling manufactured goods at prices that other producers were unable to match and bringing back the raw materials its industries needed. As a result, whole new industries like that of Lancashire cotton sprang up, while others such as Sheffield steel-making and Nottingham shoe manufacturing expanded mightily. So, too, did the demand for energy. By around 1860 Britain's consumption of coal, lignite and oil was five times that of its two closest economic rivals, Germany and the United States, and more than six times that of France.

By mid-century Britain was importing just under half of the world's raw cotton, the bulk of it from the United States. Thus the same capitalist forces that produced mushroom towns like Manchester and Bolton were transforming the American Deep South. Up to 1793, when Eli Whitney invented the cotton gin, America had exported little cotton, almost all of it being of the sea-island, long-stapled variety, growth of which was confined to the coastal regions of South Carolina and Georgia. Whitney's invention, a simple mechanism for separating out the seeds from the cotton fibre, transformed cotton production by making the cultivation of upland, or short-staple, cotton commercially viable. The effect was to give a new, frenetic quality to southern frontier expansion and an additional boost to the slave trade. Initially most of the slaves were brought directly from Africa, but after 1808, following Congress's banning of the traffic, they came largely from the Upper South, where the slave population was growing and tobacco cultivation either static or in decline.

British industry thus gave a powerful boost both to the traffic in slaves and to the development of the southern plantation system. To the extent that it represented an efficient means of mobilising labour the slave plantation was the Old South's counterpart of the British factory. Southern defenders of slavery drew attention to the parallel, contrasting the cradle-to-grave care they afforded their bondsmen with the mill owners' ruthless exploitation of their 'wage slaves'.[3] But leaving aside the question of moral equivalence, one thing that the two systems certainly had in common was that no other methods of production had been found that were capable of competing with them in terms of price and efficiency. There were parallels, too, in that each entailed a large-scale movement of labour and its concentration in particular geographical areas. This affected the two countries in unforeseen ways. In Britain it led to the creation of a proletarian working class wedded to ideas that would eventually transform the country's political system. In the United States it produced a massive shift of black population from the Upper South to the Gulf Coast and lower Mississippi Valley, a rapid increase in the value of capital tied up in the slave system, a growing intransigence on the part of the South's leaders, and an attempt at secession that almost destroyed the United States.

Cotton, however, was only one of the many factors binding the economies of the two countries together. In spite of political separation, territorial rivalry and war, ties between the two nations were, if anything, stronger in the mid-nineteenth century than they had been in colonial times. Mutual interests ensured that they took precedence over political and ideological disagreements. As an editorial in *The Times* put it on 4 July 1841:

> For all practical purposes the United States are far more closely united with this kingdom than any one of our colonies, and keep up a perpetual interchange of the most important good offices: taking our manufactures and our surplus population and giving us in return the materials of industry, of revenue and of life.

Britain was still the metropolitan power, providing the investment capital, technological know-how, manufactures, and much of the commercial enterprise, while the United States supplied the raw materials required by industry and, with the move towards free trade, a growing proportion of the nation's foodstuffs. Rather than being a simple trading relationship based on the exchange of goods, it entailed the exchange of what are commonly called 'factors of production', which is to say labour, capital, enterprise and technical expertise.

Gradually the impediments to these exchanges were removed. Until 1825, it was illegal for skilled artisans to emigrate or for industrial machinery to be exported from Britain. Such regulations, however, were difficult to enforce. Thereafter there was nothing to prevent American entrepreneurs availing themselves of British expertise, on occasion sending agents across the Atlantic with instructions to secure the services of workers with particular skills by offering them wages far above those they were currently receiving. Others took to importing and copying British machinery. Imported technology and skills thus played a crucial role in America's early industrial development. During the 1820s and 1830s, for example, Lancashire specialists were largely responsible for introducing calico printing into New England. British colliers played a similar role in opening up the resources of the Pennsylvania coalfields. As a visitor observed in 1848, 'The mining population of our Coal regions is almost exclusively composed of foreigners – principally from England and Wales, with a few Irish and Scotchmen.'[4] Up to mid-century and beyond, most of the techniques used in the wool and iron industries were modelled on those of Leeds and Sheffield.[5]

Obstacles to trade were meanwhile being gradually removed. In 1830 the United States finally gained full trading privileges in the British West Indies, allowing supplies of timber, flour and dried fish to go south to supply the plantation economies of the Caribbean, and of sugar and rum to be shipped northwards in return. US cotton had meanwhile replaced sugar as Britain's principal transatlantic import. With the removal of the hated Corn Laws, American wheat became a major commodity too, so that by 1860 King Corn was set to overtake King Cotton as America's principal export.[6] American import duties, sharply reduced in the 1830s, remained generally low throughout the period. Thus, American grain, cotton and tobacco poured into Britain, while a reverse flow of woollens, linens, ironware, books, journals, glassware, furniture and various luxury goods flowed westward to the United States. This was more than a mere two-way exchange. Others, too, were involved, notably the merchants of Latin American, the Caribbean and West Africa, whose trading systems were in turn linked to those of India and the Far East. Rather than being seen as separate economic entities, Britain and the United States might more properly be regarded as closely interrelated parts of a single fast-developing web of global credit and commercial enterprise, at the centre of which were the bankers, merchants and insurers of the City of London.

Whatever Americans might think of Britain – and the indications are that their attitudes were distinctly ambivalent – it remained the metropolitan power, and as such continued to influence their affairs in more ways than they cared to admit or perhaps were even aware.

Westward Expansion

Until the War of 1812, Native American hostility had prevented expansion into the trans-Appalachian West. Disappointing though the outcome of the war had been in other respects, Americans' campaigns against what they took to be Britain's Indian allies had succeeded in opening up the lands east of the Mississippi to settlement. Meanwhile, the

Table 3.1 Population of Britain and the United States, 1800–2000 (census figures in thousands)

	Britain	United States
1800	10500	5308
1810	11971	7240
1820	14092	9638
1830	16261	12866
1840	18534	17069
1850	20817	23192
1860	23128	31443
1870	26072	39818
1880	29710	50156
1890	33029	62948
1900	37000	75994
1910	40831	91972
1920	42769	105711
1930	44795	122775
1940	n/a	131669
1950	48854	150697
1960	51284	178464
1970	53979	204766
1980	54286	226500
1990	54889	248710
2000	55000*	281422

Note: *Estimated.
Sources: Central Statistical Office, *Annual Abstract of Statistics*; US Bureau of the Census, *Historical Statistics of the United States*.

United States had virtually doubled its geographical size by acquiring, through the Louisiana Purchase of 1803, a vast new region, extending from the Mississippi River to the Rocky Mountains.

So, with the way cleared and their new governmental system firmly in place, Americans turned their attention to exploring, mapping and occupying the West. By foot and on horseback through the Cumberland Gap, by barge and canoe along the Erie Canal and the waterways of the Ohio and Mississippi, by covered wagon across the prairies, settlers turned their backs on Europe and thronged westward, intent on developing their own continent's resources. Assisted by immigration and a high birth rate, the United States' population was doubling in every generation. By the 1840s, as Table 3.1 shows, it had overtaken Britain's. There was no telling where it would all end.

What was plain was that that Americans would not long rest content with the territories they had already acquired. Politics abhors a vacuum, and most of North America remained, if not unclaimed, at least unsettled. Although the term 'manifest destiny' was not coined until the 1840s, the idea that the United States was somehow singled out by Providence to occupy and develop the whole of the North American continent was familiar long before. That certainly seemed the way things were going. Spain and Portugal lost their possessions on the Latin American mainland in the aftermath of the Napoleonic Wars. Mexico declared its independence in 1821 and became a republic two years later, but, apart from a scattering of mission stations, the vast territories in the Southwest and Far West to which it laid claim remained largely unsettled. In its current state of economic and military decrepitude Mexico was plainly in no state either to develop them or to repel American encroachments. France was no longer a major player in New World affairs. Russia never had been a major player and its hold on remote Alaska, deriving from its interest in sea-otter pelts, was in any case tenuous. Britain alone had the energy and strength to resist United States expansionism and a motive for doing so.

In a sense Britain was merely employing in an American context what had traditionally been its policy towards Europe, which was to prevent the domination of the continent by any single power. In its wars with the Hapsburgs, and latterly with Napoleon, Britain had always been able to rely on the assistance of allies. In the Americas it had to act on its own. Not that British and American interests were entirely at odds. It was to America's advantage that Britain should continue to police the seas. Both powers welcomed the establishment of the independent republics of Latin America. The Monroe Doctrine of 1823 arose out of a suggestion by the British Foreign Secretary, George Canning, that Britain and the US issue a joint declaration to forestall any attempt at their reconquest. It was only the fear that a joint statement might be taken as implying that the two nations had equal authority in the hemisphere that, on the urging of his Secretary of State, John Quincy Adams, Monroe adopted a unilateral approach, warning that any attempt at recolonisation could not be viewed 'in any other light than as the manifestation of an unfriendly disposition toward the United States'. Quite what the United States would do in such an event was far from clear. The Doctrine did not prevent Britain's seizure of the Falkland Islands from Argentina in 1833. Only much later, with the United States' emergence as a major naval power, did the Doctrine assume significance. Meanwhile, however, there were other issues, some of them left over from the War of Independence, requiring settlement.

Territorial Rivalry

Most obviously there was the problem of agreeing on the boundary line separating US from British territory. That meant determining the ownership of the islands in the Bay of Fundy, the precise location of Maine's northern border, and, at the extreme north-west tip of the territory ceded to the US by Britain in 1783, the line connecting the western end of Lake Superior with the Lake of the Woods. More important in the long term, because it involved much larger areas of territory, was the problem of dividing up the still unsettled trans-Mississippi West, in particular that of determining the ownership of the Pacific Northwest.

Any one of these issues could have led to war. Indeed, there were moments when war seemed imminent. What gave rise to these crises, however, was not so much the intransigence of the two countries' negotiators as the impact of unforeseen events and the volatility of popular opinion. One such crisis arose as a result of a minor rebellion in 1837 in Upper Canada. The cause was twofold: French Canadian opposition to British rule, and the demand of Canadians of British stock for democratic institutions like those south of the border. Having been defeated by government forces, the rebels fled to Navy Island in the Niagara River where American sympathisers supplied them with food, arms and additional recruits. Like many Americans, upstate New Yorkers felt that a continuing British presence on their borders was unnatural, if not positively threatening. They were moved to fury, therefore, when, on the night of 29 December 1837, Canadian militia crossed the river, killing an

American and burning an American-owned steamer, *Caroline*, used for supplying the rebels. Troops were mobilised on both sides and there were American calls for an invasion of Canada. In Washington, the authorities reacted more calmly and the crisis passed, although its repercussions continued to bedevil Anglo-American relations for a number of years.[7]

In 1839 another conflict broke out, this time on the Maine–New Brunswick border, when lumberjacks clashed in disputed territory. An American land agent sent into the area with authority to expel the Canadians was promptly arrested by the New Brunswickers. Again, both sides mobilised for battle. Maine dispatched 10 000 militia to the border and Congress voted $10 million and agreed to a force of 50 000 men being mobilised. The so-called Aroostook War, however, proved a bloodless affair. General Winfield Scott, sent to negotiate on the United States' behalf, succeeded in persuading the New Brunswick authorities of the extreme danger of the situation. The two sides agreed to establish a joint commission whose findings served as a basis for the Webster–Ashburton Treaty of 1842.[8]

This agreement, made possible by a change of government in both countries, also laid to rest other outstanding issues that had arisen regarding America's north-eastern boundaries. The Maine–New Brunswick border was established in its present form by a sensible trade-off between the claims of the two powers. Adjustments were also made at the head of the Connecticut River, at the north end of Lake Champlain, on the Detroit River, and at the western end of Lake Superior. As noted in the previous chapter, the disagreements that might have arisen regarding the northern limits of the Louisiana Purchase, the area lying to the west of Lake Superior and east of the Rockies, had already been resolved by the Convention of 1818, which set the boundary at the 49th parallel. Thus, by 1842, there was a mutually agreed line dividing British from United States territory that extended all the way from the Atlantic to the Rocky Mountains.

That left the troublesome question of the Pacific Northwest, the area then known as Oregon, extending from the northern border of California to the southern border of Alaska. Following Spain and Russia's renunciation of their claims to this territory, Britain and the United States had agreed to leave it open to settlers of both countries in the expectation that time would determine where the boundary should be drawn. Unlike the situation further east, there initially appeared little chance of local complications as, apart from Native Americans and a few fur traders, the whole area was virtually devoid of population. In the early 1840s, however, this changed as American settlers began arriving by way of the Oregon Trail. For twenty years the United States had indicated its willingness to set the border at the 49th parallel, but the British had persistently refused the offer in the hope of staking a claim to the Columbia River basin.

The question acquired a new urgency with the election of James K. Polk, a fervent expansionist. In his 1845 annual message to Congress, Polk claimed the whole of Oregon right up to the Alaskan border for the United States, whereupon Americans took up the cry 'Fifty-four Forty or Fight' and Congress passed a resolution terminating joint occupation. Again it looked as if war was imminent. While these matters were pending, however, a war actually *did* break out, not with Britain, but with Mexico. While all this was happening, Britain took the unprecedented step of repealing its Corn Laws, thereby opening up its market to US grain exporters. Swayed by these events, Polk submitted a proposal to Congress based on the United States' original offer to extend the continental line along the 49th parallel, with the addition of Vancouver Island. Despite angry protests from expansionists, Congress agreed, and Britain, relieved that war had once again been averted, lost no time in accepting the proposal.

That did not quite put matters to rest. During the 1860s, hordes of American miners, only too ready to defy British authority, repeatedly swarmed northward into Canadian territory. In California, and elsewhere south of the border, they were accustomed to having their own way, and, as the areas where gold was discovered were generally remote and unsettled, neither state nor federal agents had hitherto felt much inclination to restrict their activities. This was characteristic of the way American expansion occurred. It was not, as was commonly the case with the British, a matter of the military leading the way and of traders and settlers following on behind. In America the impulse came primarily from individualistic frontiersmen in search of lands, timber, metals and other resources. To have prevented this movement was beyond the power of any central authority, certainly that of the Federal Government in far-away Washington. American expansion could thus be regarded as a natural, even democratic, process. It was not the American Government that was responsible but the American people responding to the call of Providence. Often those involved were violent and lawless, but however violent and lawless they were towards one another and the Native Americans they encountered, it hardly constituted a threat to United States interests, still less to American sovereignty.

This was very different from the experience of the British, whose imperial ambitions commonly involved imposing their authority on Ashantis,

Sikhs, Afghans and other indigenous peoples much more robust and numerous than the gold miners of California and the tribes of the American West. It also required defending their territories, often with inadequate resources, against rival colonising powers, including the United States. The defence of British imperial interests, in other words, was not something that could be left to settlers acting on their own initiative. It depended on imposing authority from above. Formidable though it appeared, the British Empire was a far more fragile construct than the American Republic.

When, therefore, American miners swarmed across the border in search of gold, beginning with the Fraser River stampede of 1857, police and troops were rushed to the area.[9] In British Colombia Governor James Douglas promptly took charge, delivering orders, one observer remarked, 'as if the machine of state could only be kept in motion by his delivering commands, with head erect, and with that rotund and peremptory utterance characteristic of British colonial officials'.[10] Not surprisingly, this led to friction. Yet, once Douglas and his subordinates had made plain their intention of maintaining British sovereignty and preserving law and order, the miners proved remarkably docile. As Douglas commented in a report to the British Colonial Secretary, 'The general feeling is in favour of English rule on Fraser's River, the people having a degree of confidence in the sterling uprightness and integrity of Englishmen, which they do not entertain for their own countrymen.'[11] Whatever the truth of this, there was less casual violence in Canada than was commonly the case south of the border. A generation later, when American miners invaded Canada's Northwest Territories, similar differences were observed. No American nineteenth-century law-enforcement agency enjoyed a reputation for honesty or efficiency to equal that of the largely British-manned Canadian Northwest Mounted Police.[12]

British Views of America, American Views of Britain

From the viewpoint of the likes of Governor Douglas, American lawlessness and violence were hardly cause for wonder. Liberty and licence were two sides of the same coin. Frederick Marryat, the former sea captain and writer of popular novels, who visited the United States in 1837, attributed both to the Federal Government's inability to guarantee 'that adequate punishment for vice so necessary to uphold the morals of a people'.[13] What surprised Tories like Marryat was not American lawlessness but that the United States did not descend into total anarchy. The events of the French Revolution had engraved themselves on the consciousness of the British upper class as incontrovertible evidence of what happened when liberty was given free sway. To be sure, nothing so startling had as yet occurred in the United States. Nevertheless, to those who took it as axiomatic that a well-ordered society depended on the impulses of its lower orders being held in check by the propertied and well-educated classes, Jacksonian America could not but appear disorderly and vulgar. They disapproved of the familiarity with which they were accosted by total strangers, American politicians' way of appealing to the sympathies of the multitude, the tone of the popular press, the lack of social refinement, not to mention Americans' offensive habit of chewing tobacco and spitting in public – all of which, as they saw it, bore testimony to the topsy-turvy principles by which the country was governed.[14]

Their disapproval is hardly surprising, given that Jacksonian politics were based on the proposition that America's history was a continuing struggle by the common man against just such people as themselves. It was, as Jacksonians saw it, a struggle that had begun with the overthrow of British rule and continued ever since in the form of resistance to office-holders, rich merchants, land speculators, bankers, supporters of the American Whig Party and anyone else claiming privileged status or assuming attitudes of superiority in the way the British had formerly done.[15]

What condescending Tories commonly failed to note, however, was the extent to which democratic principles actually contributed to social stability – a point that more astute commentators like Alexis de Tocqueville were quick to grasp.[16] A political and social system that reflected the wishes of a majority was less likely to suffer from political instability than one dedicated to preserving the privileges of a minority. Tocqueville, who toured the country shortly before Marryat, believed that he could detect in America's present a prefiguration of Europe's own future, America being the most advanced example to date of a long-term democratic revolution that was sweeping the West, and had triumphed earlier there because it encountered less in the way of entrenched interests. Marryat took a contrary view. According to Marryat, 'the experiment has been made and it has failed'.[17]

As always, what observers found depended very much on the assumptions with which they started out. To British radicals of Marryat's generation, the America of the Age of Jackson was an unfailing inspiration. Their demands for the reform of British society were shot through with references to American achievements. To Jeremy Bentham, whose vision was unclouded by first-hand experience of life in America, the United States was a land where 'all is democracy; all is regularity, tranquillity, prosperity, security . . . no aristocracy; no monarchy; all that dross evaporated'.[18] In speeches, pamphlets and newspaper articles, reformers constantly cited the American example as proof of the practicality of the measures they advocated. The People's Charter was essentially a proposal to reorganise British politics along American lines by introducing universal manhood suffrage, biennial elections, secret ballots and equal electoral districts. As the movement's journal, *The Charter*, put it, 'The inhabitants of the United States are governed on the principles of Chartism, the consequence of which is that all legislation is bent towards the welfare of the many, and not of the few.'[19] America was ruled by the people, as opposed to 'a few hundred land robbers, and a few thousand profit-mongers, with the addition of a gilded, powerless, puppet, dubbed Queen'.[20]

In Britain, as in Europe generally, these were highly subversive views. The early nineteenth century was a time of political reaction. Yet political rigidity, as the French experience had also shown, also had its dangers. The British prided themselves on their pragmatism. The answer was to find ways of managing change. Prior to 1832 approximately one adult male Englishman in twelve had the right to vote. More to the point, because of political patronage and the outdated distribution of parliamentary seats, roughly half of the members of the House of Commons were not in any meaningful sense elected at all, simply being appointed by whatever local patron controlled the seat. The most that could be said for such a system was that it worked after a fashion. Responding to intense political pressure, the Whig Government in 1832 changed it by passing Great Reform Bill, abolishing the rotten boroughs and enfranchising portions of the middle class.

But milestone though this was in British political history, in terms of political representation it still left Britain lagging far behind the United States, where by the 1830s most states had already moved from representation on the basis of taxpaying and property owning to universal white manhood suffrage. Viewed from across the Atlantic, Britain could not but appear politically antiquated. Most Americans, of course, had never visited Britain, but that did not prevent them from having strong views, including a deep-rooted aversion to what they regarded as Britain's dominant traits, namely upper-class snobbery and lower-class subservience. These were qualities which, so they believed, Britain had attempted to foist on to America. Their national existence had begun with the rejection of the principles of hierarchy and hereditary privilege, along with notions of government as something imposed from above. They were citizens, not subjects; the authority their government exercised came from the people, not from someone set above them. Theirs was, as Lincoln famously put it in his Gettysburg Address of 1863, a 'government of the people, by the people, for the people'. No fourth of July celebration would have been complete without a denunciation of British tyranny. America, in short, was what Britain was not, a land of the free. To be American in the full sense virtually required a display of Anglophobia.

Yet in this, as in many other respects, American views were far from consistent. Among the more literate and educated there was a keen awareness of the nation's cultural debt to Britain. 'See what books fill our libraries', observed Emerson. 'Every book we read, every biography, play, or romance, in whatever form, is still English history and manners.'[21] Southerners, who liked to think of themselves as descended from the seventeenth-century Cavaliers (unlike New Englanders, whom they claimed were descendants of the Roundheads), were entranced by Sir Walter Scott's tales of medieval chivalry. Dickens's readers gathered on the dockside to learn the fate of Little Nell (much as British viewers of *Dallas* a century and a half later awaited news of who shot JR). Despite their views of the British as corrupt, decadent and weighed down by obsolete institutions, Americans remained remarkably sensitive to British criticism. They were stung by Frances Trollope's *Domestic Manners of the Americans* (1832), not surprisingly, as the burden of her account was to show that Americans *had* no manners. Plainly, she had a sharp eye for people's shortcomings. But to compare the manners of Cincinnati, then little more than a frontier town, with those of English polite society was hardly fair. Had she chosen Oldham or Sunderland rather than London high society as her point of comparison her findings would doubtless have been different. Nevertheless, Americans took her strictures to heart. When Dickens himself visited the United States ten years later and reported less than flatteringly on what he observed, they were similarly nettled.[22]

Their eagerness for British approval may be attributed to a sense of insecurity, for despite their brash claim to lead the world on account of having discovered the only true basis for government, there were things the country patently lacked, among them ancient institutions and a long-established culture. This could, of course, be seen as an advantage. Starting anew, it could be claimed, freed them from the detritus of history. Theirs would be a purer society, purged of the folly, tyranny and corruption of the Old World. Yet they were in the fortunate position of being able to have it both ways. Noah Webster, the author of the first American dictionary, believed that what the English dismissed as vulgar Americanisms were, in fact, correct seventeenth-century usages. As a new nation, he claimed, the United States was in the fortunate position of being able to adopt a standard form of English more in accord with its historical roots than the debased version currently spoken by Englishmen.[23]

Admirable though such notions were in theory, many were attracted to the Old World precisely because it was a treasure house of historical lore and legend. As citizens of a new nation, born of the Enlightenment and based on rational principles, created in the full light of historical day, they were uneasily aware that certain things were wanting, most notably a sense of a past rooted in the land they trod. America was a land of the present and the future, a busy society of farmers and homesteaders, of engineers and labourers, of bankers and lawyers. Its great days lay ahead. Its past, however, was in Europe. Particularly for writers and artists of a romantic disposition – and this was, after all, the Romantic period – America's lack of ancient legends, ivy-covered ruins and tales of historical wrong raised questions as to whether the New World possessed materials enough to be worthy of their and their readers' attention. As compared with what Europe had to offer, life in America was raw, thin, everyday. Admirable though hard work and enterprise were as governing principles, a society dedicated wholly to their service provided little nourishment for the spirit and imagination. As Henry James later commented with regard to Hawthorne, 'his sense of the life of his fellow mortals would have been almost infinitely more various' had he been born into the 'denser, richer, warmer' society of Europe, because 'it takes such an accumulation of history and custom, such a complexity of manners and types, to form a fund of suggestion for the novelist'.[24]

Aspiring American painters like Gilbert Stuart and Benjamin West had travelled to Europe in the eighteenth century, both to learn their trade and establish reputations that would stand them in good stead when they returned home.[25] Writers followed in their footsteps. Washington Irving set sail for England in 1815 and spent the next 17 years regaling his fellow countrymen with picturesque vignettes of places and events illustrative of the life and history of the Old World. He described London, Oxford, Stratford-upon-Avon and Edinburgh, incidentally establishing itineraries which American tourists have continued to follow up to the present day. Dark satanic mills did not feature in his account, nor did informed comment on the social and political issues of the time. Factory acts, poor-law legislation, municipal reform acts, public health acts, the reports of parliamentary commissions, virtually everything that characterised what we now call the 'Age of Reform', were passed over. Instead, the image that he and his successors, of whom there have been many, projected was of a bucolic nation steeped in the traditions of the past, a land of castles, cathedrals, roast beef, village greens and country squires – in short, a land that was in almost every respect the antithesis of the United States. This fitted in precisely with Americans' preconceived notions, for if the United States represented the future, it logically followed that Britain stood for the past.[26]

Americans were thus presented with a highly inaccurate image of a nation that had lately defeated Napoleon and was pioneering the application of steam power to industrial production. If the shape of the future was to be seen anywhere, it was surely in Britain. At some level, of course, Americans could not but be aware of this in that they depended on it for their manufactures and investment capital. Yet, for all that, the notion of Britain as a backward-looking nation remained entrenched in Americans' consciousness. When Redburn, in Herman Melville's novel of that name, arrives in Liverpool with an old gazetteer given him by his father he is astonished to find that European cities were no more unchanging than American ones. Americans were similarly surprised when Queen Victoria and Prince Albert announced Britain's intention of mounting the Great Exhibition of 1851 as a celebration of the world's achievements in the fields of commerce, industry and science. It was preposterous, noted the *New York Herald*, to think that a country

> overwhelmed with a national debt of a magnitude almost beyond compilation, with a government of the most expensive description, with a nest of non-producers in the shape of aristocrats, eating away at its vitality, with corruption pervading every fibre and muscle of the body politic can compete with a young, vigorous, athletic republic like the United States.[27]

In the event, the United States failed to fill the area allocated to it in the Crystal Palace, giving rise to a certain amount of jocularity concerning 'America's wide open spaces'.[28]

Whether the British were any better informed as to the character of Americans is questionable. Accounts by returning visitors attributed them with practically every trait under the sun. Often these were merely different ways of describing the same thing, as when what some praised as Americans' directness others viewed as their impertinence. More perhaps than in the case of American visitors to Britain, their comments reflected their individual idiosyncrasies and personalities rather than the need to perpetuate a national myth. There were, however, certain things on which British visitors agreed, among them the generosity of Americans' hospitality, the flimsiness of their wooden architecture, their lack of servants, their energy, the absence of visible signs of poverty, their commercial enterprise and their universal concern with 'getting ahead'. When Anthony Trollope toured the States he was at pains to make amends for his mother's acerbic comments a generation earlier, but few British observers, or American for that matter, would have taken issue with his description of what he saw as being not only New York's but the nation's 'pre-eminently American' characteristics:

> Free institutions, general education, and the ascendancy of dollars are the words written on every paving stone along Fifth Avenue, down Broadway, and up Wall Street. Every man can vote, and values the privilege. Every man can read, and uses the privilege. Every man worships the dollar, and is down before his shrine from morning to night.[29]

British men and women visited the early republic for a variety of reasons. Some went on business. Frequently this gave rise to close personal and family relationships. The Webster–Ashburton Treaty of 1842 owed much to the fact that Lord Ashburton was head of Baring Brothers, a British merchant bank very much at the centre of US economic affairs. Prior to becoming Secretary of State, Webster had on occasion acted on its behalf. Frances Trollope was one of many who went to the United States with the intention of starting up a new enterprise. In her case it was in the hope of recouping her family's failing fortunes by selling British novelties to Midwesterners. This having proved a dismal failure, she turned the experience to her advantage by writing up her impressions. Her travelling companion, Frances Wright, who gave a much more favourable account, was a wealthy young radical who on an earlier visit had established an experimental colony in Tennessee, Nashoba, with a view to creating a way of life more in accord with her ideals. But this also proved a disappointment. By the time she and Mrs Trollope got there, Nashoba was on its last legs, beginning to sink back into the malarial swamp from which it had arisen.[30] Dickens later used the episode as a basis for his account of Eden, the snake-infested wilderness in which Martin Chuzzlewit unwisely invests.

Dickens set out with the specific intention of writing a travel book. In preparation for his journey he read Mrs Trollope's and other English travellers' accounts, attributing their unfavourable impressions to their having started out with their minds already made up. A trenchant critic of British society, he had long admired America from afar. He arrived, therefore, fully expecting to like what he found. He was much impressed by Boston's public and benevolent institutions and the civic effort that had gone into their creation. But soon his relations with his hosts turned sour. One reason was the United States' refusal to subscribe to international copyright conventions. Although he had many American readers, he derived no income from them. One Philadelphia publisher, Mathew Carey, went so far as to hire fast sailing boats to intercept incoming ships so that he could rush out his pirated editions a few hours before his rivals. Pirating also made it difficult for American writers to find publishers when the works of top British authors could be had for free. Dickens spoke frequently on the subject, not only on his own behalf but on that of authors in general, and was duly vilified in the press. In spite of his efforts, this remained a contentious issue until the Chace Act of 1891 made pirating illegal.[31]

What Dickens found most disillusioning, however, was the contrast between the nation's radiant ideals and its actual performance. The longer he stayed the more he found the crowds that flocked to see him vulgar and intrusive. American politics, so far as he could tell, were based on trickery, immorality and corruption. A British radical visiting America hoping to have his beliefs confirmed, he noted in 1842, would be apt to return home a Tory. 'I am a Lover of Freedom, disappointed – that's all. This is not the republic I came to see; this is not the republic of my imagination.'[32]

He had originally planned to stay a year; instead he returned after less than six months. His promised travel book, *American Notes* (1842), was by his standards a perfunctory performance. The real fruit of his trip appeared a year later in the form of *Martin Chuzzlewit* (1843–44), a scourging attack on all the things he most disliked about America – the gutter press, tobacco chewing, boosterism, dodgy business practices, an excessive sensitivity to public opinion, boastfulness, and, overshadowing it all, a sense of spiritual emptiness. As Dickens's travellers on their way back to England discuss how they would want to redesign the American Eagle, one of them comments: 'I should want to draw it like a Bat, for its short-sightedness; like a Bantam, for its bragging; like a Magpie for its honesty; like a Peacock, for its vanity; like an Ostrich, for putting its head in the mud and thinking nobody sees it.'[33] Not all visitors, however, were quite so severe in their comments. Dickens himself on a later visit sought to make amends by paying tribute to Americans' hospitality, their manly directness and other admirable qualities, and by noting how much the country had changed for the better since he was last there.

Abolitionist Empire versus Slave Republic

There was, however, one American institution that British commentators united in condemning, namely slavery. Slavery was abolished in the British Empire in 1834. Popular opinion had been mobilised against it half a century earlier. The fact that the British saw slavery as incompatible with liberty made its continued existence in the United States, supposedly the land of liberty, appear not merely incongruous, but grotesque. Dickens devoted the final chapter of *American Notes* to quotations largely culled from the leading abolitionist tract of the period, Theodore Dwight Weld's *American Slavery As It Is* (1839), quoting advertisements for runaway slaves, bloodthirsty threats against abolitionists and accounts of the branding, whipping and mutilation reprinted from the southern press expressed in such a matter-of-fact way as to indicate that such barbarities were an accepted feature of life in the slave states. The fact that slavery was allowed in Washington, DC cast doubt on the genuineness of the American enterprise as a whole. The point was aptly made by the poet Thomas Moore on a visit to Washington in 1804, where he watched slave gangs at work on the nation's new Capitol:

> Who can, with patience, for a moment see
> The medley mass of pride and misery,
> Of whips and charters, manacles and rights,
> Of slaving blacks and democratic whites,
> And all the piebald misery that reigns,
> In free confusion o'er Columbia's plains?[34]

Americans themselves were aware of the contradiction. From the eighteenth century on, the two nations' anti-slavery efforts were closely intertwined. In fact, it was in response to an 1783 petition from the Quakers of Philadelphia that the first British anti-slavery committee was formed. For the British, whose economy was less dependent on slavery and whose slaves were conveniently located overseas, emancipation constituted less of a problem than for Americans. Thus, it was they who initially led the way. By the 1830s, triumphant at having overthrown first the slave trade and then colonial slavery, British abolitionists looked to ways of extending their crusade to the United States. With the introduction of steamships, transatlantic travel was now much easier than in the days of sail.[35] In 1840 and 1843 they organised World Anti-Slavery Conventions, to which the increasingly militant American movement, eager to learn the methods used and for the blessing of Britain's leading reformers, sent sizeable delegations. The British, in turn, sent lecturers to the United States, bombarding their American colleagues with advice and collecting money on their behalf. Whether this helped or hindered is hard to say. The visit of George Thompson, an itinerant British lecturer, invited to the United States by William Lloyd Garrison on account of the sterling work he had done in Britain, provoked a warning from Andrew Jackson about 'foreign emissaries' sent to America's shores to stir up trouble. American abolitionists, in turn, toured Britain. Because of the popularity of *Uncle Tom's Cabin*, Harriet Beecher Stowe's visit attracted enormous popular attention. Although gratified to be lionised, the outbursts of anti-American sentiment provoked by her visit made her uneasy. Undoubtedly some of it was a tit-for-tat response to American criticism of Britain, but in part, too, it expressed public outrage at American hypocrisy. More importantly, it reflected a conviction that it was Britain's peculiar responsibility to rid the world of slavery. Whatever the sins of the past, the world could be assured that henceforth freedom would flourish wherever the Union Jack unfurled – a belief that later proved useful way of justifying some of the nation's otherwise morally dubious imperial ventures.[36]

Slavery, of course, had been an issue in Anglo-American relations long before the British emancipated their slaves. In the negotiations following the War of Independence, Britain refused American requests to return or pay compensation for the slaves who had fought on Britain's behalf. Some 3000 former bondsmen fled to Nova Scotia with the retreating British forces, most of whom were later settled in Sierra Leone. In the negotiations following the War of 1812 Britain again clashed with the United States having refused to pay for Chesapeake slaves swept up by the invasion force that burned the Capitol and White House.

These episodes, however, were soon forgotten. Much more destructive of good relations was the United States' persistent sabotaging of Britain's efforts to suppress the Atlantic slave trade. By coincidence, both countries had withdrawn from the trade in 1807–08. This had important implications from the point of view of Americas' future internal development and racial balance. It was the British, however, who had been the principal carriers of slaves, and, as the defenders of the trade had warned, their withdrawal served as an invitation to others to take their place. Besides offending moral sensibilities, the ability of planters elsewhere to go on importing slaves directly from Africa put Britain's own planters at a disadvantage. Britain accordingly set about negotiating agreements requiring the world's other maritime powers to follow its example, demanding as a surety that the Royal Navy be allowed to search, detain and arraign before international courts vessels suspected of violations. This the United States, still smarting from Britain's high-handed treatment during the French Wars, adamantly refused to do, with the result that much of the latter-day slave trade was conducted under the American flag. Slave ships were regularly seen outfitting in New York and other northern ports. Some were American-owned, but most were of indeterminate nationality, armed nevertheless with American ships' papers, copies of which could be acquired, at a price, from the American consul in Havana, and doubtless from US consuls elsewhere. Few of the slaves carried under American colours ended up in the United States, the majority going to Cuba and Brazil.

There was, however, one case involving the transporting of slaves in a bona fide American vessel over which Britain and the United States found themselves at diplomatic loggerheads. In 1842 the USS *Creole*, sailed from Hampton Roads, Virginia, bound for New Orleans with a cargo of 135 slaves. The United States' withdrawal from the Atlantic slave trade had not affected the internal trade in slaves, so this voyage, even though it entailed transportation by sea, was perfectly legal from the US point of view. The problem arose because, not long into the voyage, the slaves seized the ship, killed one of their owners, and forced the crew to sail to Nassau in the Bahamas. The US government demanded the return of the slaves as American property. British and American abolitionists responded by arguing that the mutineers were justified in what they had done and so could not be extradited either as slaves or as felons. The Nassau authorities hanged those responsible for the killing, but freed the others. As the Foreign Secretary, Lord Aberdeen, explained, 'when slaves were found within the British jurisdiction, by whatever means or from whatever quarters, they were *ipso facto* free'.[37] The case, which aroused a good deal of controversy on both sides of the Atlantic, was eventually settled by a mixed claims commission awarding the United States the not inconsiderable sum of $110 330 compensation.[38]

Because of Congress's pro-slavery and anti-British sympathies, the US Navy, in spite of legislation forbidding US citizens form engaging in the trade, was largely inactive. Not until the 1860s, following Lincoln's election and the advent of an anti-slavery Congress, were the two navies permitted to undertake effective joint action. To drive home the message that the new administration's attitude was different from that of its predecessors, laws on the statute books were for the first time implemented. On 7 February 1862, a slaver captain, Nathaniel Gordon, convicted of slave trading on the Congo, was hanged in New York.[39] That April, a formal Anglo-American agreement, ostensibly put forward at the United States' suggestion but in fact at Britain's, prepared the way for the final elimination of a traffic that had lasted more than 300 years.[40]

Less serious than America's recalcitrance over the slave trade, but also annoying to Britain, was the requirement of southern states that British black seamen be detained in prison while their vessels were in port. These so-called Negro Seamen's Laws reflected southerners' fear that black visitors would spread subversive ideas or assist runaways. As the seamen were lodged at the expense of ships' captains, there were cases of captains decamping with their debts unpaid, leaving British-born subjects to be sold into slavery, ostensibly to cover the cost of their temporary lodgement. Protests to the US Secretary of State got nowhere as these were deemed state rather than federal matters. Consuls in the various ports were accordingly instructed to raise the issue with the individual states. As a consequence of this decidedly unorthodox approach it was eventually agreed that black seamen would no longer be gaoled providing they remained aboard their vessels.[41]

The slavery issue also affected Britain's continuing struggle to contain American expansion. When Texas broke away from Mexico in 1836 to become an independent republic Britain saw an opportunity both of curbing American expansion and establishing an alternative source for cotton. American and British abolitionists were optimistic that, in return for British loans and recognition, Texas would agree to do away with slavery. Given the Texans' wish to be annexed to the United States and the South's eagerness for more land, this seemed unlikely. But even the remote prospect of a free-soil Texas on America's southern borders, particularly if it were beholden to Britain for trade and capital, was enough to alarm the US Congress. When British and American abolitionists went as a delegation from the 1843 World Anti-Slavery Convention to urge Lord Aberdeen, the Foreign Secretary, to use his influence with the Texans, they played into the hands of southern annexationists. Aberdeen was too shrewd to commit himself. But Ashbel Smith, the Texan chargé d'affaires in London, sent highly exaggerated accounts of abolitionist skulduggery to his opposite number in Washington, who ensured that they were given a wide circulation. So far as southern opinion was concerned, the damage was done.[42] What finally tipped the scales in favour of Texan annexation, however, was not this episode but the election, in 1844, of the avowedly expansionist presidential candidate James K. Polk. Congress interpreted the result as a popular endorsement of Polk's policies and agreed to annexation even before he took office.

Up to that time the principal obstacle to annexation had been the likelihood of war with Mexico. When, following Texas's annexation, war duly did break out, Britain remained neutral. Apart from standing firm in Canada there was not much Britain could do to curb America's hemispheric ambitions. In 1850 the two countries concluded the Clayton–Bulwer Treaty, agreeing not to colonise any part of Central America and pledging equal access to any trans-isthmian ship canal should one be constructed. When, however, American freebooters subsequently occupied Nicaragua, Britain took no action. As Benjamin Disraeli explained, if Britain 'is to regard every expansion of the United States as an act detrimental to her interests and hostile to her power, we shall be pursuing a course . . . of a disastrous character'.[43] The truth was that by the 1850s the British had pretty much reconciled themselves to thinking that sooner or later the United States was destined to overrun Cuba, most of Central America, Hawaii and much else besides. They simply had to put a good face on the matter. Short of declaring war there was nothing else they could do, and, given Canada's vulnerability and the need for corn and cotton, war was hardly an option.

The Civil War

Southerners had been threatening to secede for so long that when they finally did so the British were caught unprepared. It was only when news arrived of battles and losses that the significance of what was occurring began to sink in. Many had mixed feelings. On the one hand they were appalled at scale of the slaughter; on the other, it was hard not to experience a thrill of satisfaction at America's discomfiture. For as long as they could remember they had endured the taunts of the United States and its admirers, and yet here it was tearing itself apart while Britain basked in peace and prosperity. It was a particular source of satisfaction to those who had argued all along that liberalism and democracy were no substitute for traditional notions of authority. Perhaps comparisons between the American and French revolutions had not been so far-fetched after all.

There was also good reason to think that a divided North America would be to Britain's advantage. If it broke in two it would be possible to play one part off against another. Conceivably, like the former Spanish Empire in Latin America, it would fragment into many pieces, in which case the opportunity for commercial penetration would be all the greater. In short, viewed from across the Atlantic, there were reasons for celebration as well as regret over what was happening.

Of more immediate concern, however, were worries over the impact of the war on Britain's economy. The principal issue was cotton, some 80 per cent of which traditionally came from the southern states. Without cotton the mills of Lancashire would come to a halt. Foreseeing this, Southerners had placed great faith in what they called 'King Cotton Diplomacy'. In the early months of the war, well before the North's blockade became effective and in spite of their need for funds with which to buy armaments, cotton exports were embargoed. This was done with the intention of creating a cotton famine that would bring Britain into the conflict. For want of cotton, so the argument ran, Lancashire would face ruin, workers would be laid off, and social unrest would reach unmanageable proportions. Confronted with the possibility of revolution, the British government would have no alternative but to authorise naval intervention, thereby initiating a train of events that would lead to war with the Union and southern independence.

What southerners failed to take into account were Britain's increasing dependence on northern grain and the large stocks of raw cotton already in British warehouses. The 1850s had been bumper years for cotton growers. Far from being ruined, the owners of these stocks had only to wait to see their wealth grow. That, however, was not the only problem. As cotton prices soared, so, too, did the incentive for obtaining supplies from elsewhere. British and American abolitionists had long dreamed of undercutting the South's plantation economy by importing free-grown cotton from India and Egypt. The difficulty had always been that American slave-grown cotton was the cheapest on the market. But now that it was no longer available and prices were rising other possibilities arose. As for the Lancashire cotton workers, there was little they could do but wait and hope things would improve. Many were laid off, but without parliamentary representation they lacked political influence. Their sympathy for the Union, memorably expressed in the famous Manchester

Working Men's 1863 'Address to President Lincoln', would long be remembered on both sides of the Atlantic. A statue of Lincoln, presented in the name of the American people, still stands in the centre of Manchester.[44]

Britain's avowedly anti-slavery principles affected attitudes less than might have been expected. In part this was because, initially at least, emancipation was not one of the Union's aims. But, even after Lincoln had made his intentions in that respect clear, the British response was lukewarm and in some cases positively hostile. In October 1862, according to *The Times*,

> Mr. Peacock, M. P. for North Essex, said at Colchester that the Emancipation Proclamation, even if it had been in the interests of the negro, would have been a political crime; but as . . . it was merely a vindictive measure of spite and retaliation upon nine millions of whites struggling for their independence, it was one of the most devilish acts of fiendish malignity which the wickedness of man could ever have conceived.[45]

Peacock shared the commonly-held view that southerners were a courageous minority fighting for their political freedom and that emancipation was a last desperate attempt by a defeated North to reverse the course of events by instigating a slave rebellion. Memories of the Indian Mutiny were still vivid in people's minds, as were the legendary horrors of the 1790s slave uprising in Haiti. The situation in the southern states was, of course, quite different, but the war was practically over before images of brutal slave uprisings and ruthless white retaliation ceased to haunt British imaginations. Many also shared Peacock's view of the war as a struggle for independence. Liberal opinion had supported Hungary, and more recently Lombardy, in seeking to break away from the Austro-Hungarian Empire. The Confederacy's case, many supposed, was much the same as that of the American colonists 80 years before. Above all, there was a widespread assumption that the Union was doomed, and that the North was therefore guilty of prolonging Americans' sufferings to no good purpose.[46]

From a strategic point of view there were good reasons for remaining neutral. As always, Canada remained a hostage to Britain's good behaviour. Since the War of 1812, the demographic balance had shifted decisively in favour of the United States. There was little chance that a second assault on Canada, led, as it presumably would be, by battle-hardened troops, could be withstood. The US Navy, of course, was no match for the Royal Navy, the strength of which approximately equalled that of all the other navies of the world combined, but even in that regard there were signs of the advantage having shifted.

Nevertheless, there were moments when it looked as if Britain would be sucked into the conflict. The first occurred in November 1861 when a Union warship intercepted the British steamer *Trent* off the Bahamas and removed James M. Mason and John Slidell, two Confederate representatives on their way to Europe for the purpose of drumming up support for the South. This was at a time when the North, reeling from a succession of defeats, desperately needed something to bolster its morale. Northerners greeted news of the emissaries' capture with demonstrations of wild excitement. Furious at America's high-handed behaviour, Britain demanded the agents' release. Given that the United States' offence was to do what Britain had made a practice of doing (and would do again in the two world wars), the situation was ironic. Unaccustomed to having their maritime supremacy challenged, however, the irony, was lost on the British, who insisted that the United States apologise and release the emissaries forthwith. The Royal Navy was put on the alert and preparations made to despatch reinforcements to Canada. For a moment, it looked like war. Eventually, however, Lincoln's cabinet saw the absurdity of fighting Great Britain as well as the Confederacy and released the pair, who proceeded on their way having come closer to realising the object of their mission than they were ever to do again.

This was the nearest the British came to intervening, although it was not the only time the two nations found themselves at loggerheads, the British now claiming the privileges traditionally accorded to neutrals and the United States the right to seize vessels suspected of trading with the enemy. Irritated though the British were by the North's blockade, the anger it aroused scarcely compared with northerners' fury over Britain's building of Confederate privateers to prey on American shipping. The most notorious of these raiders, the *Alabama*, was responsible for the sinking of no less than 64 Union vessels in the course of the war. Strictly speaking, there were no legal grounds for a neutral preventing a vessel being *built* for purposes of hostile operations against a friendly power, providing it was not actually *equipped* for that purpose.[47] In practice, however, the cruisers were not only built and equipped in Britain, but largely manned by British seamen. This gave credence to the widely-held belief of northerners that Britain was conniving with the rebels in seeking to dismember the United States. As will be shown in the next chapter, the

depredations of the Confederate cruisers left a bitter legacy that bedev-
illed Anglo-American relations for many years thereafter.

Although British opinion remained divided, once the war was over few
regretted its outcome. The triumph of the Union represented a triumph
for liberal nationalism, not only in North America but in the West generally. The South fought in defence of slavery and of a static, hierarchical
concept of society; the North in support of a more flexible, democratic
social order. In his supreme moment at Gettysburg, Lincoln said that the
struggle was about much more than whether the United States would
remain a single entity; it was about whether the principles of liberty on
which the nation was founded should 'not perish from the earth'. Since
the collapse of the European revolutionary movements of 1848, liberal
causes had been in retreat. By fusing together the two great forces of the
nineteenth century, liberalism and nationalism, and showing that a
nation that upheld them could survive a long and bloody civil war,
Americans had demonstrated that, contrary to what had been supposed,
democracy could be a major source of strength.[48] That, at least, was the
conclusion drawn by William Ewart Gladstone, the British Liberal
leader. As the war progressed, he noted that it had released 'a kind of vol-
canic energy not yet suspected to exist'.[49] Years later, speaking in support
of the 1884 Reform Bill, he attributed the North's victory to the fact that
'every capable citizen was enfranchised, and had a direct and energetic
interest in the well-being and unity of the State'.[50] What the Civil War
showed, he went on to argue, was that liberal democracy could be justified, not only on moral grounds in that it promoted freedom and equality,
but as a means of augmenting the power of the nation.

4 Rapprochement: 1866–1914

Economic Developments

The British Empire of the later nineteenth century was an imposing sight. By 1900 it had grown to immense proportions, embracing nearly a quarter of the world's land surface and almost one-third of its inhabitants. Not even Spain at the height of its glory had exercised control over so broad a swathe of the world's peoples. It was, of course, an empire acquired and maintained largely by force. From Waterloo until the outbreak of the First World War there was scarcely a time when British troops or their British-officered colonial auxiliaries were not in action somewhere around the globe. On occasion, as in the Boer War, they found their resources stretched. Yet for the most part these were low-cost affairs involving what would now be called Third-World peoples, and as such very different from those long-drawn-out conflicts between Great Powers that bring about major changes in the international order. Compared to the centuries that preceded and followed it, the nineteenth century, so far as the British were concerned, was a period of relative equilibrium. For the most part they were more concerned with following Adam Smith's advice and expanding commerce than acquiring vast territories, yet one thing led to another, and often it was easier simply to extend their rule than cope with troublesome neighbours or fend off rivals.

Extending their rule was facilitated by recent advances in transportation, medicine and weaponry, which had transformed the balance of power between Europeans and the rest of the world. Thanks to steamers, quinine and breech-loading weapons, Britain could undertake expeditions and assume responsibilities that a century earlier would have been deemed not merely imprudent, but wholly impossible.[1] Behind its imperial forays, therefore, lay the same mastery of science and machine technology that had made it the world's workshop and laboratory. Long before the closing years of the nineteenth century, when for a brief interval imperialism became a popular cause, the British had prided themselves on their enterprise and inventiveness. John Bull, like his nineteenth-century American counterpart, Brother Jonathan, was neither an aristocrat nor an imperialist, but a practical-minded figure. The wonders of the early Victorian age were the railways and steamships, the cast-iron bridges and paved highways, the mechanical looms and steam presses. Above all it was the industrialists and inventors – men like George Stephenson and Isambard Kingdom Brunel – whose harnessing of technology to steam power had allowed a small island that could have been fitted into the United States many times over to acquire the largest empire the world had ever seen.

By the 1860s, many of Britain's domestic problems were also well on the way to being solved. Social revolution, which had seemed an imminent possibility in the 1830s and 1840s, had been averted and the worst miseries of the industrial revolution appeared to be over. So, while the United States struggled to come to terms with the problems left over from the Civil War, it appeared as though Britain's star was still in the ascendant. In spite of constituting only 2 per cent of the world's population, it produced 50 per cent of the world's coal, 53 per cent of its iron and almost half of its cotton manufactures. The country consumed over twice as much energy as its two closest industrial rivals, the United States and Germany combined. Its merchant marine carried over a third of the world's traffic in manufactured goods, while in terms of fighting power the Royal Navy was equal to all the world's other navies put together. Britain also provided three-quarters of the world's foreign investment[2] and was the leading centre for insurance, banking and commodity dealing.[3] Not until the 1940s, by which time leadership had passed to the United States, would a single nation again possess a combination of financial, industrial, commercial and military muscle comparable to that of Britain in the 1860s.

Yet, in spite of this impressive façade, there was cause for unease. The circumstances associated with Britain's rise to world dominance were plainly exceptional. For one small nation to wield such disproportionate power was a situation unlikely to last indefinitely. And already there were signs of change. Although British manufacturing continued to expand, that of other powers, notably Germany and the United States, was growing even faster. They were, of course, starting from a lower base. Measured in absolute terms, Britain had a formidable head start. In spite of having a population marginally larger, America's share of world manufacturing in the 1860s was only a third of Britain's. Yet, even at that date, Americans were already ahead in certain respects, as in the mechanisation, standardisation and mass production of firearms. When, in the 1850s, Britain's major small-arms factory in Enfield decided to re-equip itself, it turned to two American firms in the backwoods of Vermont for its machine tools.[4] The greater part of Britain's workforce was already living in urban areas and engaged in industrial pursuits, whereas the United States was still primarily a rural and agrarian society and thus had a larger potential resource for industrial recruitment. According to the 1870 census, four out of every five Americans were rural dwellers. This was probably an underestimate, given that many of the places categorised as 'urban' (i.e. with populations in excess of 8000) amounted to little more than agricultural centres catering for the needs of their local farming communities. In short, the United States was still what would nowadays be called a developing country, most Americans still being farmers of one kind or another or engaged in occupations relating to agriculture.

Thus the United States that emerged from the Civil War bore a certain resemblance to the Britain of a century before. Yet although still largely a rural nation, and destined to remain so until well into the twentieth century, the influences of its gathering industrial strength were already being felt even in the remotest regions. Physically, and culturally, its industrial tentacles were reaching out into the agrarian hinterland. As early as 1852 the United States had about 15 000 miles of telegraph lines – more than half the world's total. Its first transcontinental railroad was completed in 1867, by which time its rail network was already three times that of Britain. Over the next few years the great buffalo herds that had roamed the plains since time immemorial were wiped out and replaced by the longhorn cattle required to feed the population of the nation's burgeoning urban centres. American agriculture too was changing, becoming more capitalistic and market-oriented, its products going increasingly to faraway markets in the cities of the East and across the Atlantic. The Jeffersonian notion of the United States as a nation of self-sufficient yeoman farmers, always something of a pipe dream, was fast giving way to a harsher reality. For generations American farmers had been flattered by politicians into thinking of themselves as the backbone of the nation; now they were waking up to the realisation that they were merely small independent producers competing in markets over which they had no control. Try as they might, they found their incomes going down decade by decade. In part this was because of overproduction but partly, too, it reflected the way rail companies, grain merchants and mortgage companies skimmed off such profits as there were. Meanwhile, banks stood ready to seize farmers' properties when hard times arrived, turning freeholders into tenants and forcing them to grow cash crops like wheat and cotton. By 1880 some 70 per cent of US cotton, which twenty years earlier had been grown on plantations by slaves, was being produced by southern whites, many of whom had been forced into sharecropping, having lost the farms they had formerly owned.

Although times were bad for American farmers, they were even worse for their British counterparts. The repeal of the Corn Laws in 1846 had opened the way for imports of US grain, but it was not until after the Civil War that British farming felt the full impact of the prairie wheat that flooded into the country. In spite of the rapid expansion of industry, farming was still the nation's single largest employer. Compared to the situation across the Atlantic, where the population was mobile and land changed hands with great rapidity, British farming had always possessed a stolid, traditional character. Farms stayed in the same families for generations. As late as the 1860s, the old rural order presided over by the squire and parson, as described by Anthony Trollope and other novelists of the period, remained largely intact. Throughout the country, spirits still tended to rise or fall depending on whether the harvest had been good or bad. But with the ever-increasing flood of imported foodstuffs, agricultural survival became increasingly difficult. In terms of bushels per acre, the British were far more efficient than Americans. The more forward-looking responded to the challenge by becoming more mechanised. But adopting American methods failed to protect them against the ever-falling prices, and no amount of wage cutting could compensate for the advantages deriving from the almost limitless virgin land available to farmers across the Atlantic.

The major constraint on how much grain a prairie farmer could grow was lack of labour. That, however, could be compensated for by mechanisation. As Americans were to demonstrate in other fields, they were adept at finding ways of substituting machines for human muscle power. In a land where labour was expensive and resources plentiful, investing in machinery had always made sense. Although much given to celebrating the virtues of the rural life, Jefferson had devoted his leisure, as visitors to his home at Monticello can still see, to inventing labour-saving contrivances. Benjamin Franklin made a speciality of dreaming up useful devices, among them the Franklin stove, bifocal glasses and the lightning rod. Along with the Declaration of Independence and the Constitution, mechanical inventiveness and entrepreneurial initiative were part and parcel of the spirit of the American Enlightenment. Nature, as Americans saw it, was something to be tamed and harnessed to men's advantage. The restlessness of American life, the drive to open up the country's vast natural resources, the willingness to break with old methods, the individual urge to 'get ahead', all combined to create a cultural ethos favourable to technological innovation. When Ralph Waldo Emerson commented that 'If a man . . . can make better chairs or knives, crucibles or church organs, than anybody else, you will find a broad, hard-beaten path to his house, even though it be in the woods' he was expressing a characteristically American notion.[5]

Beginning with the McCormick reaper and steel-blade ploughshare in the 1830s, Americans specialised in producing farming machinery that was light, easily transported and capable of being operated by a person working on his own. These were the qualities required to meet the needs of the homestead farmer. Being far in advance of anything Europe had to offer, US agricultural inventions attracted attention at international exhibitions. The introduction of Locke wire binder in the 1870s virtually doubled the amount of grain that a prairie farmer working on his own could harvest. Improved productivity, however, failed to solve the farmers' economic difficulties. As the glut of American farm produce grew, so, in turn, did the problems of rural Britain, bringing falling land values, declining incomes and rural depopulation. Arable land was turned into sheep runs and pheasant shoots. Every year tens of thousands of workers fled the countryside, bound for the slums of the city. From the 1870s onward, the best hope for young people in Britain was to get out of agriculture.[6]

Meanwhile, on both sides of the Atlantic, cities continued to expand. In Europe, large cities had existed long before the industrial revolution; in the United States, urbanisation and industrialisation went hand in hand. Americans had traditionally viewed cities with suspicion. Jefferson attributed the superior virtue of his fellow countrymen to the fact that most were small farmers, warning that should 'they get piled upon one another in large cities, as in Europe, they will become corrupt as in Europe'.[7] He even went so far as to warn young Americans against crossing the Atlantic to study in case they came to feel 'the hollow, unfeeling manners of Europe to be preferable to the simplicity and sincerity of our own country'. Cities, in other words, were un-American – dangerous, cosmopolitan places, full of smart-money men and painted women who preyed on innocent country folk.

But with agricultural prices falling and new industrial opportunities opening up, many found that there was little choice. From the middle of the nineteenth century onwards, American urbanisation proceeded at a dizzying rate, far faster than anything Britain had experienced even in the heyday of its industrial expansion. It differed from the British experience in other ways too. In Britain the flight from the land had been essentially an internal matter. Those who quit the countryside to swell the populations of cities like Manchester and Birmingham, or mining towns such as those of Durham, Yorkshire and the Welsh valleys, were displaced agricultural workers from within Britain's own borders. By contrast, American industry recruited its workforce not only from America's own displaced rural population but from the much larger reservoir of dispossessed European peasantry. Moving to New York or Pittsburgh was hardly more difficult than moving to Milan or Warsaw. Passages in steerage were cheap and wages on arrival higher. America's new industrial proletariat was accordingly much more ethnically divided than Britain's. This led to problems, and occasionally violence, as when newly-arrived immigrants acted as strike-breakers. On the other hand, being divided along ethnic lines, America's industrial workforce was less prone to the kind of class resentment that was for so long the bane of British industry.

From the 1870s until 1914 immigration into the United States increased decade by decade. By the turn of the century a million or more were entering every year. Some travelled on their own, intending to earn enough to purchase land or set up businesses back home. Most, however, arrived intending to stay, either bringing their families with them or sending for them once they became established. The majority were unskilled, ready to take whatever work was available. A minority, like the Italian immigrants who manned New Haven's arms factories, were recruited by agents and had their passages paid, but most travelled at their own expense, finding their way to wherever they were required. Like the displaced British agricultural workers of earlier times, they provided the manpower America's burgeoning industries needed. Traditionally, most had come from Northwest Europe, but from the 1870s onwards an increasing proportion came from new areas – Italy, Greece, Poland, Russia – that had not previously sent migrants to the US. By the 1890s the majority of new arrivals were from Southern and Eastern Europe. By the turn of the century four out of five residents of Greater New York were of foreign birth or foreign parentage, many of them speaking the languages and wearing the dress of their countries of origin. Boston, that bastion of Puritan endeavour, had become a polyglot city of swarming tenements, clanging streetcars and Catholic immigrants. To Americans of native stock it appeared as if their country was being taken over by aliens.

Not all the newcomers, however, were foreign in speech and appearance, nor were they peasants fresh off the land. Among them were ambitious British workmen, looking for opportunities for advancement and alert to the rewards their skills could command in America. By the late nineteenth century American industrialists were no longer as concerned with acquiring British expertise as they had been earlier. Thanks to the introduction of machinery much of the work now required could be done by relatively unskilled workers. Nevertheless, workers from Britain were still highly valued in specific areas. The worsted wool industry was almost entirely dependent on Yorkshire-trained machine operators. In hard-rock mining the expertise of Cornishmen proved equally vital. As a Michigan State official reported in 1886, 'If there is a difficult shaft to be sunk or a tunnel to be driven in hard or dangerous ground, as a general thing it is Cornish miners who are the men to do it.'[8] The American leather glove industry was largely developed by workers from Somerset. Metalworkers from Sheffield and shoemakers from Nottingham had no difficulty in finding jobs paying double the wages they had received before. Being English speaking, British immigrants did not encounter the sort of nativist hostility experienced by many new arrivals. Having acquired a little capital, many found it possible to set up businesses of their own. Some, like Alexander Graham Bell, the inventor of the telephone, and Andrew Carnegie, the steel magnate, went on to become industrial titans, proof that America was a land where hard work and talent brought rich rewards.[9]

As industrialising powers, the United States and Britain enjoyed certain common advantages, among them the protection of ocean barriers. This spared Britain the expense of maintaining a large standing army on the continental model. In spite of its imperial commitments, its regular army in the later nineteenth century was only half the size of France's and Germany's, and less than a third the size of Russia's. Set against this, however, was the enormous expense of supporting a navy capable of keeping open the sea routes on which its prosperity depended. America's defence expenditures, in contrast, were negligible. For most of the nineteenth century it scarcely had an army as measured by European standards. Except briefly, during the latter stages of the Civil War, when it possessed what was arguably the most powerful fighting machine in the world, America's army amounted to little more than a frontier police force. Numerically, it was roughly one-eighth the size of the Britain's.[10] Until the 1880s, the US Navy, although highly professional, was smaller even than that of Chile. Militarily supreme in its own hemisphere, protected by the Atlantic on one side and the Pacific on the other, and with Britain's Royal Navy to police the high seas, the US had no need of large military expenditures. With minimal taxes and no large government apparatus to support, Americans were free to concentrate on what concerned them most, namely developing their continent's natural resources.

Fortune, so the saying goes, smiles on fools, drunkards and the United States. No European nation could match America in terms of readily-accessible deposits of coal and iron, rich oilfields, forests of virgin timber, endless stretches of cultivable land, or its a huge internal market for manufactured products. The United States also enjoyed the benefits of European capital and technology, a tariff wall designed to keep out foreign products, a well-developed domestic tradition of mechanical innovation, and a flexible labour force ready to go wherever its services were needed. In short, the United States possessed everything required for the development of modern industry without the distraction of having an overseas empire to govern or aggressive neighbours to fend off. By 1890 its overall production had overtaken Britain's, and, by 1900, Britain's and Germany's combined. Nor was it in terms of total volume alone that the US excelled. Firms like Standard Oil, International Harvester, Singer, Colt, Bell and DuPont were among the most technically advanced in the world.

One area in which American industry particularly excelled was in developing mass-production methods. An early innovator in this field was Eli Whitney. Having revolutionised southern cotton production by inventing the cotton gin (gin is simply short for engine), he went on to perform a like service for his native New England by designing and building machines capable of turning out parts with such precision that they could be used interchangeably. This was arguably more important than his first achievement in that it opened the way for assembly-line production, allowing what had previously been skilled operations (in the case of muskets, each barrel and stock had had to be individually crafted and fitted) to be performed by relatively inexperienced workers. New undertakings, like the need to produce enough steel for America's railroads, similarly called for innovative industrial techniques and methods of labour management.

Starting from scratch brought other advantages. Americans, declared the British Social Darwinist Herbert Spencer in 1882, 'have profited by inheriting all the arts, appliances, and methods developed by older societies, while leaving behind the obstructions existing in them'.[11] In fact, all of the countries that followed Britain into industrialisation in the late nineteenth century grew more rapidly than Britain did.[12] In the case of America, the introduction of instalment buying and other new develop-

ments in mass marketing helped. One especially notable American contribution was the application of industrial management techniques – the
so-called Taylorian system, named after Frederick W. Taylor – based on
time-and-motion studies that co-ordinated the way materials and products flowed into, through and out of factories. This was in response to the
needs of vast enterprises like United States Steel and the Singer Sewing
Machine Company that emerged from the great industrial mergers of the
1880s and 1890s. In short, the mass-production, mass-marketing
methods characteristic of modern industrial enterprise were largely
American inventions. The American mind, wrote Henry Adams, differed
from the English mind in being remorselessly practical. It did not waste
its energies on 'eccentricities'. 'From the old-world point of view, the
American had no mind; he had an economic thinking machine which
could work only in a fixed line. The American mind exasperated the
European as a buzz-saw might exasperate a pine forest.'[13]

British visitors to the United States were awed by the display of wealth
and enterprise: the Manhattan skyline, the New York Stock Exchange,
the new department stores, the clanging streetcars, the transformation of
cow towns into metropolises, the constant talk of dollars and investments,
the headlong rush into modernity. All was bustle, verve, animation.
Arnold Bennett marvelled at Americans' vitality and wondered where
they got their energy from. Herbert Spencer noted that their lack of
leisure prevented them from enjoying the finer things in life, and worried
about the effect of overwork on their health. H. G. Wells, applying socialist principles, saw the United States as a scene of chaos, lawlessness, and
disorder, Americans having apparently not thought of applying the same
scientific planning they used in industry to society as a whole.[14] Even
James Bryce, the author of the classic study of late nineteenth-century
society *The American Commonwealth* (1888), on returning to the United
States in 1905, was astonished:

> That which most strikes the visitor to America today is its prodigious
> material development. Industrial growth, swift thirty or forty years
> ago, advances more swiftly now. The rural districts are being studded
> with villages, the villages are growing into cities, the cities are stretch-
> ing out long arms of suburbs, which follow the lines of road and
> railway in every direction. The increase of wealth . . . impresses a
> European more deeply than ever before because the contrast with
> Europe is greater. In America every class seems rich compared with
> the corresponding class in the Old World.[15]

The picture was not perhaps quite as contented as Bryce makes it appear. As in the United Kingdom, industrialisation had its downside in the form of belching smokestacks, toxic waste, polluted rivers and landscapes littered with refuse. Along with the shift from agriculture to manufacturing came widening income differentials and industrial violence on a level rarely experienced in Britain. But whatever the balance sheet of gains and losses, one thing was clear beyond doubt: America had become an industrial titan.

Imperial Expansion

Nations possessed of power are seldom at a loss to find ways of using it. Between 1865 and 1914, Britain and the United States expanded mightily. These were the years when the United States completed the settlement of the Trans-Mississippi West, overcoming what little Native American resistance remained. It also acquired Alaska, Hawaii and the Philippines. Britain's acquisitions were on an even larger scale, comprising Nigeria, Uganda, Kenya, Northern Rhodesia, Southern Rhodesia, Somaliland, South Africa, Burma, Malaya, Sarawak, North Borneo, and much else besides. Both countries fought wars against nationalist rebels, the United States in the Philippines, Britain in the Sudan and South Africa. Benjamin Disraeli proclaimed Queen Victoria Empress of India; Theodore Roosevelt seized Panama in order to build a trans-isthmian canal. Imperial pursuits, it emerged, were uniting the two countries in ways that could hardly have been foreseen a half-century earlier.

In Britain's case nothing was more at odds with the dominant beliefs of the mid-nineteenth century than the notion that it was in the nation's interest to acquire vast new colonial domains in Asia and Africa. Recalling the circumstances leading to the loss of their American possessions, British statesmen had resolved not to make the same mistake again. The British North America Act of 1867 granted Canada dominion status, effectively giving Canadians self-government and independence on the assumption that they would continue to co-operate with the mother country on matters of common concern. Similar considerations led to Australia and New Zealand also being granted independent status and, in due course, to the emergence of the British Commonwealth of Nations.

As far as the settler colonies were concerned this made good sense. Why support all the paraphernalia of empire when ties of affection, common interests, free trade and private enterprise would serve equally well? Similar considerations informed British thinking with regard to the rest of

the world. Traders were better judges of what was profitable than governments. Let people look to their own interests. If Africans and Asians
did not want to trade with Britain they could take their custom elsewhere.
Conversely, British entrepreneurs should be relieved of government regulations, taxes and other restraints. The secret to economic success lay in
freeing private enterprise from the meddlesome attentions of the state.
That had been the message of Adam Smith's *Wealth of Nations*, and it was
a view with which government ministers, Cobdenites, Benthemites,
Manchester merchants and London bankers agreed. Colonies, according
to Cobden, 'serve but as gorgeous and ponderous appendages to swell
our ostensible grandeur without improving our balance of trade'.[16]

In this respect British thinking had come around to a view remarkably
like that of Americans. It was, after all, resistance to government meddling that had led the establishment of the United States in the first place.
Americans did not need Adam Smith or Richard Cobden to persuade
them that the best prescription for prosperity was a free-market economy.
When, in 1837, John L. O'Sullivan declared that 'all government is evil,
and the parent of evil. . . . The best government is that which governs
least' he was expressing a sentiment with which few Americans would
have quibbled.[17] The worst governments, by implication, were those that
assumed a God-given right to impose taxes, order people about, and generally behave in ways contrary to the wishes of those concerned, which, of
course, was precisely what colonial governments did. From this it followed that colonialism, imperialism or any other imposition of alien rule
over subject peoples was contrary to American principles.

John L. O'Sullivan, however, is best remembered, not for his advocacy
of limited government but for having coined the phrase 'manifest destiny'
and his fervent support of American expansion. 'Our manifest destiny',
he declared in 1845, 'is to overspread the continent allotted by Providence for the free development of our yearly multiplying millions.'
Within a century, at present rates of growth, the population of the United
States would reach 250 million. Already 'the Anglo-Saxon foot' was on
the borders of California. It was only a matter of time before Canada severed its 'colonial relation to the little island three thousand miles across
the Atlantic' and followed the example of Texas by opting to join the
United States. It was all part of the 'manifest design of Providence'. The
outlines were already clear; only the timing remained to be determined.[18]

British statements on the subject of imperial expansion were similarly
infused with evocations of divine intent. It was, after all, 'at Heaven's
command' that Britain had arisen from 'out the azure main'.[19] Being

assured of their own excellence, it was the natural duty of the British to lead struggling humanity along the pathways of progress. Power implied responsibility. When troubles occurred, it was their responsibility to sort them out. Like the Pax Romana of ancient times, the Pax Britannica ensured that nations could go about their lawful business in safety. It was God's way of bringing commerce, Christianity and civilisation (the famous three Cs) to the peoples of the globe. There was no contradiction between making a profit and improving people's lives. Private commerce, disinterested benevolence and political example went hand in hand. Just as traders were expected to travel the globe to find new customers, so British missionaries would reach out in search of converts who, in turn, would be brought to understand the virtues of hard work, personal cleanliness and parliamentary government.

Americans' sense of mission, although differently expressed, was no less high-minded. Long before the War of Independence there had been those who saw it as their destiny to set the world to rights. The Puritans who settled New England went there with the intention of pioneering a form of society based on religious precepts that they would subsequently take back to England. Their failure to do so was only the first of many disappointments Americans encountered in seeking to convey their message to the world. If the blessings they enjoyed had not been granted them for a purpose then, at the very least, they were under an obligation to make known what was to be learned from their experience. By the mid-nineteenth century there could be little doubt as to what that was: the message was democracy; the mission was to make the United States an example to the rest of humanity. American expansionism, then, was not to be confused with the land-grabbing activities of other nations. When America's borders extended, so, too, did liberty. Although the conquest of the American West might *look* very much like the sort of thing Britain and other European nations were doing in Africa and Asia, it was, in reality, quite different. It was the natural fulfilment of the nation's destiny, an expression of the exuberant energies of a democratic people. Where European nations conspired to subject others to their authority, the United States merely ensured the right of free individuals to occupy and develop North America in whatever ways suited them best. The driving force behind American expansionism was not the United States government but, in O'Sullivan's words, 'the irresistible army of Anglo-Saxon emigration, armed with the plough and the rifle, and marking its trail with schools and colleges, courts and representative halls, mills and meeting houses'.[20]

To O'Sullivan, as to most expansionists, the fate of those already occupying the territories in question was a secondary matter. If the United
States stood for liberty, it was liberty of a one-size-fits-all variety. It did
not include the liberty of Native Americans to go on leading the kind of
lives they had traditionally led, at least not if it meant allowing them to go
on occupying vast stretches of territory that others coveted and could use
more fruitfully. After all, America stood for equality. Why should one
group be treated differently from another simply because of its primitive
way of life? Such thinking, current from the 1830s if not earlier, lay
behind the Dawes General Allotment Act of 1887, which provided for
the break-up of the Indian tribal relationship and the allocation of small
plots of land to heads of households on a family basis.

Similar acts of unscrupulous land-grabbing occurred throughout the
colonial world. In this respect there is little to choose between the behaviour of Americans in the West and British settlers the world over. Both
rode roughshod over indigenous peoples when it suited their interests to
do so. There were, however, differences. Much of the British Empire,
whether on account of disease, climate, or because it was already heavily
populated, was unsuited to white settlement. Although persuaded of the
rightfulness of their role as rulers, and thus of their superiority to the
peoples they encountered, the British had no equivalent ideology to that of
Americans. They made much of their loyalty to the Queen-Empress. But
they did not expect those over whom they ruled to turn into Englishmen
any more than they expected Britain's own labouring classes to become
gentry. Britain itself was a layered society. It was one thing to help people,
see that they were properly fed and housed, quite another to expect them
to become like oneself. Peoples' institutions needed to be treated with
respect, if only because failing to do so would cause trouble. They did not,
therefore, set about proclaiming highfalutin notions about 'life, liberty,
and the pursuit of happiness'. Their aim was the more pragmatic one of
leading backward people along the path to enlightenment in modest
ways. As the they saw it, the nations and races of the world were ranked
according to the stage of development they had attained. They themselves naturally headed the list; Americans came a little lower, followed
by Scandinavians, Germans, French and other Europeans, with Asians
and Africans just beginning to struggle upward from far below. These, of
course, were very approximate rankings, for within each category there
were important variations. Britain itself was a hierarchical society in
which a few still unabashedly claimed superiority to the rest. All societies,
even that of the United States, had their social gradations. Wealth, class

and education therefore needed to be ranked alongside race when it came to dividing up the world's populations – as the ready acceptance into British society of Indian maharajahs, Malay sultans and Arab emirs bore witness. The 'education of the native' was one of the principal justifications for British imperialism. Rather than speculating on the reasons why some peoples were more backward than others, the essential thing was to create conditions that would allow them, under British tutelage, to ascend the ladder of civilisation. For a start, they needed to be freed from cannibalism, slavery, debt bondage, suttee, polygamy, nakedness and other barbarous practices. Thanks to their global influence and long experience, these were tasks that the British saw themselves as uniquely qualified to perform.[21]

Improving the lot of Africans and Asians, however, was at best only a secondary consideration so far as Whitehall was concerned. With the spread of industrial technology, the balance of world power was changing. The unification of Germany and Italy gave a new edge to European rivalries, setting off a feverish race for colonies. Between 1870 and 1914 virtually the whole of Africa was partitioned among the European powers, with Britain getting the lion's share. It was, of course, convenient, when questions were asked with regard to the moral justification for these new imperial commitments, to say that Britain was suppressing the slave trade by extending its beneficent rule to those in need of its protection. But that was largely the icing on the cake. What most impressed Whitehall was rather the need to protect trade routes and forestall the activities of others. In fact, the great imperial expansion of the late nineteenth century was as much a sign of Britain's weakness as of its strength.

That, of course, was not how it was presented to the British public. The sense of imperial endeavour, expressed in the works of Rudyard Kipling and other turn-of-the-century British writers, appealed to the imaginations of the millions of city-bred readers, much as Ned Buntline's and Zane Grey's stories about adventures in the Wild West did to their American counterparts. Kipling was born in Bombay and began his literary career as a journalist in Lahore, which provided him with the material he used for his tales of intrigue, heroism and military life in India. Rider Haggard, a close friend, spent his formative years in South Africa, acquiring experiences that he exploited in *King Solomon's Mines* (1885) and other bestsellers. Joseph Conrad, who had travelled the world in the British merchant navy, described in colourful and dramatic detail the fates that befell white men in the tropics. Robert Louis Stevenson wrote of buccaneering in the South Seas, W. E. Henley about the glories of the strenuous life, G. A. Henty about heroic episodes in the British past. These and a host of other writers provided tales of patriotism and manly courage that stirred the imaginations of readers whose own workaday worlds offered little in the way of excitement. For the flag-waving British public that is largely what the Empire represented – a national adventure, life in exotic places, heroes in whose achievements they could take pride, an enterprise that added a sense of spaciousness to their mostly cramped and routine urban lives.

It was not only tales of the Empire, however, that caught the imagination of British audiences; so far as manliness and adventure were concerned, accounts of exploits in the American and Canadian West served just as well. It made little difference whether the enemy were Zulu or Sioux or the heroes British cavalrymen or American cowboys. When Buffalo Bill's Circus arrived on tour the British public flocked to buy tickets. The show included a mock Indian attack on a coach and a ranch. Queen Victoria found the spectacle 'most exciting', and the Indians 'with their feathers, & wild dress (very little of it) rather alarming'. Colonel Cody himself she thought 'a splendid man, handsome & gentlemanlike in manner'.[22] Mark Twain's Western tales (*Roughing It, Tom Sawyer, Huckleberry Finn*) were as popular in Britain as they were in the United States. Jack London's *The Call of the Wild* (1903) and *White Fang* (1906) were all-time bestsellers on both sides of the Atlantic, as were the novels of Bret Harte and Owen Wister. Zane Grey developed the Wister formula, based on the notion of the West as a moral landscape within which violent struggles are enacted, with *Riders of the Purple Sage* (1912) and its many sequels becoming the single most popular author of his day.

The period's best-known exponent of strenuous living was President Theodore Roosevelt. As a young man he bought a ranch in Dakota Territory, where he set about improving his naturally poor health by following an active career as a rancher while working on his four-volume history, *The Winning of the West* (1889–96). Like other Americans, Roosevelt saw parallels between the settlement of the American frontier and the colonisation of East Africa. On retiring from the Presidency in 1909 he embarked on a two-year African safari in the course of which, according to his account, he was continually struck by the similarity of the country to parts of Colorado and Texas. At times he could almost believe that he was back 'in the cow camps of the West, a quarter of a century ago'. The British settlers he met reminded him of 'those Western ranchmen and homemakers with whom I have always felt a special sense of companionship and with whose ideals and aspirations I have always felt a special sympathy'. In Africa, too, there were resources to be exploited in the form of land to be cultivated and copper to be mined. It was all part of the same process whereby 'Anglo-Saxons' wrested territory from the 'clutches of savagery'. To turn-of-the-century Americans – as to Ernest Hemingway a generation later – British Africa offered opportunities for heroic outdoor adventure of a kind no longer possible in the western United States.[23]

Roosevelt's most heroic, adventure was in 1898 when he led his troop of volunteer cavalry, the Rough Riders, in its famous charge up San Juan Hill, an episode which, like Winston Churchill's youthful exploits in the Sudan and Boer War at approximately the same time, helped advance his political career. John Hay, the American Secretary of State, later described the Spanish-American War as 'a splendid little war', which was how it impressed most Americans. It also heralded a new departure. In terms of population and industrial output the United States was potentially a great power. It was only natural, therefore, that the question should arise of whether to follow the other great powers of the world and expand overseas. There were economic arguments for doing so: American industry needed markets and raw materials. There were also strategic considerations.

Among the latter was US unease at Germany's growing naval strength. Americans had grown used to British naval power but were decidedly less confident about the uses to which Germany's might be put. Doubts also arose concerning Britain's capacity to go on policing the seas. The leading naval historian of the time, Admiral Alfred Thayer Mahan, a former head of the US Naval War College, had attributed Britain's rise to its control of the world's seaways. According to Mahan, history showed the strategic advantages deriving from control of the world's central oceans. Coastal defences were useless against any power with the ability to bring its entire strength to bear on virtually any point of its choosing. Logic, therefore, indicated that the United States should build a first-class, ocean-going navy.[24] For such a force to perform the role expected of it, however, would require obtaining overseas bases. In the days of sail, vessels could dock almost anywhere for food and water. Modern vessels needed coaling stations. The US already owned the Aleutian Islands, acquired along with Alaska by purchase from Russia in 1867. By 1890 it had established a presence in the Midway Islands, Samoa and at Pearl Harbor in Hawaii.

These, however, were only small beginnings; the big change came in 1898. As Joseph Conrad put it in *Nostromo*: 'On 1st of May, 1898, a gun was fired in the Bay of Manila and, in response, the skirmish line crossed the Pacific, still pushing the frontier before it.'[25] The battle of Manila Bay, a decidedly one-sided affair, led to the loss of Spain's entire Pacific fleet, with no deaths and only a small number of wounded on the American side. The United States now had control not only of the Philippines but of Guam, Wake Island, Johnston Island and a network of other bases. Effectively the Pacific had become an American lake.

In the Caribbean the story was much the same. There, too, the Spanish fleet was outgunned, and although the Spaniards fought gallantly it was all over in a matter of hours. Cut off from Europe and the hope of reinforcements, the Cuban army commander, after a largely token show of resistance, surrendered. Capturing Puerto Rico, where the colonists collaborated with the invading force, proved even less problematical. Within ten weeks of the first shots being fired the war was over.

The Spanish-American War was the most popular of all American wars. With minimal losses the US ended the rule of a colonial power that at one time had dominated the greater part of the New World. For those who formed their impressions of the war from the heroic drawings of Frederic Remington and the manly prose of the war correspondents, it seemed as if the predictions of those who had prophesied a great imperial destiny for the United States were being borne out.

In the longer term, America's victory proved more problematic. Having acquired the Philippines, the United States found itself saddled with a long-running colonial war against insurgent Filipino forces commanded by Emilio Aguinaldo, who believed, not without reason, that American rule amounted to no more than the substitution of one colonial oppressor for another. When Rudyard Kipling, in a poem addressed to Theodore Roosevelt, called on Americans to 'take up the white man's burden', he stressed the difficulties rather than the glories of the task they were undertaking. The war against the Filipino nationalists dragged on for a further three years, becoming increasingly brutal as US troops were forced into adopting similar tactics to those of their Spanish predecessors. In the event it took more troops to suppress freedom in the Philippines than it had to liberate Cuba.

The notion of establishing dominion over alien peoples in distant islands would hardly have commended itself to the nation's founders. Even in the euphoria of victory, there were those who saw it as a betrayal of the nation's principles.[26] But times were changing. To the expansionists of 1898 the acquisition of the Philippines showed that the United States was capable of keeping in step with the other great powers of the day. That the Philippines might also prove a strategic liability became evident only much later.

Anglo-American Diplomatic Relations

Britain's conduct during the Civil War had left Americans feeling angry. Although popular opinion in Britain had tended to favour the North, most northerners believed that Britain's actions favoured the South. What most incited their wrath were the activities of the *Alabama* and other cruisers constructed in Britain. These vessels had wreaked such havoc that the US merchant marine was reduced to less than a third of what it had been at the beginning. The resulting claims not only took account of the value of the shipping lost but of the length of time the cruisers' activities had supposedly prolonged the war. This amounted, according to some calculations, to a staggering two billion dollars. After much wrangling Gladstone finally agreed to let the matter go to international arbitration, which resulted in Britain agreeing to pay $15.5 million to the United States.

Canada was also a source of friction. In spite of Britain's having agreed in 1867 to grant Canadians self-government, American politicians continued to talk of annexation. Because of the influence of the Irish vote they also turned a blind eye on the activities of the Fenian Brotherhood, whose aim was to foment a war between Britain and the United States in the hope of furthering the struggle for Irish independence. Three times between 1866 and 1871 Fenian 'armies' crossed into Canada. On each occasion they were repulsed with little difficulty. Nevertheless, the casual attitude adopted by the US government towards these plainly illegal proceedings rankled.

Americans, for their part, could see no reason for what they regarded as a continued British presence in North America. They also complained vociferously of the excessive influence of British interests within the United States. Three-quarters of the foreign capital invested in the US was British, much of it in key sectors such as mines, ranches and railroads. Just as a century later the British would blame their troubles on the 'American invasion', so post-Civil War Americans blamed the British for everything from low farm prices to the way the rising value of gold increased the burden of their debts. As Kipling noted at the time, every country needed someone to denounce: France had Germany, Britain had Russia and the United States had Britain.[27]

Anglophobia reached new heights during the Venezuelan Crisis of 1895–96. For what would prove the last time, the two nations found themselves on the brink of war. That such a situation could arise over a boundary issue in an area that so far as anyone could see had no bearing on the essential interests of either, came as a great surprise, particularly to the British. Although Britain's doings bulked large in the minds of Americans, those of the United States did not do so in the consciousness of Britons. Even Americans, however, would hardly have taken issue over the ownership of a pestilential and largely uninhabited stretch of jungle south of the River Orinoco, had there not been exceptional factors involved. What made it a matter of concern was the discovery of gold and Venezuela's claim that, by extending the borders of British Guiana to include the goldfields, Britain was infringing the Monroe Doctrine. Given that the Monroe Doctrine had originally been proclaimed, partly at Britain's instigation, to discourage the recolonisation of Latin America by European powers, it required some stretch of the imagination to perceive how it related to a long-standing border dispute. As the British Prime Minister, Lord Salisbury, pointed out, there was no question of Britain imposing its system of government on unwilling subjects. In any case, he argued, the Monroe Doctrine, although cherished by Americans, had no standing in international law.[28]

President Cleveland responded by sending a message to Congress calling for a commission to look into the matter. Although hedged about with qualifications, it clearly implied that should the commission find Britain appropriating territory that rightly belonged to Venezuela it would be the duty of the US to resist it 'by every means in its power'.[29] These were fighting words, and a wave of jingoism swept the country. The New York *Sun* ran the headline, 'WAR IF NECESSARY'. Irish Americans lined up to volunteer, and there was even talk of invading Canada. Then the stock market took fright, prices plummeted, and within a matter of days the excitement subsided. Nevertheless, alarmed by the extreme American reaction, Britain hastily backed down. In a famous speech, Joseph Chamberlain, the Colonial Secretary, made it plain that Britain did not covet a single inch of American soil, and looked forward to a day when the two countries would unite 'in defence of a common cause sanctioned by humanity and justice'.[30] Salisbury made a similar statement in the House of Lords, explaining that, while he did not see the relevance of the Monroe Doctrine, he fully appreciated that the US had reason to feel concerned over events in the region. Within weeks Britain and Venezuela agreed to international arbitration, with the result that an agreement was reached accepting most of Britain's claims.

The principal significance of the Venezuelan Crisis was not Britain's vindication but that it marked a watershed in Anglo-American relations.

As long as its maritime primacy remained unchallenged it was possible for Britain to dispense with alliances; but now that other nations were building navies splendid isolation was no longer an option. For the first time since the defeat of Napoleon, the British felt the need for friends. This was brought home when, at the height of the Venezuela Crisis, they learned of a telegram the German Kaiser had sent to the President of the Boer Republic, Paul Kruger, congratulating him on having foiled an attempt by British freebooters to seize the South African goldfields without having to call on Germany for assistance. Few doubted that Jameson's raid was an act of criminal folly. However, the idea that Germany, which they regarded as an upstart European nation, should so much as contemplate intervening in the affairs of South Africa enraged the British far more than Cleveland's message to Congress. Suddenly the significance of the Germans' naval expansion seemed clear: they were bent on challenging Britain's control of the seas. Quarrelling with fellow Anglo-Saxons in the face of a Teutonic menace that threatened the interests of both countries was absurd. Thanks to the Reform Acts of 1867 and 1884, Britain could now claim to be a liberal democracy much like the United States. Germany, in contrast, was an autocratic power, governed by a militaristic elite, bent on overturning a world system long taken for granted. Thus, a growing sense of insecurity, deriving largely from uncertainty as to Germany's intentions, inclined the two nations towards amity.

The change in mood was reflected in the demonstration of pro-American feeling with which, in June 1898, the British greeted the news of the outbreak of the Spanish-American War. They had heard accounts of the barbarous treatment of the Cubans by Spain; now, Cuba was to be liberated by a nation that shared Britain's civilised values. Officially, Britain declared its neutrality, but while the rest of Europe expressed disapproval it made its sympathies clear. A rumour even circulated that at the battle of Manila Bay a squadron of the Royal Navy contributed to the US victory by stationing itself between Admiral Dewey's fleet and a German flotilla that threatened to intervene on the side of the Spanish. Although not strictly true, the fact that Americans believed it showed that their attitudes were changing as well. Meanwhile, there was no doubt as to Germany's ambitions in the Pacific, as shown by its eagerness to establish a naval base in Samoa. This was one reason why Britain supported America's annexation of Hawaii and the Philippines. Having ventured on to the world stage, Americans were reassured to know that they had British support.

A year later, the British were grateful for the assistance they received from the US Government during the Boer War. American popular opinion, as might be expected, was on the side of the 'gallant little Boers'. The administration, on the other hand, did not stand in the way of Britain's turning to the New York money market for funds. This was a matter of convenience rather than a necessity as the extra money could have been raised in London, although at the cost of adding to the national debt, something the Chancellor wished to avoid at that particular moment.[31] Still, it created a precedent. Britain also turned to the United States for war supplies, including 200 000 pack mules and hundreds of thousands of pairs of boots.[32] Given that the United States itself was still actively engaged in suppressing the Filipinos, the problems the two countries were facing had more than a little in common.

Capitalising on the goodwill it had established, the US hastened to resolve other outstanding issues, the most important being the building of an isthmian ship canal. In 1850, the two countries had agreed, under the Clayton–Bulwer Treaty, that any canal linking the Atlantic and Pacific would be a joint Anglo-American venture. As an aspiring world-class naval power it was now more important than ever that the United States be able to move its ships from one ocean to the other without their having to go all the way around Cape Horn. However, as a quid pro quo for agreeing to abrogate the treaty, Britain insisted that the US agree to a settlement of a dispute that had recently arisen concerning the Alaskan–Canadian border.

Like so many of the geopolitical difficulties of the period, the Alaskan boundary question had arisen as a result of the discovery of gold, in this case along the Klondike River. Being in the Canadian interior, but without ready access except by sea, prospectors had to pass through the Alaskan panhandle to get there. In support of their case, the Canadians invoked the Anglo-Russian treaty of 1825, claiming it gave them control of the land at the head of the inlets. Americans, on the other hand, maintained that the border ran along the highlands overlooking the bays and inlets, so entitling them to control of all the ports and harbours leading into the Yukon and the northern sections of British Columbia. Canada, they claimed, was trying to cut off overland communication between the northern part of Alaska and the panhandle, while the Canadians argued that the US was bent on barring lateral access from the sea.

Theodore Roosevelt, who embodied the new American imperialism, saw no reason why the US should agree to moderate its claims out of deference to either the British or the Canadians. So far as the Isthmian

Question was concerned, he believed the strategic importance of a two-ocean navy so great that the United States should be prepared to act unilaterally. Aware that in the end the Americans were bound to win, the British agreed to their building, operating and if necessary fortifying a canal on condition that it remain open to the ships of all nations. This left the problem of reaching agreement with an appropriate isthmian state. Finding Colombia dilatory, Roosevelt hastened matters along by organising a political coup in Panama, Colombia's northernmost province, and proclaiming it an independent republic. In return for a grant of $10 million and an annual fee of $250 000, Panama's new ruling junta agreed to give the US full sovereignty over a ten-mile-wide zone across the isthmus. Work on constructing the canal began almost immediately and was completed in 1914.

Having acceded to all of America's demands regarding the canal, Britain was not prepared to sacrifice its goodwill over the matter of the Alaskan boundary. It agreed to put the matter to a judicial commission made up of two Canadians, three Americans and one British representative. Much to Canada's irritation, the British delegate consistently voted with the Americans. This was plainly a political manoeuvre that reflected Britain's need for America's support rather than a fair-minded interpretation of the evidence. The dispute was thus settled on America's terms, effectively excluding Canada from the ocean inlets of the panhandle. Understandably, many Canadians felt betrayed. But it was to Canada's interest no less than Britain's to cultivate good relations with the United States, a fact recognised four years later, in 1908, by the signing of a treaty defining once and for all the entire boundary between the two nations from the Atlantic to the Pacific.[33] After three centuries of engagement, Britain at last felt justified in withdrawing its forces from North America.

Americans were meanwhile asserting themselves in other ways. In 1899, Cipriano Castro had become military dictator of Venezuela, plunging the country into financial chaos. When Venezuela reneged on its debts, Germany declared that it intended sending gunboats. Anxious that this should not be a unilateral German action, Britain agreed to mount a joint coastal blockade, reassuring Roosevelt that no permanent occupation of Venezuela was contemplated. Roosevelt replied that the US was not prepared to provide a guarantee to any state against punishment for misconduct, and that he did not regard their action as a violation of the Monroe Doctrine. The Anglo-German blockade quickly persuaded Castro to agree to arbitration, as a result of which the Hague

Tribunal in 1904 awarded Britain and Germany, as the blockading powers, preferential treatment in settlement of their claims. Venezuela, however, was not the only New World country caught up in a cycle of revolution and debt default. Realising that this would encourage further European intervention, Roosevelt used his 1904 Annual Message to Congress to proclaim what became known as the Roosevelt Corollary to the Monroe Doctrine, turning what was originally a policy aimed at discouraging intervention by European powers into one justifying intervention by the US in the event of what he termed 'chronic wrongdoing'. In fulfilment of this doctrine, and to protect its investments, the United States over the next few years intervened in the Dominican Republic, Haiti, Honduras, Nicaragua and Mexico.

The US was also making its presence felt elsewhere. The Open Door Policy, first promulgated in 1899 in response to what it perceived as efforts by Japan and the European powers to partition China, heralded a growing American concern with trade and investment in the undeveloped world. Having more miles of railway than any other nation, Americans saw themselves as well equipped to build railways in Latin America and Asia as a first step towards tapping their wealth and turning them into markets for American goods. As the country's business leaders saw it, the future health of America's own economy depended on forging links with the outside world.

There were also strategic reasons for adopting a more outward-looking policy. The acquisition of the Philippines meant that the United States now had an interest in maintaining the balance of power in that region. In 1905, Roosevelt assumed the role of mediator in the Russo-Japanese War, an act for which he was subsequently awarded the 1906 Nobel Peace Prize. At the same time, his Secretary of War, William Taft, on a visit to the Philippines, concluded an agreement with the Japanese Foreign Minister (the Taft–Katsura Memorandum), which stated that the US would not interfere with Japanese activities in Korea, in return for which Japan renounced any territorial ambitions it had entertained with regard to the Philippines. In 1907, Roosevelt helped organise the Algeciras Conference, which affirmed the independence and territorial integrity on Morocco. As Roosevelt's successor, Taft eagerly promoted American commercial enterprise by persuading American bankers to join in various commercial projects in China, including the setting up of an international railway consortium. At diplomatic conferences and other international gatherings around the world, Americans were making their presence felt more than ever before.

Cultural and Economic Relations

To Britain's increasingly uneasy statesmen and politicians there was consolation to be had in the fact that at least one the newly emerging world powers was both English-speaking and friendly. At the very least, it was assumed, Americans could be relied on to maintain civilised standards of behaviour, unlike the Germans and Japanese – or for that matter Britain's traditional enemies the French, regarded as antagonistic, unreasonable, and possibly hostile. Language, of course, was a key factor, anyone whose native language was English being regarded as being at least half British, besides which there were genuine family and cultural ties. The 'rich American uncle' whose death or sudden advent transformed the fortunes of a struggling British family became one of the literary clichés of the period. British families tended not to have German or French, let alone Japanese, uncles.

Other changes were also bringing the two countries closer. By the late nineteenth century transatlantic travel was no longer the formidable undertaking it had once been. The large Cunard and White Star liners were floating palaces where life was organised on strictly hierarchical lines. In steerage, so called because passengers were housed in the nether regions of the ship, conditions were still fairly primitive, but for those on the upper decks there were all the amenities of a luxury hotel: shops, hairdressers' salons, clubby smoking rooms, even winter gardens and palm-court orchestras. For first-class passengers there were private suites with bedrooms and sitting rooms that could well have been taken from a contemporary Victorian house. Throughout the day there were deck games, and in the evenings theatrical performances. Those judged sufficiently important would be invited to dine at the captain's table, and after dinner there would be a chance to play cards or discuss business and politics over brandy and a cigar. In short, ocean travel offered opportunities for relaxation and social intercourse not available to earlier generations of transatlantic passengers or, for that matter, to the air travellers of today.[34]

Ease of travel also helped contribute to a spate of transatlantic marriages. This was a new phenomenon. In the early nineteenth century there had been few American fortunes to compare with those of the British peerage. By the standards of London Society, life across the Atlantic appeared pretty rough and ready. This changed, however, with the great surge of American industrial expansion following the Civil War. By the end of the century the fortunes of the wealthiest Americans far exceeded those of their British counterparts, a fact of which British land-ed families, labouring under the shadow of the agricultural depression, took note. New York now had its own social season, presided over by the hardworking ladies of the Vanderbilt and Astor families, ably assisted by Ward McAllister, the Beau Brummell of the day. Instead of taking the traditional Grand Tour of Europe, enterprising young Englishmen now had the option of visiting the United States, an added incentive being the possibly of rescuing their family fortunes through the acquisition of a wealthy American bride. Their presence, in turn, was much sought after in the summer mansions of Newport, Rhode Island, and the winter salons of New York and Philadelphia. Between 1870 and 1914 no less than 60 peers married Americans, among them both the 8th and 9th Dukes of Marlborough.[35] So, too, did a number of aspiring statesmen of the period, among them Joseph Chamberlain, Randolph Churchill and George Nathaniel Curzon. Besides replenishing family coffers, this sud-den influx of wealthy American women introduced a breath of informal-ity into hitherto rather stuffy British elite circles.

Nobody has described these encounters with more insight than Edith Wharton and Henry James. It is worth remembering that their tales reflect events that were actually occurring at the time they were writing. In certain respects, although at a vastly different social level, the way American heiresses entered London Society resembled the manner in which European migrants became Americans, not least in respect of the key role played by the first wave of arrivals. Once some had established a foothold, others followed. Fannie Assingham, who in James's *The Golden Bowl* is shown inducting a succession of young American women into the mysteries of the London marriage market, could well have been modelled on Minnie Paget, who did precisely that. Among the progeny of such unions were some of Britain's future leaders, including two prime minis-ters, Winston Churchill and Harold Macmillan.

The British upper class was in any case becoming more broadly based around the turn of the century with the arrival of increasing numbers of nouveaux riches, among them eager Canadians, Australians and South Africans anxious to make their mark. For as long as anyone could remember young Britons had sought careers in the Empire; now their descendants were returning with the intention of buying their way into British public life. This was a milieu into which Americans readily fitted. Whatever their origins they were regarded as classless, and so welcomed into circles where many Britons of similar background would have found it hard to gain acceptance.

Although the political structures of the two nations differed, the outlook of the liberal and progressive elites that ran the two countries had
much in common. In theory, the monarchy was still the basis of the
British social and political order. Supposedly Britons obeyed the law, not
as Americans did because of a social contract or because it protected their
natural rights, but because they were subjects and must do what the
monarch told them. In practice, however, the people now told the
monarch what to tell them, which came to much the same thing. The two
systems were alike, too, with regard to many of the problems they confronted – urban squalor, crime, prostitution and the social evils arising
out of unregulated industrial competition. The British academic and
jurist, James Bryce, whose *The American Commonwealth* (1888) provides the
best contemporary account of the American politics of the period, felt
equally at home in British and American elite circles.[36] Fabian Socialists
like Sidney and Beatrice Webb looked to American Progressives like Jane
Addams and Henry George for inspiration and vice-versa. Gradually the
two nations were establishing a network of linkages bringing them closer
together.

This was perhaps most clearly evident in the world of letters. Practically
all of Britain's leading turn-of-the century writers resided at various times
in the United States, some for long periods. Several, Robert Louis
Stevenson and Rudyard Kipling among them, acquired American wives.
American writers, in turn, flocked to Britain. Henry James, arguably the
most distinguished American writer of the period, wrote most of his novels
in England, eventually becoming a British subject. A more colourful visit-
or was Bret Harte, famous for *The Luck of Roaring Camp* and other accounts
of life in the American West. Harte was so taken with England that he
transformed himself into a London dandy, joined the Royal Thames
Yacht Club, and was to be seen about town decked out in a monocle and
yellow gloves. Stephen Crane, author of *The Red Badge of Courage*, lived for a
time in Sussex, where he attracted attention by going about wearing a six-
shooter. Ambrose Bierce, also a writer of Civil War tales and close associ-
ate of both Bret Harte and Mark Twain, lived in England from 1872 to
1876. Twain himself spent various periods in England, where he was
received with even more enthusiasm than in America, and was inordinate-
ly proud to be awarded an honorary doctorate. by Oxford University.
American writers, especially those writing in the vernacular, valued the
prestige conferred by European recognition, while British writers, now
that the copyright issue had been resolved, were mindful of the financial
rewards that could be reaped across the Atlantic.[37]

In the age of the steamship and railroad, fees could be earned and sales usefully promoted by means of lecture tours. Dickens and Thackeray inaugurated the practice in the 1850s, and from the 1860s on – when the big lecture agencies were established – a succession of authors, including Twain, Bierce, Charles Kingsley, Wilkie Collins and Matthew Arnold, were whisked around the two nations' lecture circuits. The young Oscar Wilde arrived in New York in 1882 with the intention of 'gathering up the golden fruits of America', and did so. He arrived at an opportune moment. The taste for high aestheticism, brought over from Europe, was just catching on, and the newspapers lapped up his camp posturing. He had, Wilde said, come for the purpose of civilising America, the country having gone from barbarism to decadence, having omitted the usual intermediate stage. As he told the miners of Leadsville, Colorado, 'let there be no flower in your meadows that does not wreathe its tendrils around your pillow, no little leaf in your Titan forests that does not lend its form to design'. They had never seen anything like him, but took it all in good part and raised a cheer when, at the end of a dinner in his honour, he lit a long cigar.[38]

Although the two countries were becoming more alike in some respects, they remained very different in others. In contrast to Great Britain, where the extension of the franchise in 1884 revolutionised politics by opening the way for political activity by the trade unions, the United States never developed a mass socialist, labour or social democratic party. Socialism there remained only a marginal force, the high water mark of its achievement being the 6 per cent of the national vote gained in 1912. That socialists did so poorly in what was rapidly emerging as the most advanced capitalist society in the world was partly a reflection of the country's social fluidity and ethnic diversity. As new immigrants arrived, eager to take any jobs available, opportunities opened up for those already settled to move up the occupational ladder. There were better ways of getting ahead in America than by soaking the rich.[39]

Middle-class reformers, on the other hand, increasingly found common ground with the American Progressive movement, which sought to curb business excesses, combat political corruption, and make government more democratic. On issues such as women's suffrage, antitrust legislation, industrial regulation, tax reform and workmen's compensation their approaches were similar. The British labour movement, however, increasingly took the view that Americans had little to teach them. So far as trade unionism was concerned, it was rather the other way around, with Americans looking to Europe for inspiration. The most militant of the American unions, the Industrial Workers of the World (IWW), known as the Wobblies, dreamed of seizing control of the nation's industries and overthrowing capitalism. Essentially, it was an American version of the movement that around the turn of the century was behind much of the labour unrest in Europe, the aim being to overthrow democracy by direct action and establish in its stead a corporate society controlled by trade unions and workers' co-operatives. Although the IWW won a number of successes, and perhaps as many as three million workers passed through its ranks, its active membership at any one time probably never exceeded 150 000. Throughout its existence it was subjected to such unremitting harassment from police and corporation hirelings that its strength was eventually broken. Management had no compunction about using strong-arm tactics or resorting to trumped up charges.

As seen by British labour, the United States exemplified all the worst features of capitalism – plutocracy, sweatshops, strike-breaking, unsafe working conditions, factory towns, lack of social provision, and a corrupt legal system. The muckraking journalism of the period helped reinforce the impression that a country that had started out as a noble experiment in liberty had taken a wrong path. Instead of being a beacon of freedom, it had become a nation where the laws intended to protect the liberty of the individual had been reinterpreted in a way that granted corporations the freedom to ride roughshod over the interests of the people at large. Along the way, it had acquired an urban elite that aped the lifestyles of the European upper classes and prostituted its daughters for the sake of noble titles. It was, in short, an example of what could happen even to the best of societies if capitalism were allowed free rein.

This, needless to say, was a highly biased view. Comparisons are difficult, because what is done at the national level in Britain is often the responsibility of individual states in America. But at local, state and national level American businesses were constrained in their activities far more than America's overseas critics supposed, as, for example, with regard to safety in the workplace, the location of factories and the quality of their products. Well-established businesses on both sides of the Atlantic mostly supported regulation, partly for the sake of their reputations but also as a means of fending off the challenge of small competitors less able to bear the additional costs involved.

One result of America's rise to industrial pre-eminence was that the English-speaking people now exercised a disproportionate influence on the world's affairs. 'We are a part, and a great part, of the Greater Britain which seems so plainly destined to dominate this planet', declared the *New York Times* on the occasion of Queen Victoria's Diamond Jubilee.[40] That the two nations found themselves in a position appropriate to such self-congratulation most modern commentators would put down to a combination of historical and geopolitical circumstances – in other words, to cultural attitudes, available resources, ready access to markets, levels of education, technical skills, and the like. But, with Social Darwinian ideas in the ascendant, nineteenth-century commentators preferred other explanations. Was it entirely a coincidence that the English-speaking nations were at the forefront of civilisation's onward march? Might it not be more logical to attribute their success to their inherent qualities rather than external influences? After all, the circumstances associated with Britain's rise to maritime pre-eminence were very different from those that led to America's winning of the West. In short, drawing analogies with what happened in the animal kingdom, surely the simplest explanation was that 'Anglo-Saxons' were simply superior people? Darwin himself did not invent the term 'survival of the fittest' (Herbert Spencer did), and would never have approved of its being applied to cultural phenomena, still less to business competition, as was a common practice at the time. Darwin's concern was the survival of *species*. Nevertheless, for those seeking to account for the almost effortless way people of British descent had succeeded in taking over so large a portion of the world, it provided a ready-made explanation. Who could doubt that they were the most energetic, capable, ethical, talented and advanced of all the races – the very highest twigs in the tree of evolution? Some of the more extreme Social Darwinists, like the Ohio minister Josiah Strong, prophesied a future in which, perhaps with the fate of the Native Americans in mind, the less fit would be supplanted and physically disappear. A more generally held view, however, was that of Senator Beveridge of Ohio, who declared: 'God has not been preparing the English-speaking and Teutonic peoples for a thousand years for nothing. . . . No! He has made us the master organisers of the world to establish system where chaos reigns.'[41] Hearing of the US victories in the Spanish-American War, and carried away by the euphoria of the moment, Joseph Chamberlain, the expansionist British Colonial Secretary, even went so far as to call for an alliance between the world's two great Anglo-Saxon peoples.[42]

Americans, though, remained mindful of Washington's and Jefferson's warnings concerning the dangers of involving themselves in Europe's affairs. Elsewhere, it was true, they had allowed their interests to expand mightily. They now regarded the whole of the western hemisphere, along with the Philippines and much of the Pacific, as falling within their sphere of influence, but any kind of alliance with Britain, formal or informal, was out of the question. Unlike the British, they did not feel beleaguered. Their star was still in the ascendant. Protected by vast oceans, with an expanding population, huge natural resources, and now a first-class navy, the United States was in a stronger position in relation to the rest of the world than ever before. America had no need of allies; even if the balance of power was changing it did not follow that the policies that had served it well in the past would not continue to do so in the future.

5 The Great Divide: 1914–1920

At the beginning of the twentieth century the balance of power in the world was shifting. Britain still had the largest battle fleet, but its control of the seas was no longer something to be taken for granted. Germany, the United States, France and Japan now had sizeable battle fleets that, collectively, outgunned Britain's. More disturbingly, the cost of naval weaponry had escalated. Gone were the days when Britain could patrol the seas and guard the outposts of empire at little cost to the taxpayer. Between 1870 and 1911 Britain's naval budget had increased from £9.8 million to £40.3 million, and expenditure on the army by almost as much.[1] Weapons were not only becoming more expensive; they were becoming obsolete and needing replacing sooner. Around the middle of the nineteenth century a ninety-gun warship could be built for as little as £100 000; by 1912–13 the cost of one of the new Dreadnoughts ran to some £2.5 million. As the Spanish had discovered in Manila Bay, an antiquated navy stood no chance against properly equipped modern fighting ships; either a country kept up with technological change or ceased to be a great power.

Apart from a handful of Little Englanders, no one proposed that Britain take the latter course. The long-term trends, however, were worrying as it became increasingly clear that Britain was losing its industrial edge. Economic growth had been sluggish ever since the 1870s, having declined from 4 per cent in the early part of the century to a mere 1.5 per cent in its closing decades. Its lead in such key fields as steel, chemicals and machine tools had been whittled away. For the first time in its history it had become a significant importer of manufactured goods. The picture was not uniformly gloomy. Thanks to the steady expansion of global commerce, the City of London flourished as never before, as did shipbuilding. Measured in absolute terms, established industries, such as iron, coal and textiles, continued to expand. Still, from the way in which Britain's share of the world's manufacturing capacity dropped from 32 per cent in 1870 to 15 per cent by 1910, and of world trade from 25 per cent to 14 per cent, the long-term trend was disturbing.

Something of the sort, of course, was bound to happen as industrial knowledge spread. Britain could not prevent the secrets of its industrial

success from leaking out, and with improved communications news travelled faster. Formerly, the United States had looked to Britain both for
manufactures and industrial know-how. It still looked to Sheffield for certain types of steel, even though it had long since overtaken Britain in overall steel production. But increasingly the process was reversed as the
British looked to the United States for new developments in such fields as
chemicals, car manufacture, electrical appliances and industrial management. Among the signs that times were changing was the ease with which
American companies had begun penetrating the British market. Singer,
the sewing machine manufacturer, which opened up a factory outside
Glasgow in the 1860s, was the first American company to begin production in Britain. Henry Ford opened his first British factory, in Trafford
Park outside Manchester, in 1908. Soon F. W. Woolworth was revolu-
tionising the retail trade and H. J. Heinz the market in tinned foods.[2] The
British also found themselves relying increasingly on European countries,
particularly Germany, for essential machine components like ball bear-
ings. One way in which the British might have maintained their lead was
by concentrating on research and development, but here, too, they
lagged behind.

The reasons for Britain's industrial weakness remain a matter for
debate. Other countries, of course, possessed advantages that Britain
lacked in the form of easily mined minerals and readily available timber
supplies. Social factors were also presumably involved. Some have
argued that the imperial aspirations of Britain's upper classes and the
socialist leanings of its industrial workforce combined to create a culture
unsuited to industrial efficiency. Correlli Barnett, in *The Collapse of British
Power* (1972), pins the blame on the romantically idealised outlook of late
Victorian educators for inculcating values hostile to business and industry.[3] Whatever the truth of this claim, the same could hardly be said of
Americans who, if late-nineteenth-century visitors to the United States
are to be believed, thought of little else.

Other things being equal, there was no way that a small island like
Britain could compete with a continental power like America. The British
Empire, however, was another matter. In 1914 it contained a grand total
of 425 million inhabitants as compared with America's 100 million. It
could be roughly divided into two parts: the 'white' empire, with a population of some 59 million, made up of Britain itself and the four self-governing dominions of Canada, Australia, New Zealand and South Africa; and
the 'non-white' empire consisting of India, the West Indies, much of
Africa, and various possessions in the Far East, where the other 366 mil-

lion were located, and which was governed directly from London. How much value Britain derived from this 'non-white' empire is debatable. It was rich in resources, but with certain notable exceptions, such as rubber and tin in Malaya, oil in Trinidad, and copper and tungsten in Rhodesia, remarkably little had been done to develop them. The most treasured of all Britain's possessions was India, whose population (along with that of Burma) totalled 316 million and accounted for over three-quarters of the Empire's total. It had been to protect the seaways to India that much of the rest of the Empire had been acquired. Yet, in spite of India's pride of place in the imperial scheme of things, as a field for British investment it occupied a position well below the United States and only slightly above Argentina. The dominions had done rather more in the way of developing their resources, but even there the record was patchy. Partly this was due to lack of population. Although Canada's land area was roughly equivalent to that of the United States, its population of 7.6 million was scarcely larger than London's. Australia and New Zealand, with populations of 4.7 and 1.1 million respectively, were even less fully settled. Impressive though it looked in terms of land mass, the British Empire was an assemblage of pieces, accumulated at different times for different purposes, scattered across the face of the globe. Compared to the fast-growing and thoroughly modern United States, the British Empire, for all its pomp and ritual, was plainly something of a ragbag.

The Changing Balance of Power in Europe

Nevertheless, like other great powers before it, Britain regarded its position as the world's leading nation as part of the natural order. Who could doubt the superior character of its culture and system of parliamentary government? Surely no other people were so well endowed with the qualities necessary for extending the benefits of civilisation to the rest of mankind. All the same, it was becoming evident to the country's statesmen and politicians – if not yet to the general public – that they could no longer regard the affairs of Europe with the same lofty indifference as their mid-Victorian forebears. In earlier times it had been Britain's aim to prevent any single power dominating the continent. That had been the fundamental issue in a succession of wars, first with Spain and later with France. Since the defeat of Napoleon, however, that had not been a problem. Now, however, the situation was changing.

The principal destabilising factor was the rise of Germany. Not that Germany was intent on launching a war of European conquest, although some suspected that might be the case. But whatever the conscious intent of Germany's leaders, there was no doubt that they expected to be treated with the deference appropriate to their nation's newly acquired status as a great power. It was plain also that they resented the way the British and French had stolen a march on them by creating colonial empires that left little room for German overseas expansion. What most alarmed the British, however, was their naval building programme. If Germany lacked overseas possessions, why did it need a large navy? Germany was essentially a continental power. It had no need of an ocean-going navy unless – and this was the suspicion – it intended behaving in ways that challenged British interests. As Winston Churchill shrewdly commented, 'our claim to be left in undisputed enjoyment of vast and splendid possessions, mainly acquired by violence, largely maintained by force, often seems less reasonable to others than to us'.[4] Plainly the Germans' view of their rightful place in the world differed from that assigned them by the British.

Matching Germany's naval building programme, however, was no easy matter. Germany had a larger population, and by 1900 had overtaken Britain in key areas like steel, electrical machinery and chemicals.[5] Negotiations aimed at limiting naval building proved unavailing. Britain refused to countenance any changes likely to affect its maritime dominance, while Germany insisted on a role consonant with its growing industrial strength.[6]

If Germany's advent on the world scene made the British uneasy, it frightened Germany's immediate neighbours even more. The French had particular cause for alarm. Having been humiliated in the Franco-Prussian War of 1870, when they were obliged to give up Alsace-Lorraine and pay Germany an indemnity of five billion francs, they naturally looked to Britain and Russia for support. This led to Germany's feeling encircled and to its allying itself with Austria-Hungary. Alarmed at the prospect of fighting on two fronts at the same time, the German Army General Staff drew up the so-called Schlieffen Plan, which provided that should war break out, regardless of the cause, Germany would immediately strike west through Belgium so as to neutralise France before turning to confront Russia in the east. Simply to mobilise was enough to provoke conflict, for, as the Franco-Prussian War had shown, the army that took the field first had a decisive advantage. Europe had become a powder keg. As the rickety arrangement of alliances, understandings and contingency plans grew, so did the possibility of a single spark setting off an explosion that would blow the structure sky high.

American Responses to the Outbreak of War

The chain of events leading up to the outbreak of the Great War has been described too many times to need recounting. In spite of uncertainty as to the exact degree of culpability attaching to the various powers involved, one thing on which all authorities agree is that the United States cannot be held responsible. Europe was behaving much as it had always behaved, only on a larger scale. Neither the American people nor their government had any clear idea of what it was all about except that it confirmed what their leaders from George Washington onwards had told them about Europe. When President Wilson called on Americans to be impartial in thought as well as in action, voices were not raised in dissent.

Despite the President's injunction, a majority of Americans favoured the Allied cause. Whatever the origins of the war, Germany's violation of Belgian neutrality was plainly an act of aggression. Allied propagandists made other charges, some untrue, concerning the treatment of Belgium's civilian population. These claims were widely believed, not least on account of the autocratic tone of Germany's denials – public relations not being a forte of the German military. What principally predisposed Americans towards the Allied cause, however, was the sense that Britain and France were democracies facing a brutal, militaristic power.

Wilson himself was of English ancestry, loved England, and admired the British political system. His first book, a study of British parliamentary government, drew attention to the many advantages it had over the tripartite American system with its division of powers between the legislature, executive and judiciary. The son of a Presbyterian minister, he adopted a moralistic approach to politics, preferring the dictates of his conscience to the advice of others. High-minded, liberal, self-righteous, he strove to reconcile the irreconcilable by upholding American interests while keeping the country out of war.

Not all Americans favoured the Allied cause. Jewish Americans were not disposed to look favourably on any alliance that included Russia. Irish Americans, who had long regarded Britain as their enemy, hoped that a German victory would help promote Irish independence. At the very least they hoped to see Britain humiliated. Some began drilling in readiness for the day when, with German help, they would return to fight their oppressors. German Americans were more divided. Some simply felt pleased to have escaped involvement, others opposed what they saw as German militarism, although a vocal minority joined the Irish in proclaiming their support for the Central Powers. A few even went so far as to commit acts of sabotage in dockyards and munitions factories, a policy that did little physical damage, but helped discredit the cause they were intending to promote.[7]

Most Americans, however, still traced their cultural, if not their ancestral, roots back to Britain. They had been brought up to think of Chaucer, Shakespeare and Dickens as being as much a part of their culture as of England's. Above all, America's liberal ideology inclined them towards Britain and France. Thus, from the outset, Americans, especially those in the higher echelons of government, hoped for an Allied victory. Pro-Allied feeling was especially marked in the case of Wilson's intimates, among whom were his personal adviser, Colonel Edward House, the First Counsellor at the State Department, Robert Lansing, and the US Ambassador to Britain, Walter Hines Page. So passionate was Page's identification with the Allied cause that in addition to his official dispatches he bombarded the President with personal letters pleading that America provide more active assistance. It is significant that in spite of Wilson's regarding him as 'more British than the British', and of much press criticism on that account, he was not recalled.[8] There was, however, one member of the administration who did not share in the prevailing Anglophilia, namely Page's immediate superior, Secretary of State William Jennings Bryan. In contrast to Wilson and Page, Bryan was for peace at any price. A religious fundamentalist and ardent pacifist, his views reflected the attitude of many in the Midwest. Bryan's fear, fully justified by what later transpired, was that as a result of a sequence of events over which it had no control the United States would be inveigled into intervention against the wishes of a majority of the American people. Thus, when the war broke out, he had the State Department issue a statement to the effect that for American bankers to make loans to foreign nations at war would be inconsistent with the nation's policy of strict neutrality. As he informed the President:

> Money is the worst of all contrabands because it commands everything else. . . . The powerful financial interests which would be connected with these loans would be tempted to use their influence through the newspapers to support the interests of the Government to which they had loaned because the value of the security would be directly affected by the result of the war. We would thus find our newspapers arrayed on one side or the other, each group supporting a financial group and pecuniary interest. All of this interest would make it all the more difficult for us to maintain neutrality.[9]

At that early date Britain had no need of loans, having large holdings of American assets it could dispose of in return for supplies. Nevertheless, the President felt obliged to go behind Bryan's back and authorise Lansing to let bankers know privately that the administration would not look unfavourably at the granting of credits to belligerents so long as they were represented as grants in furtherance of trade rather than as loans. Bryan was, of course, right in supposing that the President was being less than impartial. The loans were bound to favour the Allies, who controlled the seas, rather than the Central Powers. Relations between the President and his Secretary of State finally broke down in May 1915 following the sinking of the *Lusitania*, when Bryan refused to sign a stern note of warning to Germany, drafted by Wilson, upholding the right of Americans to travel on belligerent vessels. Unwilling to risk war over such an issue, Bryan resigned and joined the peace movement. Lansing succeeded him, although in effect Wilson became his own Secretary of State.

The Struggle to Maintain American Neutrality

In August 1914 the general expectation was that the war would soon be over. This was based on the experience of the brief Franco-German conflict of 1870 rather than on the long-drawn-out American Civil War of 1861–65, which, in its latter stages, foreshadowed the trench warfare of 1914–18. So far as relations between Britain and the United States were concerned, however, the parallel was rather with the Napoleonic wars. Once more the US was the world's leading neutral mercantile power, and, as before, the belligerents sought to prevent their opponents importing goods that might assist their war efforts. Americans still claimed the right to trade freely with belligerent countries in time of war. In theory this left them as free to trade with Germany as with Britain, but in practice Britain's naval dominance, financial reserves, and close links with the US money markets meant that the Allies benefited far more than the Central Powers. As German spokesmen continually complained, American neutrality was anything but even-handed.

Neutrality also raised once again the thorny question of maritime rights. As before, the combatants declared the waters around each others' coastlines a war zone. One important difference, however, was that whereas in Napoleonic times the United States had been a minor power on the world's periphery, it was now an industrial giant. Whatever it did or did not do was bound to affect events. The British, foreseeing that if the war became a long-drawn-out affair they would necessarily become dependent on America for war supplies, moved cautiously. One option available to the United States was to do what Jefferson had done in 1807 and cut off trade with Europe. However, with the US economy already showing signs of sliding into recession the loss to the nation's industries would have been serious. America needed the economic boost that Allied war purchases would provide. Britain tactfully delayed imposing its blockade until the revivifying effects of its purchases had begun to be felt. Germany, too, moved with deliberation, hoping for a quick knockout blow in the land war and uncertain about the legality and adequacy of its principal maritime weapon, its fleet of 28 submarines.

Maritime law, even more than usual, was in a state of flux. For a blockade to be legitimate, according to the traditional view, it had to be effective, which is to say maintained by a force sufficient to prevent access in the great majority of cases. This was more than Germany's U-boat fleet was capable of achieving so far as the coastal waters of Britain were concerned. During the American Civil War, the British had not demurred when the United States extended the right to intercept vessels to include those bound for neutral ports on the grounds that they might be carrying war materials destined for the enemy. On the other hand, there was no agreement about what constituted war materials – so-called 'contraband' – now that the conduct of war was increasingly dependent on industrial production. Broadly enough defined, practically anything relating to industry – even food supplies destined for workers and their families – could be placed under that heading.

What maritime law made no allowance for was the introduction of *new* weapons. Immediately following the declaration of war, Britain announced that Germany had violated international law by laying mines in the open waters of the North Sea, and invoked the right to take retaliatory measures. Encouraged by a United States' statement that it did not object in principle to mine-laying so long as it did not interfere with neutral shipping, the British proceeded to lay minefields around the German coast. The whole North Sea, it declared, was a military zone into which it was unsafe for neutrals to venture without guidance from the Royal Navy. As in Napoleonic times, there thus began a process of escalation involving measures and counter-measures of increasingly doubtful legality – such as requiring all neutral ships arriving from the western hemisphere to dock at British ports before proceeding to their destinations. While in port, their cargoes were closely examined and any mail they were carrying was routinely opened and read. So well enforced was this policy that between January and July 1915 over 85 per cent of vessels destined for neutral ports were stopped and searched by the Allies.[10]

The United States protested, arguing that these practices went far beyond what was required for Britain's defence. The British replied that, on the contrary, they were entirely necessary, and proceeded to add further items, including foodstuffs, to their contraband list. More provocatively, they compiled a blacklist of American firms with which British nationals were forbidden to do business on account of their being suspected of trading with the Central Powers. The justification given for this policy was that it discouraged blockade breaking, but many Americans suspected, not without reason, that the real aim was to benefit British firms. The overall effect of the war, however, was to enrich the United States at the expense of the United Kingdom. Between 1914 and 1916 American exports to Britain quadrupled, more than making up for any loss of trade with the Central Powers. So, although Americans had cause to feel resentful at British high-handed behaviour, there were strong arguments against their adopting retaliatory measures. As the British Ambassador to the United States, Sir Cecil Spring-Rice, reported, '[T]he prosperity of the country increases, and it seems to be in a fair way of gaining the whole world, whatever other thing it may lose.'[11]

Irritating though Allied restrictions undoubtedly were, the anger they caused did not compare with that aroused by Germany's decision of 4 February 1915 to resort to submarine warfare. The pretext for this action was that it was in retaliation for Britain's creation of a war zone around the coast of Germany. Germany, accordingly, declared a war zone around the entire British Isles into which it warned that neutral shipping would enter at its peril. This was unprecedented. It was one thing to stop and search neutral vessels, as blockading navies had always done, quite another to torpedo them without warning, irrespective of what cargoes they were carrying or where they were destined. In retrospect, Germany's action appears perfectly understandable: the U-boat was a new weapon that depended on its invisibility for its effectiveness. On the surface it was virtually defenceless, even against lightly-armed merchant vessels, and with Germany's main battle fleet afraid to venture from harbour, short of leaving the Allies in undisputed command of the world's oceans, Germany had no alternative.

The US response, however, was to hold Germany to 'strict accountability' for any loss of American lives or property arising out of U-boat action. What this meant in practical terms Wilson did not specify, although the phrase plainly implied some fairly drastic action. The implications of Germany's new policy soon became clear with a succession of sinkings, culminating, on 7 May 1915, with that of the British passenger liner *Lusitania* off the southern coast of Ireland with the loss of 1,198 passengers and crew, among whom were 128 Americans. Such was America's outrage that there were calls for a declaration of war. The President, however, sought to calm the situation. 'There is', he said, 'such a thing as a man being too proud to fight. There is such a thing as a nation being so right that it does not have to convince others by force that it is right.' One response would have been to forbid Americans from travelling on belligerent ships. However, the United States had come to regard itself as a major power, and having taken such a high moral line it was difficult now to back down. Wilson, therefore, demanded an assurance from Germany that it would henceforth adopt measures guaranteed to safeguard American lives and American shipping.

This was a fateful step. Effectively it took the decision over whether the United States would enter the war away from Congress and put it in the hands of the German High Command. For four months Germany hesitated, during which time more American lives were lost. As the Germans saw it, America was being hypocritical, prattling on about neutrality while supplying Britain with arms and munitions for the purpose of killing German soldiers. On the other hand, there was growing doubt as to whether, with only some forty submarines currently in service, the damage they were capable of causing justified bringing America into the war. Accordingly, in September 1915, Count von Bernstorff, the German Ambassador in Washington, gave Secretary Lansing an assurance that German submarines would in future refrain from attacking 'liners'.

Nevertheless, Germany remained determined to do what it could to prevent America from supplying its enemies. Early in 1915 it had dispatched Franz von Rintelen, an international banker and naval reserve officer, to organise sabotage networks in the United States. 'I'll buy up what I can and blow up what I can't', he told the German Admiralty on the eve of his departure.[12] Once in America, he was soon busily at work bribing dock workers to place time bombs in departing munitions vessels and organising demonstrations in support of the German cause. A briefcase stolen from the German Commercial attaché by the American Secret Service revealed clandestine payments to Irish-American and German-American organisations. So extensive were these activities that rumours began to circulate of a possible armed uprising. By way of countering these efforts, British intelligence created a network of agents, mostly immigrants from central Europe, to infiltrate German-American organisations and businesses, so that it was soon better informed about German espionage and covert operations than the US Government. The most spectacular German escapade occurred in July 1916 when agents succeeded in detonating two million pounds of explosives awaiting shipment in a New York freight yard, creating a large crater and rattling windows in Brooklyn and Manhattan. Such activities, however, were entirely counter-productive. Germany's crassness in this regard more than offset the anger felt by many Americans at Britain's ruthless crushing of the 1916 Easter Rising in Dublin. The German cause also suffered as a result of British agents spreading often invented stories of wrongdoing, such as the famous tales of German soldiers raping Belgian nuns.[13]

As the war progressed, Britain's dependence on the United States increased. The problem was that its need for munitions, foodstuffs and other commodities far exceeded America's demand for British goods. To make up for this shortfall, the British Treasury depleted its gold reserves and began selling off the dollar securities accumulated over the years by British investors. To prevent the flight of American capital it found itself having to maintain high interest rates. More and more, however, it had to borrow on the American money market, not, as at the time of the Boer War, for the sake of convenience, but out of necessity. It found a valuable ally in J. P. Morgan, the son of the famous financier and an ardent supporter of the Allied cause, who used his extensive contacts in American industry to negotiate deals on Britain's behalf. In order not to alarm the anti-war lobby or alert Germany to the Allies' growing dependency, Morgan moved discreetly, liaising with London through Morgan Grenfell, the Morgan Bank's British partner company, and placing orders without telling the suppliers who was purchasing the goods they produced.[14]

Thus, as William Jennings Bryan had warned, a symbiotic relationship developed between the British Government and US financial interests, the one seeking to stave off military defeat, the other to maintain the buoyancy of the American economy. In the process, New York emerged as the world's leading financial centre. No longer did Americans have to go on bended knee to London financiers; now it was the other way around. For the first time in its history the United States found itself a creditor nation. Ambassador Page, in spite of his fervent support for the Allied cause, could not conceal his glee: 'These English are spending their capital, and it is their capital that continues to give them their vast power . . . . The great economic tide of the century flows our way. *We* shall have the big world questions to decide presently.'[15] The balance of world power was shifting. The United States would, indeed, have the big questions to confront, although whether it would welcome having to do so was quite another matter.

Meanwhile, as orders for war matériel continued to pour in, the American economy continued to grow. So, too, did the need for workers. The effects of the demands being made on the economy was especially noticeable in areas such as New Jersey and Delaware, where the Du Pont Corporation had its munitions plants, and in steelmaking towns like Pittsburgh, Toledo and Birmingham. Shipbuilding and textile production also expanded. In Bridgeport, Connecticut, where the Remington Arms Company established a new factory producing rifles and bayonets, hordes of new workers transformed what had previously been a rather staid New England community into a thriving factory town. Because immigration from Europe had virtually ceased on account of the war, the demand for workers accelerated the northward migration of African Americans. Agriculture also profited. With men away at the front and Allied farm production disrupted, Europe's need for American imports increased driving farm prices upward. Cotton, that had sold for 12 cents a pound in 1913, was soon selling for more than double that figure; corn prices jumped from 70 cents a bushel to $1.50. Although the cost of living also went up, real incomes kept well ahead. Americans were earning more and spending more than ever before. Between 1914 and 1917 automobile production quadrupled, rising from 460 000 to 1.8 million. Well before the President's war message to Congress, neutrality had become a decidedly relative concept.

Nevertheless, the great majority of Americans remained adamantly opposed to involvement. Wilson ran for re-election in 1916 on the slogan 'He kept us out of war', narrowly defeating the Republican candidate, Charles Evans Hughes. The slogan was particularly helpful in garnering him votes in the isolationist Midwest and in those Western states where women had recently been granted the vote. Irish-American and German-American groups, on the other hand, voted for Hughes on the grounds of Wilson's supposedly pro-British sympathies.

Wilson, however, was becoming ever more exasperated with Britain. 'I am, I must admit,' he wrote to Colonel House in July 1916, 'about at the end of my patience with Great Britain and the Allies. This Black list business is the last straw. . . . I am seriously considering asking Congress to prohibit loans and restrict exports to the Allies.'[16] He was also angry that the British had failed to take advantage of on offer of mediation he had made through Colonel House to the British Foreign Secretary the previous February.

Almost immediately on his re-election, and presumably with his approval, the Federal Reserve Board issued a warning to banks that it was not in the nation's interest to encourage investing in foreign bonds. This led to a run on sterling and an abrupt fall in the value of British Treasury bills. Wilson's evident intention was to use America's economic muscle to bring the Allies to the negotiating table. Well-meaning though this doubtless was, the British made plain that they had no intention of agreeing to an arrangement that would raise popular hopes of peace or lead to their having to make concessions to Germany. They also found Wilson's apparent assumption that there existed any sort of moral equivalence in the behaviour of the two sides deeply offensive. Germany, after all, was the aggressor, as its invasion of Belgium showed. It was a militaristic power bent on imposing its authoritarian values on Europe, unlike Britain and France (Russia, the other leading member of the Alliance, was not mentioned in this context), who were fighting for freedom and democracy – surely values that Americans, of all people, should understand. King George V reportedly wept over America's lack of appreciation of the sacrifices Britain was making.[17]

Fortunately for the Allies, Wilson was dissuaded from carrying out his threat of cutting off loans. As in previous continental wars, Britain had assumed the burden of paying not only for the maintenance of its own armies, but for those of its allies as well. Because of the Treasury's pressing need for dollars, it was given the power to requisition and sell off private overseas investments. By early 1917, however, the situation had become desperate. Britain was spending £150 million a month on the war, £60 million of which had to come from the United States, more than a third of it in the form of loans. Its gold and dollar reserves were about to run out. When they did there would be only two possibilities left: either the American public would have to triple its contributions, which seemed improbable, or the Allies would have to reduce their expenditure. Effectively the American people were paying for the war; if they stopped, the Allies would in all probability have to sue for peace. To make matters worse, Russia was now in the grip of revolution, creating a likelihood that Germany's eastern forces would shortly be moved to the Western Front. In short, it began to look very much as if Germany was about to win.[18]

Germany, however, was also hard pressed. Neither side had prepared for a long-drawn-out war of attrition or for the cost of modern weaponry. The Allies' great advantage was their ability to draw on America's resources. Unaware of the likelihood that this arrangement might be about to collapse, the German High Command made a fateful decision. On 7–8 January 1917, it determined to expedite matters by resuming unrestricted submarine warfare despite the almost certain knowledge that it would bring the United States into the war. Like other authoritarian leaders over the years, Hindenburg and Ludendorff, Germany's supreme military commanders, mistook the workings of American democracy for a lack of effective political leadership. The American public's determination to remain out of the war also helped give credence to the belief that, should the US become involved, it would be on a strictly limited basis. Given that American industry was already fully mobilised in support of the Allies, would a formal declaration of war make much difference,? Like the Japanese thinking that led to the attack on Pearl Harbor a generation later, this was a gross misreading of the situation. Plainly, Germany had underestimated the additional resources, material and psychological, that Americans were capable of bringing into play once their anger was aroused. Still, even if the US did decide to bring its full strength to bear, raising an army would take time. By unleashing its now much-expanded U-boat fleet Germany could still hope to bring the Allies to the negotiating table well before Americans in any significant numbers reached the Western Front.

Germany made its formal announcement on 31 January 1917; Wilson broke off diplomatic relations three days later. While Americans waited to see what the effect of Germany's declaration would be, news of another development provoked their ire. On 17 January, the German foreign minister, Arthur Zimmerman, sent a message to Germany's Washington embassy for onward transmission to Mexico City offering an alliance with Mexico in the event of war breaking out between Germany and the United States. The Zimmerman telegram, as it became known, also offered to return Texas, New Mexico and Arizona to Mexico in the event of a German–Mexican victory. The message was intercepted by British intelligence, which, unbeknown to the United States, had been tapping America's Atlantic cable. Unwilling to admit that they had been reading US as well as German diplomatic traffic, the British were initially uncertain how to exploit this coup. They succeeded in covering their espionage activities, however, by obtaining a second copy of the message from an agent in Mexico City. On 24 February, Arthur Balfour, the British Foreign Secretary, summoned Ambassador Page to the Foreign Office and presented him with a copy. Page promptly forwarded it to Wilson, who was furious at Germany's duplicity, particularly as he had done

Germany the favour of allowing it to use the US cable, but the more so as it occurred while he was still trying to bring the Allies and the Central Powers to the negotiating table.

When the text of the telegram appeared in the press the American public was even more outraged than it had been by the news of the invasion of Belgium or the sinking of the *Lusitania*. Invading neutral countries and endangering lives at sea were bad enough, but never in their wildest dreams had Americans imagined that a foreign power might go so far as to contemplate dismembering the United States. German sympathisers claimed that the telegram was a British forgery, but doubts as to its authenticity were removed when Arthur Zimmerman accepted full responsibility. British code-breakers were not displeased when, in the subsequent flurry of news stories about how copies of the telegram had been obtained, it was popularly assumed that American agents had been responsible.[19]

America Enters the War

Much to Britain's relief, Congress declared war on Germany on 6 April, and on Austria-Hungary the following day. Having lost all faith in Germany's good intentions, and faced with a growing list of American shipping losses, Wilson felt he had no alternative. In a memorable speech to Congress he mentioned the Zimmerman telegram and condemned 'Germany's irresponsible government which has thrown aside all considerations of humanity and is running amok'.[20] Although the immediate precipitating factor was German maritime policy, he was able to exploit the growing feeling that the United States simply could not allow an autocratic country like Germany to take control of Europe.

So far as the Allies were concerned, the announcement came none too soon. The war on the ground had been going badly. Successive assaults along the Aisne and in Champagne had ground to a halt, eroding morale and leading to mutinies in the French army. Shipping losses, which reached a peak of 881 000 tons in April, far exceeded the Allies' capacity for replacement. Despite enormous casualties, a series of British offensives in Flanders, beginning in June 1917, won little ground. In July, the long-hoped-for Russian offensive was decisively smashed by the Germans, giving rise to an upsurge of peace sentiment and the collapse of the Provisional Government. Then, in the autumn, came the crushing defeat of the Italians at Caporetto and the loss of the whole of north-eastern Italy to the enemy. The only hope the Allies had of staving off defeat, it was becoming clear, was intervention by the United States.

One effect of America's entry into the war was to give the Allies full access to America's resources. Not surprisingly, American shippers had been refusing to risk their vessels in submarine-infested waters, the result being that at the time of Wilson's declaration Britain had less than six weeks' food supply on hand. Alarmed at the possibility that the Allies might collapse and the United States be left to fight Germany on its own, the US Navy was instructed to move 31 of its 56 destroyers to British ports to assist in hunting U-boats in the eastern Atlantic. Convoy operations, introduced largely on the initiative of the United States, cut down shipping losses. So effective did this system prove that not a single American soldier was lost in transit to Europe. The US Navy also assisted in closing off the North Sea to submarines by laying a huge mine barrage. By the end of 1917 shipping losses had declined to half their former level.

Thanks to the stimulus of Allied war purchases, the United States had had almost three years in which to build up its armaments industry. Under the direction of Herbert Hoover and Bernard Baruch, organisations were established to take charge of allocating resources. Eventually an Inter-allied Council on War Purchases and Finance was set up in Washington to oversee not only weapons production and distribution but the shipping of food. In Europe, a whole series of inter-allied councils took on the task of co-ordinating the various aspects of war finance, maritime transportation, munitions allocation, food distribution and naval policy. Although the United States was officially only an 'associated power' – a distinction Wilson was at pains to stress – America's organisational know-how contributed significantly to the streamlining of effort.

Within a few months of America's entry into the war it was clear that the Germans had miscalculated. Had Hindenburg and Ludendorff studied the American Civil War they would have had a better idea of what to expect. Nevertheless, it was more than a year before American troops made their presence felt on the Western Front. In early 1917, the US Army had consisted of a mere 200 000 men – a tiny force by European standards. Britain alone had already *lost* roughly double that number in battle and France more still. By the time the war ended, however, the US Army had expanded to approximately four million, of whom some two million saw service in France. The first contingent arrived in late June 1917 but did not take up positions at the front until late October. Their commander, General John J. Pershing, rejected a British suggestion that in view of their having a common language American brigades be mixed in with British. Instead, at his insistence, they were given their own sector of front in an area just west of Verdun.

The first time American troops were involved in major military action was in March 1918 when the Germans launched a massive attack along the Somme with the intention of capturing Dunkirk and Calais. When the Allied lines began to crumble, American reinforcements were thrown in and managed to stabilise the situation. In May and June they played a decisive part in stemming the second phase of the German spring offensive, which broke through Allied defences on the Marne and at one point seemed in danger of capturing Paris. Germany had gambled on putting all its resources into a massive offensive in the hope of ending the war before more Americans arrived. By midsummer, a million American soldiers were on French soil with thousands more arriving by the day. In July 270 000 of them took part in the Allied counter-offensive which drove the now exhausted Germans out of the areas they had just occupied. The tide of war had turned. Germany's allies, Austria-Hungary, Bulgaria and Turkey sued for peace. In September, 1.2 million Americans took part in the last great battle on the Western Front, capturing Sedan and cutting one of the key railroad links used for supplying Germany's forces. The following month the German front line began to give way along the entire 200-mile segment stretching from Alsace-Lorraine to the North Sea. With the morale of their troops collapsing, Germany's generals urged the Chancellor to ask for an armistice. Rather than negotiate with the Allies, from whom he could expect harsh terms, he appealed to Wilson. The Allies, not surprisingly, were furious, but at that late stage there was little they could do. Their people were war-weary, and there was a growing fear of a westward surge of Bolshevism unless peace came soon. In any case, there was no possibility of their continuing to fight if, as Wilson threatened, he withdrew US forces on the grounds that it was wrong to support the efforts of countries that did not share America's war aims.

In later years the British expressed bitterness that it took the United States so long to come to their assistance. At the time they found it galling that America was put in a position to dictate the terms of the armistice. The battle casualties of the American Expeditionary Force amounted to 49 000 dead, a formidable figure, but hardly one to compare with the 750 000 Britons and over one million Frenchmen who had lost their lives. For three terrible years the Allies had held the Germans at bay while America prospered. On the other hand, there was no gainsaying the fact that had US forces not arrived, the Allies would most likely have lost the war. It was American resources that had enabled them to go on fighting for as long as they did and American reinforcements that helped stop Germany's final desperate onslaught.

There was consolation also to be had in the tough terms Wilson was persuaded to impose on the Germany. In return for agreeing to an armistice, he required that the German army give up the lands it had occupied, withdraw beyond the Rhine, and abandon vast quantities of war matériel. This was enough to satisfy the Allied military commanders, although Pershing, with the precedent of the American Civil War in mind, would have preferred unconditional surrender. Wilson also contributed to the overthrow of the Kaiser by urging the German people to adopt a democratic form of government. At least the Germans were left in no doubt that they had lost the war. Most people were simply glad that the fighting was over.

Negotiating the Peace Settlement

Because of the almost accidental way in which the Allies had stumbled into war, apart from stemming the German advance they had no very clear idea of what they were fighting for. In due course specific agreements were reached regarding the confiscation and redistribution of Germany's overseas possessions, but until the Bolsheviks leaked news of them, these were kept from public knowledge. In view of the sacrifices being demanded, it had been thought best to avoid mention of territorial considerations. Far better, it had been decided, to dwell on freedom, country, God, an end to future strife and other ideas of an uplifting nature. Thus, when Colonel House met with Allied representatives in Paris in late 1917, it soon became clear that, apart from their being intent on defeating the Central Powers, there was little common ground other than a conviction that Germany would have to be permanently weakened. House informed Wilson that since the Allies did not have a plan for the post-war world the United States had better formulate one.

This was something Wilson had been turning over in his mind. As he had made plain in his war message to Congress, America was going to war, not on account of her own economic needs, nor to gain any territorial advantage, but because its vessels had been attacked by the Imperial German Navy. Yet for the United States to cast aside the precepts of the Founding Fathers and involve itself in Europe's struggles at the cost of thousands of American lives could hardly be justified on those grounds alone. There had to be great moral principles involved. The American people needed to be assured that they were committing themselves to a cause worthy of the sacrifice they were making. Germany's attack, therefore, needed to be seen, not simply as an attack on American shipping but as an attack on 'all nations' and 'a warfare against mankind'. The United States was not declaring war on the people of Germany but on their autocratic leaders, men whose principles constituted a threat to the rights of all men everywhere. The strategy might have changed, but America's objectives were essentially the same as they had always been: to promote the safety and happiness of mankind as a whole. Americans must dedicate themselves to making the world 'safe for democracy', by setting up 'among the really free and self-governed peoples of the world such a concert of purpose and action' as would henceforward ensure that the principles of peace and justice be universally observed. As inhabitants of the New World, untainted by the sins of the Old, it was incumbent on them to adopt a different approach from that of the other belligerents. Not for the first or last time, the United States had gone to war for one reason, but declared that it was fighting for quite another.[21]

That this was more than mere political rhetoric was clear from Wilson's refusal to identify America's war aims with those of the Allies. In spite of his admiration of British liberal culture, he suspected Britain of imperial ambitions. The public adulation that greeted him in London on his way to the Paris peace conference failed to melt his icy demeanour. At a dinner in Buckingham Palace he was unfavourably impressed by the sumptuous display of royal opulence. In his after-dinner speech, he pointedly rejected the references to the bonds of language and history linking the two nations traditionally evoked on such occasions.

> You must not speak of us who come over here as cousins, still less as brothers; we are neither. Neither must you think of us as Anglo-Saxons, for that term can no longer be rightly applied to the people of the United States. Nor must too much importance in this connection be attached to the fact that English is our common language. . . . No, there are only two things which can establish and maintain closer relations between your country and mine: they are community of ideals and interests.[22]

The ideals and interests he had in mind were encapsulated in the Fourteen Points he had outlined in a speech to Congress on 8 January 1918. These included open agreements openly arrived at, free navigation of the world's oceans in time of peace and war, encouragement of international trade, the readjustment of borders along clearly recognisable national lines, the right of national groups to self-rule, reductions in armaments, and the creation of an assembly of nations with the power to adjudicate future international disputes. These constituted, in his view, the only possible basis for a just and lasting peace. High-minded, democratic, they offered a characteristically American solution to the world's problems, although quite what 'self-rule' would mean in the context of a polyglot and ethnically divided Europe was far from clear. Nevertheless, Wilson's Fourteen Points had much in common, with Britain's war aims as outlined by the Prime Minister, David Lloyd George, in a speech delivered only three days before. There were differences of emphasis. One was that, as an island empire and the world's leading naval power, Britain did not wish to enter into any arrangement that would limit the Royal Navy's freedom of action in time of war. But freedom of the seas in wartime, as subsequent events would demonstrate, was an outmoded concept anyway. There were also disagreements over war reparations and indemnities, as well as over what should be done with Germany's former colonies. On most issues, however, Britain and the United States saw eye to eye, including the need for an international organisation to limit the future production of armaments and reduce the chances of war.

It was on the basis of Wilson's Fourteen Points that Germany had asked the United States to intercede with the Allies in arranging an armistice. Wilson, in turn, insisted that they constitute the framework for discussion at the forthcoming peace conference, and that the arrangements for setting up his proposed League of Nations be written into the final treaty. As the leader of the only belligerent to emerge from the war not only unscathed but with its power substantially augmented, he was in a position to ensure that his proposals receive attention. Although the fighting had ceased, the Allies still depended on the US for food and other essentials. Outside the conference hall, many regarded Wilson as a New World Messiah come to right the wrongs of the Old. Inside, many began to suspect that this was also Wilson's own view. Having started out as a convinced isolationist, he now saw it as his – and America's – destiny to create a new liberal world order. Tense, self-righteous, he burned with a cold flame, indifferent to other men's advice, including that of his own delegation.

The Versailles Conference began in early January 1919 and ended with the signing of the final Peace Treaty on 23 June. While the delegates conferred, troubles accumulated. In Britain, there were confrontations with the trade unions. Demobilisation was delayed because, in theory at least, the war had merely been suspended on a month-by-month basis. This led to discontent and even signs of mutiny. In Russia, the struggles between the Bolsheviks and White Russian forces continued, bringing stories of battles and atrocities. Following the collapse of the Turkish and Austro-Hungarian empires, the Balkans and much of Eastern Europe were in turmoil. In Germany, parts of the military were refusing to admit defeat, while radicals under Bolshevik influence fought to gain control of the streets. Against this turbulent background, the delegates struggled as best they could to reconcile their differences and redraw the world's political boundaries, while remaining mindful of the aspirations of those to whom they were answerable back home. Despite the bullying language they used towards Germany, it was increasingly doubtful whether America and the Allies would dare resume hostilities should Germany prove recalcitrant.

So far as their own particular interests were concerned, the British had little cause to feel let down by the final Treaty. With the U-boats gone and the German High Seas Fleet scuttled, Britain's Royal Navy was in a stronger position than ever – except, of course, that it was now rivalled by the US Navy. In the colonial sphere, Britain took over a number of Germany's former possessions. The key issue, however, was what happened to Germany itself. Wilson and Lloyd George, their countries protected by ocean barriers, saw it as important not to punish Germany so severely that it would be unable to play a full part in the new and prosperous world order they were hoping to create. The French, having lately suffered two German invasions, took a different view, arguing that Germany's power be reduced so drastically as to remove any possibility of military revival.

These differences came to the fore in the discussions over reparations. As Germany was held responsible for having started the war, popular opinion in Britain and France favoured its paying all the costs arising out of the conflict. Many Americans took the same view. On Wilson's insistence, however, the Alliance delegates agreed to exclude punitive damages from their calculations, limiting their demands to payment for the actual damage inflicted. But what exactly constituted 'damage', and how was its value was to be assessed? Ideally, Wilson would have liked to do away with reparations altogether. America, after all, had done well out of the war. Realising, however, that that would be unacceptable to others, some of whom had suffered severely, he was prepared to concede a figure of around $30 billion. France, on the other hand, produced claims ranging as high as $200 billion. The figures put forward by the British fell between these two extremes. What would have eased the situation would have been for the United States to renounce the $10 billion in loans it had advanced to the Allies. Wilson, on the advice of American bankers and the US Treasury, ruled this out (thereby, as we will see, storing up much trouble for the future). Finding the reparations issue so contentious, and reluctant to delay the signing of the Treaty any further, the parties agreed to refer the setting of a specific sum to a Reparations Commission for further examination.

The one point on which Wilson was unwilling to compromise concerned the setting up of the League of Nations. The League, as he saw it, was the centrepiece of the Treaty, the one sure guarantee that there would be no recurrence of the horrors lately experienced. Under Article 10 of its Covenant, the League would be granted the power to mobilise its members to use economic and military sanctions against future aggressors. At its heart would be a Council consisting of the Big Five (Britain, the United States, France, Italy and Japan), together with four other nations, selected from among the League's members to serve in rotation. Unlike the five permanent members of the United Nations Security Council, the Big Five would not have a power of veto. For the first time in the world's history there was to be a permanent body, to which all nations would be entitled to belong, with the power and moral authority to settle international disputes.

Not everyone shared Wilson's confidence that such an arrangement would work. Still, although they lacked his enthusiasm, the other leaders at the peace table were anxious to appear conciliatory. It was not, therefore, from the hard-bargaining Europeans that the principal opposition to Wilson's measures came, but from his fellow countrymen. Irish Americans took exception to the fact that his insistence on national self-determination did not extend to the Emerald Isle. The British press did not help matters by playing down America's contribution to Germany's defeat. What most exercised Americans, however, was their traditional fear of foreign entanglements, particularly the possibility that the United States would find itself committed to policies – perhaps even involved in wars – contrary to the wishes of Congress and the American people. America's determination to stand aloof, temporarily abandoned in the passion of the moment, now reasserted itself. Much of the responsibility for America's rejection of the League, however, attaches to Wilson himself for assuming that the dictates of his conscience and the beliefs of the American people were one and the same.

Colleagues and other delegates in Paris alerted him to the danger.[23] He received further warnings in February 1919 when he returned briefly to the States, the Republicans having meanwhile gained control of both houses. Wilson's long-standing opponent, Henry Cabot Lodge, now chaired the key Senate Foreign Relations Committee. For the United States to enter the League, the Peace Treaty would first have to be ratified by a two-thirds vote in the Senate. While in Paris, Wilson had been confident that regardless of Congress's views, once the Treaty had been drafted the American public would rally round. Back in Washington, however, he found he could no longer shrug off the fact that his dream of substituting the League of Nations for traditional sphere-of-influence politics conflicted with the Monroe Doctrine and the Roosevelt Corollary. A more adroit leader would have foreseen the difficulties ahead and at least taken the precaution of including Republicans in his delegation. But, as a former university professor, he was accustomed to doing his own thinking. The high opinion of America and its ideals that he so cherished did not extend to its elected representatives, whose limited vision and parochial concerns, as he saw it, stood in the way of their appreciating virtues of the new international order that existed in his mind's eye.

Back in Paris, however, all this was put aside. Nevertheless, closeted with Lloyd George, and the French and Italian leaders, Georges Clemenceau and Vittorio Orlando, he found the ground slipping away under him. If the United States had non-negotiable demands, so too did other countries. Clemenceau, in particular, was sceptical as to the League's capacity to handle future crises. By way of reassurance, Britain and the United States offered to enter into a commitment to come to France's assistance in the event of an unprovoked attack by Germany. This was an unprecedented step. Had it been honoured it might well have changed the course of twentieth-century history. It is unlikely, however, that the US Senate would have agreed to such an arrangement, which, in the event, was lost sight of in the battle over ratification.

At the end of five months of arduous negotiation, the document that finally emerged was far harsher than Wilson would have wished. It required Germany to admit its war guilt, stripped it of its colonies, returned Alsace-Lorraine to France, gave the French temporary occupation of the coal-rich Saar Basin, and readjusted Germany's eastern borders, leaving large numbers of ethnic Germans under Czech and Polish rule. The terms so shocked the German delegation that it produced 443 pages of criticism aimed at showing the extent to which they violated the Fourteen Points on the basis of which Germany had approached Wilson eight months before. A few changes were made, but not enough to satisfy Germany, which finally agreed to sign only under military duress. In 1921 the Reparations Commission resolved that Germany owed the Allies $33 billion.

In retrospect, it is plain that the Treaty was a disaster. It left the German people with an abiding sense of resentment and a burden of debt far beyond their capacity to pay. Liberals, too, were shocked. The most prescient comment made about it was Lloyd George's observation that 'We shall have to do the whole thing over again in twenty-five years time at three times the cost.'[24] The League of Nations, on which Wilson had set his heart, survived, but only in an emasculated form. His desperate attempt to persuade the American people to share his vision of a new world order presided over by the United States constitutes a tragic epilogue to what had started out as a noble crusade. But Americans had had enough of noble crusades, at least for the time being. On three separate occasions the Senate took up the question of joining the League, and each time voted in the negative. Wilson, incapacitated by a stroke, was dissuaded from seeking a third term. In the presidential election of 1920 the Democratic nominee, James M. Cox, ran on a party platform promising unequivocal ratification of the Treaty of Versailles with only such reservations as were required under the US Constitution. He was decisively beaten by his Republican opponent, Warren G. Harding, a run-of-the-mill Midwest politician, who promised an end to America's attempts to direct the destinies of the world and a return to 'normalcy'. It may not have been very good English, but it was plainly what the American people wanted.

6 The Inter-War Years

The First World War and the Versailles Treaty represented a watershed. The old world order had gone; a new one was taking shape. So far as the Anglo-American relationship was concerned, the United States was now clearly the stronger partner. Four years of bitter struggle had depleted the resources of the one and greatly augmented those of the other. Now the United States was the leading creditor nation and New York the world's financial centre. America's industrial production exceeded that of Britain, France and Germany combined. Contrary to what many had anticipated, the US had shown itself capable of raising vast armies and deploying them in a distant theatre. Its President had largely set the agenda at the Peace Conference.

Yet, in spite of all this, there was little jubilation, still less any glorying in the prospect of Americans assuming the kind of world leadership role that Wilson had envisaged. They had had enough of world responsibilities. In rejecting the League, they effectively shrugged off the moral obligations that stemmed from their having become one of the world's great powers. Whether they chose to exercise it or not, they now had the capacity to determine the outcome of world events. But playing the role of world leader was not what they wanted. Their aim was to return to the security they had enjoyed in pre-war days. Time would show that this was impossible, but only after it was forced on their attention in a manner they could hardly ignore.

Much that is clear in retrospect, however, was far from evident at the time. This applied to the British no less than to Americans. Although Britain had emerged from the war with its powers much impaired, the appearance belied the reality. After all, it was one of the victors. Its two principal pre-war rivals, Germany and Russia, would not be in a position to threaten its interests for many years. Meanwhile, the area over which it held sway had grown by some 27 per cent with the acquisition of vast new regions in the Middle East and Africa. These included Iraq and Persia, both of which contained valuable oil reserves. In Africa, the confiscation of Germany's former possessions gave it control of an uninterrupted swathe of land stretching from Cairo to the Cape. The Indian Ocean was virtually a British sea. With the advent of the telephone and air travel, communication with the dominions and colonies was easier than ever before. Not even in its Victorian heyday had the Empire presented so glittering a spectacle.

Its population and natural resources far surpassed those of the United States, as did its land area. Ever since the 1890s there had been those who dreamed of turning it into a similar sort of federation. Between 1914 and 1918 the 'white' empire had raised 1.3 million men, 141 thousand of whom had lost their lives in battle. Their contribution had added considerably to Britain's fighting strength and to a belief in the unity of the so-called 'family of English-speaking nations'.[1] The contribution of the rest of the Empire, relative to population, had been less impressive. Even so, there were those who dreamed of transforming the whole into a single great transoceanic union, bound together by common interests and loyalty to the Crown. But although such aspirations inspired the dreams of imperialists, such as Milner, Beaverbrook and Curzon, serious practical problems stood in the way of their realisation. For one thing, there was a strong body of opinion against the further strengthening of imperial ties, as became clear in the imperial conferences of 1926 and 1931 where it emerged that the white dominions were more concerned with developing their own regional interests than acting like so many transoceanic Californias and Wyomings. In the case of Britain's non-white possessions and protectorates there was the further problem of containing nationalist movements, the stirrings of which were already being felt in India and Egypt. Important though the contribution of the Empire had been to its war efforts in 1914–18 – and was destined be again in 1939–45 – there was plainly a world of difference between Britain's miscellaneous assortment of dominions and colonies and the relatively homogeneous and compact United States.[2]

Yet, rickety construct though the Empire was, it was what justified Britain's claim to be not merely *a* leading power, but *the* leading power of the day. Priority was accordingly given to protecting trade routes, and thus to the financial demands of the Royal Navy and the newly-founded Royal Air Force rather than to those of the army. This was in spite of the fact that it was the army that had borne the brunt of the fighting in the last war. To have maintained an army capable of making a significant contribution to another war on the European continent, however, would have required conscription, something the government could not well afford and the public would not tolerate in peacetime. In any case, during the 1920s there appeared no immediate likelihood of any threat from that quarter. If, eventually, one did arise, it was assumed that, as in 1914, the French would hold the field long enough for the British to mobilise. Low on Britain's list of priorities, therefore, was any provision for coping with a European land war arising out of German revanchism. Traditional attitudes thus reasserted themselves in ways that obscured the true sources of danger to the nation's security.

In this respect, British and American thinking had much in common. After all, the war had been 'a war to end all wars'. Its horrors were still fresh in people's minds. Why start preparing for another war when the last one was barely over? The first priority was to avoid doing anything that might invite a recurrence. As in the past, Britain's geographical position guaranteed it a measure of protection. The Channel, of course, was not as effective a barrier as the Atlantic, and as an imperial power, unable even to feed its own largely urban population, isolationism on the American model was plainly not an option. But what the British could do, and actively attempted to do so far as circumstances allowed, was to return to the splendid isolation of former times, leaving Europe to its own devices and relying on the navy and air force to maintain the network of trade routes on which the nation's well-being depended.[3]

Naval Rivalry

Yet, even on the basis of this parsimonious approach to national security, finding the necessary resources was a problem. The war had called for sacrifices from civilians as well as the military. Now that it was over, the political emphasis was on meeting domestic needs rather than providing for imperial defence. What people demanded, and their elected representatives sought to provide, were jobs and houses, not airplanes and battleships. An additional problem was the escalating cost of modern weaponry. Whereas previously the Royal Navy had been the equal of the next three or four navies combined, it was now hard-pressed to remain in first place. Even had the nation's priorities been different, there simply was no way in which it could maintain naval primacy in the Atlantic, the Mediterranean and the Far East all at the same time, or even cope effectively should crises arise in any two of those areas.

The principal challenge to Britain's naval pre-eminence came, of course, from the United States. America's maritime interests, however, were much the same as Britain's. The territorial disputes that had formerly been a dividing factor were now settled. In fact, the whole of British strategic thinking ever since the 1890s had been predicated on the assumption that conflict between the two nations would not arise. The overriding desire of both peoples was for a period of equilibrium that would allow them to put aside thoughts of conflict and get back to domestic concerns. On the other hand, it was not difficult to imagine circumstances in which, as in 1812 and 1914–17, they might find themselves at odds over questions of maritime rights. One issue that worried the United States was Britain's naval alliance with Japan, an agreement negotiated in 1902 at a time when Britain had begun to feel alone in what it saw as an increasingly hostile world. Although the US had no cause to distrust Britain it was altogether less complacent about Japan, whose imperial aspirations it saw as a growing threat to America's Pacific interests. The Japanese, for their part, could see no reason why they should not have colonies just like the Western powers. They also resented Americans' assumption of racial superiority, as exemplified by talk of the 'yellow peril' and US restrictions on Japanese immigration. To allay American fears, Britain insisted on inserting a new clause into the Anglo-Japanese treaty to the effect that it could not be invoked in relation to any conflict to which the United States was party. Still, the possibility remained that uncertainty over the matter would lead to a naval armaments race which, in view of America's far greater resources, Britain was bound to lose.

The issue was finally resolved, at least to the satisfaction of Britain and the United States, at the Washington Conference of 1921–22. The success of the meeting owed much to the initiative of Senator William Borah of Idaho and other isolationists who regarded a reduction in armaments as a means of preventing future wars. In his opening address, Secretary of State Charles Evans Hughes startled his audience by proposing a ten-year moratorium on the building of warships of over 10 000 tons and the systematic scrapping of vessels already in commission, leaving the navies of the three principal naval powers, the United States, Britain and Japan, at a ratio of 5–5–3 in terms of capital ships (battleships and aircraft carriers). More specifically, he called for the destruction of 845 000 tons of American, 583 000 tons of British, and 480 000 tons of Japanese shipping. The British Admiralty, already concerned that its resources were overstretched, was naturally aghast, but the politicians present, taking a wider view, quickly saw the advantages that were to be gained by accepting the proposal, which would relieve Britain of the strain and embarrassment of competing in a race that would weaken its economy and that it could not possibly hope to win. In a speech even more momentous in its implications than Hughes's, the British Foreign Secretary, Arthur Balfour, observed that, although the 'solid, impregnable, self-sufficient'

United States 'was wholly immune from the particular perils to which, from the nature of the case, the British Empire is subject', he was prepared to accept the idea of naval parity.[4]

Working out the details took longer. France, because of its fear of Germany, refused to have land armaments put on the agenda. It did agree, under pressure, to having its ratio of capital ships set at 1.7, but refused to allow any limitation on its cruisers, destroyers and submarines. Italy, too, accepted a 1.7 ratio. Britain, which relied mainly on vessels of smaller tonnage for policing the world's seaways, also refused to agree to restrictions on overall tonnage, and so in practice gave away less than Hughes's 5–5–3 ratio suggests. Critics in the United States seized on this as evidence that Americans were once again being hoodwinked by Perfidious Albion. But, in a symbolic sense if in no other, the Washington agreements represented a concession to the United States of a kind that in all the centuries of its maritime history Britain had never before made to a foreign power. They also provided a graceful way of escaping the Anglo-Japanese naval treaty.

Inter-Allied War Debts

A less easily resolved question was adjudicating the various debts left over from the war. In earlier conflicts, in which Britain had usually acted as paymaster, it had been the practice to agree to a general cancellation of debts once the war was over. The burden of indebtedness acquired as a result of the Napoleonic wars had led to an increase in the national debt so enormous that for decades its servicing took up over half of the nation's budget. The American approach was different. Fighting as part of a coalition was a new experience. What Americans were familiar with was business; theirs was a business culture, and, as Wilson, the bankers and public opinion made clear, when they lent money they expected it to be paid back.[5]

In all, the United States had loaned the Allies some $10 billion. As it happened, that was almost exactly the sum that Britain had loaned to its allies. To do so, however, Britain had increasingly been obliged to look to the New York money market, acting, in a sense, as middleman on behalf of those lacking contacts or unable to provide the security American bankers required. By the end of the war its debt to the United States totalled $4.3 billion, France's $3.4 billion, and Italy's $1.6 billion. The result was that while the United States emerged as an overall creditor, owing nothing to anyone, the other powers struggled to cope with a spider's web of debt, amounting, in all, to some $26.5 billion. Sorting out these overlapping claims was not easy. Although Britain was theoretically a creditor, much of what it had loaned – for example, the sums advanced to Russia in the hope of keeping it in the war – was unrecoverable.

It would have been to Britain's advantage, and to that of the other Allies, if the settlement of their debts to the United States could have been linked to the reparations owed them by Germany, thereby making the Germans – purportedly the aggressors – the debtors of last resort. In view of Germany's war guilt, it was argued, this was not only equitable but an effective way of ensuring that for want of resources Germany would be unable to make trouble in the future. In 1921, after lengthy deliberation, reparations were put at $33 billion. Had such a sum been available for immediate distribution it would have solved the problem. But how the Germans, in their state of post-war disarray, were to raise such a staggering amount – or any money at all – was far from clear. In any case, the United States steadfastly refused to acknowledge any connection between reparations and Allied debts, which it saw as having been incurred on a normal commercial basis. Business was business: those who borrowed, regardless of the circumstances, were under an obligation to pay back. If others owed them money, that was their problem.

As the British saw it, this was not only unjust but short-sighted. In 1915 the Allies had agreed to unite their military and financial resources with a view to ending the war as soon as possible and in the expectation that adjustments would be made once the war was over. Relative to its financial resources, Britain had contributed more generously to the defeat of Germany than had the United States, which, as the overall figures showed, had actually profited from the war. But this was not an issue to be measured in financial terms alone. Britain – and to an even greater degree France – had contributed far more than America in terms of blood spilled. In terms of sacrifice, there was simply no comparison. If, as President Wilson had claimed, the war was a crusade 'to make the world safe for democracy', it was the Allies who had done most of the crusading.

But what in the British view made the American attitude wrong-headed was not simply its injustice but its potentially disastrous effect on the world's economy. The mechanisms governing international finance were not like those of a business. Loading Europe with a burden of unpayable debt was not to anyone's advantage. Having hitherto been largely responsible for setting the terms of international trade, Britain was quick to realise that its effective management required the provision of easy credit and ready access to markets. The long prosperity of the Victorian

era had been made possible by Britain's adherence to free-trade principles, the gold standard, and the free circulation of money. Now financial pre-eminence had passed to the United States, which, having a
larger internal market, was less concerned with issues of world trade.
More important, unlike Britain, it kept its markets tightly closed The
Fordney–McCumber Tariff of 1922 was one of the highest on record,
raising the level of imposts on both manufactured and agricultural goods
to levels that made selling to the US virtually impossible. It was bad
enough demanding that Europeans pay their dollar debts, but worse still
to take such a stand while denying them the opportunity of obtaining the
dollars with which to do so.[6] World trade was not a zero-sum game.
There were profits for everyone. But if dollars were to replace pounds as
the medium through which world trade was conducted, there had to be
opportunities for earning them. What the United States needed to do,
according to the British, was to cancel the debts, throw open its markets
to foreign competition, and free up world trade so that everyone, including the United States, could gain.

Americans took a different view. Until the United States itself entered
the war, the money raised on behalf of the Allies had been lent by private
citizens and institutions in the expectation of their receiving a fair return
on their investment. All subsequent remittances, spent on joint efforts to
defeat Germany and post-war relief, came from the US Treasury. If
Allied debts were cancelled, the result would be that responsibility for the
private debts would need to be assumed by the US Government, and the
entire cost of repayment, capital and interest, would have to be met by
the American taxpayer. Instead of external credits, the United States
would have internal debts. Looking back on the war and the post-war
wrangling over the peace treaty, Americans had begun to wonder if their
intervention had been wise and if Germany really had been a threat to
American interests. It had never been their wish to assume the mantle of
world leadership, and it was not their aspiration now. The whole question
came down to ethics: the Allies had incurred contractual obligations and
now they were trying to renege on them.

There were, however, ways of easing the situation, at least in the short
term. Thanks to its change of status from debtor to creditor, the United
States was increasingly a net exporter of capital and goods. As businesses
expanded, the profits earned at home were used to invest abroad, either
by taking over existing concerns or establishing new ones. Also, more
Americans were going abroad, profiting from easier ocean travel and
favourable rates of exchange. Dollars were, therefore, in circulation and

could be earned. This was not the way in which the international economy had formerly operated, but so long as Americans continued to spend dollars abroad it was possible for Europeans to balance their books.

Americanisation and the Image of the Good Life

Just as Victorian Britain had been the dominant cultural force in the nineteenth century, so the United States set the standards for the newly-emerging consumer societies of the twentieth. Remarkable though the effects of other economic revolutions have been, it is doubtful whether technological change ever transformed people's lives more rapidly or more fundamentally than in the America of the 1920s. With the advent of electricity and the internal combustion engine, not only were cars becoming widely available for the first time but so were radios, refrigerators, record players, telephones, washing machines, vacuum cleaners, synthetic fabrics, and a host of other new products. The problem was no longer producing goods, but persuading people to purchase them. Instalment buying was one solution. So, too, was advertising, which played an increasingly important role in economic and cultural life, not only boosting the sales of particular brand names but creating an image of a society in which happiness was achieved through mass consumption. Freedom came from the ownership of a motor car, health from the consumption of fruit juice, sophistication from smoking cigarettes, beauty out of a bottle. Advertising also exported urban ways to rural people. Through Sears Roebuck catalogues, farmers and their wives on remote homesteads could order practically everything they needed, from farm equipment and dungarees to clothes modelled on those worn by Hollywood stars.

Because the United States led the consumer boom, the rest of the world had difficulty distinguishing what was essentially American from what was simply modern, because the two generally went together. When the British flocked to the cinema or listened to gramophone records, as often as not it was to see American films or listen to American popular music. The 1920s are remembered as the Jazz Age because jazz was quintessentially American and because, like America, it was new, vibrant, individualistic and exciting. The foxtrot was American; so, too, was the Charleston. Above all, the United States represented the future. A century earlier, that had also been the view of British radicals, but the future they had envisaged was very different from the one that now caught the world's imagination. Then it had been the homespun rural democracy of Andrew Jackson; now it was the culture of the big city, easy money, consumer goods, automobiles. 'The future of America', wrote Aldous Huxley in 1927, 'is the future of the world. Material circumstances are driving all nations along the path in which America is going.'[7]

In Britain, similar processes were at work. Twenties Britain, however, lacked the brash assertiveness of twenties America. London had its Art Deco architecture, but nothing on the scale of New York's Radio City Music Hall or the Chrysler and Woolworth buildings. The counterparts of Scott Fitzgerald's flappers were Evelyn Waugh's Bright Young Things, the sons and daughters of wealthy families who shocked their tweedy elders by going to parties and getting drunk.[8] Insofar as the British had aspirations to grandeur, they were more apt to find expression abroad – for example, in Sir Edward Lutyens's new imperial capital at Delhi, which trumped even Pierre Charles L'Enfant's Washington – rather than in Britain itself. At home, the old social order might be crumbling, but overseas registers of social precedence grew longer as the pageantry of empire grew ever more elaborate. The more Britain's troubles multiplied, the more extravagant its imperial rituals became. In displays of a theatrical splendour that far surpassed anything that Hollywood could have matched, African kings, Malay sultans, Nigerian emirs and Indian maharajas swore fealty to the King-Emperor, George V.[9] However, it was not the pomp of empire but the democratic energy of America that set the tone of the new age. The United States had the tallest buildings and the longest bridges. The world's best boxers were American; the first transatlantic flight was by an American. American athletes dominated the Olympics (gaining 255 points in the Paris Olympics of 1924 as compared to Britain's 85). Even in Britain there was a growing sense that empires were old-fashioned. The future was individualistic, fast-moving, streamlined. It was in America that all the exciting, trend-setting things were happening.

American consumerism impinged on the consciousness of Britons in all sorts of ways. There were advertisements urging housewives to emulate American lifestyles, go out and buy the latest products, spend money on carefree holidays, adopt the new flat-chested boyish outfits popularised by Mary Pickford, Clara Bow and Lilian Gish. Stars such as Douglas Fairbanks Snr, Rudolph Valentino and Theda Bara had their British fan clubs. So that women could enjoy the benefits of 'The Make-Up of the Stars', the American cosmetics manufacturer Max Factor set up factories in Britain. In towns across the country Alhambra-style movie palaces sprang up where audiences followed the fictional exploits of their American film idols, whose real-life romances and luxurious lifestyles they read about in the tabloids.[10]

Because so much of what was new in the British culture of the 1920s was a spillover from the United States, the more traditional minded urged that steps be taken to provide suitable British alternatives. In 1927, when Parliament passed the first of many bills aimed at promoting British films, only 5 per cent of those shown in Britain were actually made there. By setting quotas the British proportion was increased, but many were so poorly made that few audiences would pay to watch them, and there was no prospect whatever of exporting them abroad. In any case, as with other foreign-made products, the United States kept its doors tightly closed, so that even if British films had been better made it is doubtful whether the Big Five that controlled the networks would have allowed them on to America's screens. Elsewhere in the English-speaking world, it was the American products that audiences preferred. When His Majesty's subjects went out for an evening's entertainment in Toronto or Canberra, Bombay or Lagos it was Hollywood films they watched. Thus, this most modern of visual media became the flagship of American-style capitalism, providing alluring glimpses of wealth and luxury far removed from people's ordinary lives. Many deplored the films' influence, claiming that they stirred up false expectations by making people discontented with what they had. Others claimed that they were corrupting the young, distracting them from more intellectually arduous pursuits. In the days of silent film much of what was shown was simply knockabout fun reminiscent of the music hall and circus, the entertainment fields from which many of the early stars came. Hollywood took care to ensure that the films it produced were suitable for family viewing. The plots it favoured were for the most part of a predictable kind: celebrating the triumph of good over evil, typically represented by the cowboy who saves the homesteaders, or the poor boy who resists the temptations of the big city and wins the heart of the boss's daughter. Naturally, the image of the United States they projected was distorted, giving the impression that it was disproportionately populated by cowboys, gangsters, and the very rich. It was a fantasy world that British moviegoers encountered as they paid their shillings and took their seats in the stalls, but it was an *American* fantasy world, one in which, when the talkies came along after 1927, the heroes and heroines spoke in American accents.

Economic Contrasts and Connections

What the movies conveyed, and Britain plainly lacked, was that feeling of buoyancy and optimism that was the hallmark of 1920s America.

Although Britain had won the war it hardly felt like victory. Nine per cent of men between the ages of 18 and 40 had been killed and almost 20 per cent wounded. How far this contributed to the sluggishness of Britain's post-war recovery cannot be measured, but plainly a significant proportion of the nation's talented youth had been lost. Unlike France and Belgium, Britain had suffered virtually no direct physical damage, but in other respects it had fared badly. Two-fifths of its merchant fleet had been lost to enemy action. The financing of the war had increased the national debt from £650 million to £7,828 million. Throughout the 1920s, debt servicing consumed some 40 per cent of the nation's budget.[11] Parliament, therefore, was hard pressed to find the additional funds required for maintaining the nation's defence capabilities, improving its infrastructure, and alleviating the lot of the unemployed, whose sufferings were a burden on the nation's conscience throughout the post-war years. Paying for the war had also meant disposing of around 10 per cent of Britain's overseas investments. In addition, a further 5 per cent had been lost through physical destruction or, as in the case of Russia, through outright confiscation. In short, the country emerged from the war feeling that it had little to celebrate.[12]

Adding to this sense of disillusion was the knowledge that while they had been otherwise occupied, Britain's commercial rivals, most notably the United States and Japan, had taken over markets formerly regarded as British preserves. Japanese manufacturing had leaped by 75 per cent during the war years thanks largely to the expansion of its textile exports. Latin Americans now looked to the United States rather than Britain for manufactures and investment capital. Canada, Brazil and Argentina, formerly accustomed to importing manufactured goods from Britain, had taken advantage of the hiatus caused by the war to develop their own industries. China and India, which had played a key role in the pre-war British economy, were now making most of their own textiles.

All this would have mattered less if Britain had been able to resume its former role as soon as the war ended, but the years of struggle had left its economy in disarray. Because of the loss of overseas markets, the textile industry suffered from massive over-capacity, which drove up prices and made competition difficult. Steelmaking, shipbuilding and coal, having expanded far beyond normal peacetime requirements, were in a similar condition. Either they had to contract or find new customers. Not all sectors were so badly placed. The demand for motor vehicles, railway rolling stock and machinery remained buoyant. So did that for chemicals and electrical goods, but the British were slow to respond and soon found themselves trailing behind their German and Scandinavian competitors. Overshadowing everything was the way the old staple industries, like coal, textiles and steel, which Britain had pioneered and to which it remained disproportionately committed, were slowly dying.[13]

The United States was not immune from such difficulties. Its great advantage was having a vast internal market, protected from overseas competitors, which encouraged it to develop a full range of newer industries. America exported only 10 per cent of what it produced, as compared with the 25 per cent exported by Britain. Although some industries went into recession, others expanded to take their place. The sheer size of the American market also made possible economies of scale of the kind from which Britain had profited a century earlier. That was when it had been the world's leading industrial nation and Americans had had no choice but to come to it for manufactures. Now, the roles were reversed, and it was Britain that felt unable to compete with a nation with double its population and almost four times its industrial base.

Building on the industrial feats of the war years, American industry continued to register impressive increases in productivity. Instead of slowing down, the pace of economic change perceptibly quickened as the decade advanced. Except for a brief period at the very beginning of the 1920s, unemployment and inflation remained low. Previously the settlement of the West and the building of the railroads had absorbed much of the nation's energies; now the city was the principal locus of change. What most impressed visitors to the United States were no longer its natural wonders like Niagara Falls or the Rockies but the New York and Chicago skylines, the technology of steel girders, concrete and plate glass, the great asphalt highways linking the nation's metropolises. Across the land a new urban culture was taking shape, based on the automobile, the elevator, the telephone, assembly-line production, and instalment buying. American cities, rapidly changing, pulsating with a commercial energy, were qualitatively different from the cities of Europe.

Not everyone, needless to say, approved of what was happening. Many thought it mindless and vulgar. In the early 1920s there was the Red Scare and the Volstead Act (Prohibition). Practically all of America's aspiring young writers, taking advantage of the dollar's high exchange rate, fled abroad. America might be the land of the modern, but Europe was the land of modernism. One thing that became clear only much later was how much the experiences of these expatriates would transform America's own artistic scene when they eventually returned home. Instead of being merely a sub-category of English literature, American writing (and the same applied to painting, dance and music) ceased to be provincial and became part of a far wider enterprise, international in scope.[14]

Of those Americans who stayed at home, by no means all profited from the 1920s boom. As in Britain, those in long-established industries, such as coal miners and textile workers, suffered hardship. Farmers, too, after the prosperous war years, experienced hard times. And, as always, the South lagged behind the rest of the nation. In general, it was those who were already better off who reaped the benefits of the 1920s bonanza, and the unskilled and those without capital who fared least well. Yet, unevenly distributed though the benefits were, the economy was plainly growing at a rate that European nations simply could not begin to match. Whereas the number of cars on Britain's roads had barely reached one million by 1929, the number on America's jumped from 8 million in 1920 to just under 23 million nine years later, which is to say one car to every 4.5 Americans as compared with one to every 50 Britons.[15] Like the family telephone, the family car was something to be taken for granted. By the mid-1920s the American automotive industry had emerged as the country's largest enterprise, consuming 90 per cent of its petroleum, 80 per cent of its rubber and 20 per cent of its steel. To cope with this parade of vehicles, new roads were needed. In 1921 the nation's legislators passed the first of what was to prove a series of federal highway acts to encourage road building. In the West, burgeoning cities like Los Angeles were constructed on the assumption of universal car ownership. For some, having a car was more important than having a bathtub. In the East, middle-class Americans increasingly quit the noise and congestion of the city by moving their families out into the suburbs. By 1925 more than half the homes in the country were lighted by electricity. Just as the first industrial revolution, based on coal and steam, had transformed the lives of the British a century earlier, so this second revolution, driven by oil and electricity, was changing living patterns even in the remotest and least favoured parts of the American nation. Whether or not they enjoyed the benefits of this transformation, Americans could at least pride themselves on belonging to the most technologically advanced country in the world.[16]

By comparison, Britain's economic performance was lacklustre. Only once, and then only briefly, did unemployment dip below 10 per cent. In 1927, by which time the volume of world exports was 18 per cent above pre-war levels, the British proportion had dropped by almost a third. Rather than speeding up, the economy actually seemed to be slowing down. The Balfour Committee on Industry and Trade (1929), like earlier inquiries, castigated manufacturers for their out-of-date attitudes. British entrepreneurs, it noted, were less ready to scrap old machinery than those in United States and Germany. In the workforce, too, conservative habits of mind prevailed, leading 'many workmen and some of their Trade Unions to cling tenaciously to obsolete trade customs and lines of demarcation and thus preventing them from co-operating to the full in getting the best value out of machinery at the lowest cost'.[17] The report went on to castigate the educational system for the poor provision of technical training it provided. The problem was not simply that old Victorian industries were in decline, but that people were set in their ways. Unlike Americans and Germans, they were failing to adapt to the changes brought about by science and technology. All the war had done, it seemed, was to increase the rate of Britain's long-term industrial decline.

Not only were Americans displacing the British in markets abroad, they were busily taking over large segments of Britain's own economy. From an investment point of view, Britain appeared a safer bet than most. It had a stable government, and thanks to a common language firms could use the same sales techniques and advertising materials as back home. When Hoover began selling its wares in Britain, trainee salesmen were taken to America to be inducted into the company's culture and sales methods. So successful were their techniques of high-pressure salesmanship that 'hoover' entered the British vocabulary as a noun and a verb for vacuum cleaners and vacuum-cleaning in general. As in America, Henry Ford's Model T dominated the car market in the early 1920s. When Parliament sought to protect British car manufacturers by placing a 33 per cent tariff on imports, Ford set up a Detroit-style factory in Dagenham in east London, mass producing vehicles for the British market and for export to Europe and the Empire. General Motors and the big tyre manufacturers, Firestone, Goodrich and Goodyear, followed suit.

Although happy to use American household appliances and drive American cars, the British public was uneasy at the prospect of the whole of industry passing into American hands. When General Electric of America set about buying up Britain's electrical manufacturing industry, it sought to conceal its identity by registering its acquisitions in the name of a sympathetic British industrialist, Dudley Docker. Although it failed to acquire its namesake, General Electric of Britain, it did succeed in swallowing up practically everything else, merging its holdings to form AEI (Associated Electrical Industries). Americans also began buying up power stations in a piecemeal fashion, using the distinguished lawyer and politician Lord Birkenhead as a front. No one was fooled, but in 1936, when it emerged that funds were being siphoned off to support ailing operations back home, government pressure was brought to bear and power generation was returned to British ownership. Hurtful though it was to national pride that American capital and expertise were required to modernise British industry, British consumers benefited. Americans were simply providing a service that in former times the British themselves had provided in North America and elsewhere.[18]

The Great Depression

Like the causes of the First World War, the causes of the Depression are much clearer in retrospect than they were at the time. As always, there were warnings, and those who uttered them appeared very wise after the event. But when are there not Cassandras telling of troubles ahead? Unfortunately there exists no ready formula for distinguishing those with a genuine grasp of the perils of a situation from the general run of nay-sayers. It was particularly difficult in late-1920s America on account of the growth in productivity over the preceding 17 years. America was now producing close to half of the world's manufactures. In 1927, to encourage the public to go out and buy what the economy was producing, the New York Federal Reserve Bank cut its interest rate from 4 per cent to 3.5 per cent. Much of the consumer boom of the preceding years had been fuelled by buying on credit; now credit was easier than ever to obtain. The good times seemed destined to roll on for ever.

This was very different from the situation in Britain, where growth had remained sluggish ever since the war. What happened to Britain, however, was no longer a matter of major concern to anyone except the British themselves. It was the United States economy that was the great engine on which the prosperity of the world depended.

What made America important was not so much the size of its industry or the scale of its overseas trade but the fact that New York now occupied the position at the centre of the spider's web of credit and debt formerly occupied by London. In 1924, and again in 1929, efforts were made to ease the problem of the debts left over from the war, first under the Dawes Plan and then under the Young Plan. German reparations were reduced to $8 billion, repayable at 5.5 per cent over 58 years. Meanwhile, Britain, France, Italy and other former Allies struggled to keep up their payments. With American markets effectively closed to them, they relied largely on tourism and on reparations paid to them by Germany, while

Germany, in turn, obtained the currency it required by borrowing dollars from the United States. So long as this merry-go-round continued, payments could be made. If it stopped, so, necessarily, would the payments.

What brought it to an abrupt halt was the American stock market crash of 1929. Over the preceding two years Americans had begun investing in Wall Street stocks as never before. Dividends no longer mattered; people simply bought shares expecting that their value would go up, as by and large it did. Between 1925 and 1929 the total market value of all stocks rose from $27 billion to $87 billion. As the speculative frenzy gathered momentum, so did the scale of the profits that could be reaped. Investors increasingly availed themselves of the generous terms offered by stockbrokers to buy on credit. Providing the market continued going up, debts could always be repaid. So an enormous *internal* merry-go-round was created which, like its external counterpart, was capable of maintaining its momentum only so long as new money kept on being added.

When that ceased, as in October 1929 it did, and people began withdrawing money realising that the market had ceased going up, the whole system went into reverse, starting the downward spiral leading to the Great Depression. Alongside the orgy of speculation on Wall Street, American manufacturers had been producing goods in excess of what customers were able to afford. In the panic that followed the fall in the value of shares, people stopped buying, inventories grew, workers were laid off, and spending power fell still further. Plainly it was a time for economic retrenchment, but that only made matters worse. Where the spiral would end, no one knew – if indeed there would ever be an end.

Americans were thus unwilling to go on lending the dollars needed for the repayment of war debts. To make matters worse, they began withdrawing funds to meet their obligations at home. One by one the rickety pillars on which the world's post-war economy had been built collapsed. In 1924 Britain had returned to the gold standard in the hope of resuming its former role as the world's banker, but with minimal reserves and a run on gold its position soon became untenable. On assuming office in 1929, the Labour government under Ramsay MacDonald had agreed to increase the benefits paid to the unemployed. As the number of unemployed doubled, a budget deficit opened up leading to a run on sterling. MacDonald appealed to J. P. Morgan for help, but was told that this would only be possible if steps were taken to balance the budget. Unwilling to agree on cutting payments to the jobless, the cabinet split and an all-party government was formed under MacDonald to carry through the necessary economies. Even these, however, failed to suffice, and on 21 September 1931 the pound was allowed to float, with the result that its value almost immediately fell from $4.86 to $3.50.

Europeans naturally blamed the United States for what was happening. It, however, was suffering as much as anyone. Americans, for their part, found it hard to believe that they were responsible for the economic blizzard now sweeping the markets. Since the foundation of their nation they had been taught to believe that the world's troubles emanated from Europe, yet these troubles showed every sign of having originated in the United States. Nor could their sufferings be accounted for by some egregious departure from the laissez-faire capitalist principles. There had never been a stauncher defender of rugged individualism than Herbert Hoover, except possibly his two immediate Republican predecessors Warren G. Harding and Calvin Coolidge. It was Coolidge who famously remarked in a speech to the Society of American Newspaper Editors in 1925 that 'the business of America is business'. It was Hoover, however, who was the more adept at describing what he called 'the American system'. As he put it in a campaign speech of 1928:

> By adherence to the principles of decentralized self-government, ordered liberty, equal opportunity and freedom of the individual, our American experiment in human welfare has yielded a degree of well-being unparalleled in all the world. It has come nearer to the abolition of poverty, to the abolition of the fear of want, than humanity has ever reached before. The progress of the past seven years is the proof of it.[19]

Yet this was the system that had collapsed. All Hoover came up with in response was an appeal to the business community for assistance, meanwhile urging the American public to put their faith in self-help and local initiatives. In spite of his repeated assurances that prosperity lay 'just around the corner', the downward spiral appeared unstoppable. When he left office on 4 March 1933 the gross national product had shrunk to well under half what it had been four years earlier and a quarter of the workforce was unemployed. He had, as H. L. Mencken put it, been well and truly 'fried, boiled, roasted and fricasseed'.[20]

Britain fared less badly. Having suffered more than most during the preceding decade, the downturn of the early 1930s came as less of a shock. Banks did not collapse as in the United States, and few wealthy families found themselves suddenly penniless. As always, those who suffered most were wage earners in traditional industries like coal mining, textiles and shipbuilding. Salaried workers, and the middle class generally, fared relatively well. Over the decade as a whole, average real income per capita rose by 17.7 per cent. There were also signs that British labour productivity was improving as compared with that of the United States and Germany. Although the proportion of the workforce unemployed never fell below 10 per cent, the workforce itself expanded as more people, an increasing proportion of them women, entered the labour market, so that by the end of the decade more people were at work than ever before.[21]

The onset of the Depression pointed up the absurdity of the international debt situation. Between 1924 and 1931 Germany had borrowed considerably more from Britain and the United States than it had paid them in the form of reparations. Britain, on the other hand, had been remarkably conscientious, paying the United States close to half of what it owed. By June 1931, however, economic forces beyond anyone's control made further payments impossible. Hoover took the initiative by proclaiming a 'one-year moratorium, emphasising that this was only as a temporary measure and that he expected payments to be resumed as soon as the crisis abated. At Lausanne the following year the European powers agreed to write off 90 per cent of Germany's debt on condition that their own creditors, namely the United States, agreed to a satisfactory settlement. This naturally led to cries of rage from the US Congress, which responded by declaring it illegal for any American to lend money to a government in default of a debt to the United States. After a number of token payments Britain finally defaulted, having paid $2.2 billion out of an original debt totalling $4.3 billion, a far higher proportion than was paid by France, Belgium or any of America's other major debtors.[22]

Britain's failure to meet its financial obligations would long be remembered. Many Americans attributed the Depression to the refusal of Europeans to pay their debts. How was it possible, they wondered, that with all their colonies, wealthy aristocrats and royal baubles, the British were too strapped for cash to behave like honest citizens? Once again, it seemed, Perfidious Albion was up to its old tricks. Matters were exacerbated when, following America's example, Britain resorted to protectionist measures. This was an important break with the past. Ever since the 1840s, when Britain had finally succumbed to the thinking of the Manchester School, it had relied on its ability to compete on equal terms with foreign manufacturers. That was when it had been the workshop of the world and free trade had been to its advantage, but as other countries caught up, keeping their domestic markets tightly closed to foreign competition, that ceased to be the case. The turning point came at the 1932

Commonwealth Conference in Ottawa when it was agreed to establish a system of imperial preference involving the levying of higher tariffs on goods imported from outside the Empire. Having always argued for the open door, except with regard to their own domestic market, Americans were furious at finding the tables turned. Henceforward the world economy was effectively divided into competing blocs based on various currencies, the two largest blocs being those based on sterling and the dollar. Despite repeated American protests, the British refused to give way unless the United States changed its own tariff policy, which it adamantly refused to do. So far as Congress was concerned, opening America's markets to foreign competition in the depths of the Depression was unthinkable. That, however, did not prevent Americans resenting Britain's refusal to admit their exports or to allow them access to the Empire's resources of rubber, zinc and other essential raw materials. Imperial preference remained a bone of bitter contention, and was not resolved until after World War II.

The Road to War

Although the United States can absolved from any responsibility for the outbreak of World War I, the same cannot be said with regard to World War II. Its part in the drafting of the unworkable Treaty of Versailles, its failure to join the League of Nations, the resentment it stirred up over the repayment of war debts, the Wall Street crash and the world-wide depression that followed, above all its refusal to exercise the authority that its wealth and military potential might have commanded, helped create a world situation in which destabilising forces arose and flourished. Not that the United States' record was uniquely bad in this respect. Britain's was scarcely better. Where the United States chose isolation, Britain opted for appeasement, hoping to buy off the world's troublemakers with concessions, only to find that in practice this merely led to further demands, until eventually it became clear that nothing short of war would end the cycle.

The reluctance of the democracies to face up to these challenges owed much to their experiences in World War I and their fear of doing anything that might lead to a repetition. Although the doughboys on the Western Front saw action for a mere four or five months, Americans had found the experience as disillusioning as the British. There was, they discovered, nothing glorious about modern war. They were also increasingly persuaded that they had been misled by their government and that intervention had been a mistake. For all the patriotic fervour and talk at the time of glory and sacrifice, the real issues they now suspected had been the very things against which the nation's founders had warned them – greed, ambition, and European intrigue. The prevailing sense of disillusion helps explain the Kellogg–Briand Pact of 1928, by which 62 nations, partly at the instigation of the US Secretary of State, Frank B. Kellogg, agreed to outlaw war as a method of resolving disputes.

It also found expression in many memoirs and novels of the period, such as John Dos Passos's *Three Soldiers* (1921), Robert Graves's *Goodbye to All That* (1929), Ernest Hemingway's *A Farewell to Arms* (1929) and Erich Maria Remarque's *All Quiet on the Western Front* (1929). The Germans, it belatedly emerged, were not the monsters they had been depicted. As the provisions of the Versailles settlement unravelled, it became increasingly clear that Germany had been dealt with unfairly. In any case, with their economies in a state of collapse, it was hardly a moment for the democracies to start flexing their muscles. The irony is that had they been prepared to spend more on preparing for warfare and less on welfare war might have been averted, but that was not how it appeared at the time.

Surprisingly, it was the United States that took the lead in calling for a response to the first challenge. Back in 1900, the US had demanded of Britain and other mercantile powers the right to trade with China on equal terms. Like the Monroe Doctrine, the so-called Open Door notes had no perceptible influence at the time.[23] Since then, however, America's trade with the Far East had grown, and it had become the principal sponsor of missionary effort in China. When, therefore, Japan invaded northern China in 1931 and established a puppet regime, the US called on it to remove its troops, invoking both the Open Door agreement and the Kellogg–Briand Pact. Japan remained unmoved. Hoping to mobilise the support of world opinion, Hoover's Secretary of State, Henry Stimson, repeatedly called on the British Foreign Secretary, Sir John Simon, to join him in issuing a declaration condemning Japanese behaviour, only to receive a dusty answer. As the British saw it, there was never any question of the United States being prepared to do more than upbraid Japan. All one ever got from Americans were words. As Neville Chamberlain noted,

> We ought to know by now that the USA will give us no undertaking to resist by force any action by Japan short of an attack on Hawaii or Honolulu. She will give us plenty of assurances of goodwill especially if

we will promise to do all the fighting, but the moment she is asked to contribute something she invariably takes refuge behind Congress.[24]

For Britain to fight Japan all on her own over events in far away Manchuria was plainly out of the question. Stimson interpreted Britain's response as pusillanimity. The fact of the matter was that, struggling as they both were to cope with the effects of the Depression, neither was prepared to risk a confrontation with Japan over an issue it perceived as being far removed from its vital interests. The League eventually agreed to condemn Japan's action, whereupon the Japanese withdrew from membership. The slide towards war had begun.[25]

As the decade progressed it gathered momentum. Hoover's successor, Franklin Delano Roosevelt, was well versed in international affairs. He had supported the Allied cause in the Great War, opposed the subsequent drift towards isolation, deplored the Republicans' high tariff policy, and mocked the naiveté of the Kellogg–Briand Pact. Unlike Britain's leaders, he was quick to see that Hitler was intent on war. Having served in the Wilson administration, however, he was conscious of the need to cultivate the support of Congress, which, as crisis followed crisis, showed itself ever more determined to ensure that the US remain neutral.

As the likelihood of war increased, Congress passed a series of Neutrality Acts, framed with a view to preventing circumstances such as those that had led to American intervention in World War I recurring. In doing so it drew heavily on the findings of historians, and on the evidence amassed by a special investigating committee chaired by Senator Gerald P. Nye of North Dakota, which had been charged with looking into the part played by US banks and munitions manufacturers in financing and arming the Allies. Particularly during the Depression years, conspiratorial theories featuring capitalist plots were widely believed. In 1935, a well-documented study by Walter Millis, *Road to War: America, 1914–1917*, purportedly proved that Americans had been inveigled into fighting by war profiteers and capitalists whose financial interests rendered it essential to stave off an Allied defeat. Accordingly, the neutrality legislation of 1935–37 forbade both the extending of loans to foreign belligerents and the export of arms and ammunition in time of war. It also sought to prevent any repetition of the *Lusitania* episode by making it unlawful for American citizens to travel under a belligerent flag.

Roosevelt signed the Acts with reluctance, arguing that they made no distinction between victims and aggressors and actually encouraged warmongering by assuring those bent on aggression that their victims would be denied the means of defending themselves. Such arguments fell on deaf ears. Recalling Wilson's behaviour, Congress took the view that the judgement of the executive on such matters was not to be trusted. In 1938 a motion calling for a constitutional amendment that would have required a national referendum before any declaration of war except in cases of actual attack was rejected, but only by a narrow margin.

In spite of mounting evidence to the contrary, Britain's leaders clung stubbornly to the notion that peace could be preserved through concilia- tion. Overstretched as Britain's forces were, there appeared no alterna- tive. Until the Japanese invasion of Manchuria in 1932 the government's working assumption had been that no major conflict would break out for at least ten years. By the late 1920s spending on defence had fallen to 2.5 per cent of gross national product, a level even lower than in the peaceful years at the beginning of the century. In 1931 Germany began rearming. For Britain to follow suit was difficult, both on account of the increasing demand for social spending and the country's massive trade deficit. The choice, according to the Treasury, was between remaining militarily weak and going bankrupt. There were other constraints, among them the widespread popular assumption that once an arms race began war would somehow ineluctably follow.

Yet in spite of this, military expenditure did increase, rising to 5.6 per cent of gross national product in 1937–38. Even that, however, came nowhere near providing the sort of global capability required if Britain were to meet the challenges posed by Japan, Italy and Germany all at the same time. As Sir Thomas Inskip, the minister in charge of co-ordinating defence, told the Cabinet in early 1938, 'the plain fact which cannot be obscured is that it is beyond the resources of this country to make proper provision in peace for defence of the British Empire against three major powers in three different theatres of war'.[26] Germany alone had a larger population than Britain and a broader industrial base. Whether the Royal Navy could match the Japanese navy in the Pacific, given that Japan had launched a massive naval building programme, was extremely doubtful. The hope was that in any general conflagration the dominions would once again rally to Britain's support, although in view of their growing regional interests there was no guarantee that they would do so. On the other hand, the dominions made plain that they counted on Britain for their defence should it be required. But even had their whole- hearted support been assured, it seemed unlikely that the situation could be contained. As matters worsened, the tone of the military assessments submitted to the Cabinet grew increasingly gloomy.

History has not dealt kindly with the appeasers. The Munich agreement of 1938 is remembered as particularly shameful, albeit no more so than US isolationism. Yet the cast of mind that led to Munich is understandable. Britain was ill-prepared to fight Germany, least of all in Eastern Europe, an eventuality for which it had made absolutely no provision. Because of the priority given to building up the air force and navy, even its capacity to help France was questionable. Imperial commitments, financial constraints, moral idealism, domestic considerations, and an inability to comprehend the nature of the lawless forces now at work all combined to render Britain unready to respond to the situation that now confronted it.[27] America's neutrality legislation indicated that no help was to be anticipated from that quarter. When, in January 1938, Roosevelt sent a secret message to Neville Chamberlain offering to call a conference in Washington to discuss the international situation, he was politely rebuffed on the grounds that it would interfere with delicate negotiations then in progress aimed at recognising Italy's conquest of Abyssinia in return for a pledge of Italian friendship. Whether anything useful could have been salvaged from such a conference is doubtful. But that an offer from the United States was refused in order to achieve a morally suspect agreement with Mussolini indicates not only Chamberlain's desperation, but the depths to which Anglo-American relations had descended.

In spite of having his offer rejected, Roosevelt did not cease to believe that American interests were at stake. The problem was that with his hands tied by Congress there was not much he could do. Americans regarded rearmament with even more suspicion than the British. Nevertheless, he pressed ahead as best he could with plans to strengthen the country's defence posture, and even consented to secret talks being held between US and British naval staff officers. He also confessed his growing concern to the Senate Military Affairs Committee. When, however, word leaked out that he had told them that 'America's first line of defence is in France', he felt obliged to issue an official denial.[28] Although humanitarian sentiment in the country increasingly turned against Germany because of its bombing of Spanish cities and persecution of Jews, and against Japan for its blatant aggression against China, isolationist sentiment showed little sign of diminishing.

Britain's leaders finally realised that Hitler's ambitions could not be contained when he occupied Prague in March 1939. Until then it could be argued that he was merely intent on undoing the Versailles Treaty and reincorporating German-speaking populations into Germany. If Germans wanted to be part of Germany that was their affair. But the taking over of Czech-occupied lands was another matter. This time there were no flag-waving crowds to greet his invading forces. Who now could doubt that he was an imperialist or that Poland was next in line? Without even so much as preliminary discussions between their respective military staffs Britain agreed to a military assistance pact with Poland. It was, of course, a calculated gamble. There was nothing that Britain or France could do to help the Poles directly. The hope was that, even at that late stage, Hitler might be deterred by the fear of starting a wider conflict. It was now up to Germany to decide whether or not Britain went to war.

7 World War II and the Grand Alliance

When Hitler launched his invasion of Poland he did not, of course, know that he was starting a world war, still less that he was starting a conflagration that would eventually engulf Germany itself. Emboldened by his successes to date and the feeble responses of the democracies, it seemed he had little to fear. The might of the *Wehrmacht* would soon overwhelm the ill-equipped Polish army. The Soviet Union, the only power in the region with an army comparable in size to Germany's, was now an ally and had agreed to co-operate in Poland's dismemberment. Whether Britain and France, which had backed down over Czechoslovakia, would prove any more resolute on this occasion remained to be seen. In any event, there was not much they could do. Within weeks they would be faced with a fait accompli. Later on perhaps some agreement could be worked out. For a resurgent Germany they were heady times.

Britain was ill-prepared for war. Although it had begun rearming in 1936, its expenditures had failed to match Germany's. There was also the usual inter-service wrangling. Because of the fear of aerial bombardment (greatly exaggerated as it proved), priority was given to supplying the Royal Air Force with bombers on the assumption that the only effective means of deterring Germany from bombing British cities was to have the means of bombing German cities in return. Not only was this strategy ill-conceived, but most of the effort expended was wasted as the bombers in question lacked the ability to reach German targets from British bases. Only late in the day, thanks to the deployment of radar, itself a recent British discovery, and the building of squadrons of Spitfires and Hurricanes, did the country set about creating an effective fighter force.[1]

In opposition to what seemed to them the excessive demands of the RAF, the heads of Britain's army and navy fought to defend their respective spending progammes. As always, the army fared worst. Its chiefs pleaded for a sufficient increase in forces to allow them to support the French in the event of a ground war, but to little effect. Remembering the Great War, the very idea of another British Expeditionary Force was enough to terrify the public. In February 1939 a target was set for 1942 for 32 divisions – 6 regular and 26 territorial army. Conscription was introduced the following month, but did not gather momentum until after war was declared. Even then, the contribution to the defence of the Western Front was much less than it might have been in view of Britain's population and industrial capacity. As late as May 1940, the British contingent in France amounted to only 10 divisions, none of them armoured, as compared with France's 104, Belgium's 22 and Holland's 8.

The declaration of war automatically committed India and the other colonies to the support of the mother country. The dominions – Canada, Australia, New Zealand and South Africa – followed Britain's lead by issuing their own declarations. Even before German troops entered Warsaw the British Empire stood arrayed for action. Yet for the next nine months virtually nothing happened. Being reluctant to force matters, the Allies, by mutual agreement, did not attack Germany, and being otherwise occupied in Poland, it did not attack them.

Prelude to Global War

During this strange hiatus, the United States, for the third time in its history, found itself grappling with the problem of how to remain neutral in a world bent on war. In a fireside chat on the evening of the day Britain and France declared war, Roosevelt expressed the hope of most Americans by reaffirming his determination to keep the country out of war. Unlike Wilson, he did not call on Americans to be 'impartial in thought as well as in action'. Too much was already known about Nazi policies for that to be expected. 'Even a neutral', he declared, 'cannot be asked to close his mind or his conscience.'

As the law required, he invoked the Neutrality Acts of 1935–37 that forbade the sale of arms, ammunition and weapons to belligerents. This was plainly disadvantageous to Britain and France. Determined to stave off the possibility of their being defeated, the President called for a special session of Congress to amend the law to the extent of placing the traffic in arms on a cash-and-carry basis. Isolationists in Congress, backed by such national figures as Charles Lindbergh and Herbert Hoover, claimed that Roosevelt was bent on leading the country into war. Anxious to allay the fear that he was following in Wilson's footsteps, he prohibited US citizens from travelling in belligerent ships and requested Congress for the power to forbid American merchant ships from entering combat zones. A national poll, taken in October 1939, revealed that although American opinion was overwhelmingly on the side of the Allies, fewer than a third would favour US entry into the war even if Britain and France were on the point of defeat.

Perceptions changed as a result of the dramatic developments of the following spring and summer. On 9 April 1940 Germany attacked Denmark and Norway. In spite of British troops being sent, both were quickly overrun. This led to Chamberlain's resignation and the appointment of Winston Churchill as prime minister. No sooner had Churchill assumed office, however, than German armoured units, outflanking France's Maginot Line, swept through Belgium, and within a week had thrust deep into northern France. Britain's forces, accompanied by remnants of the French army, unprepared for the swiftness of the German advance and in imminent danger of encirclement, made their way to Dunkirk, and were ferried back to Britain, leaving virtually all of their equipment behind. Remarkably, almost the entire British Expeditionary Force escaped, but there was no disguising the fact that Britain had suffered a major military catastrophe.

The fall of France and the expectation that an invasion of Britain would shortly follow alerted Americans to the danger of their own situation. With all of Western Europe under Hitler's control, it would presumably not be long before US interests were challenged. Roosevelt's immediate response was to appoint a National Defense Advisory Commission to take stock of the country's military needs, meanwhile calling for a billion-dollar increase in defence appropriations and the production of 50 000 warplanes. Popular alarm led to growing support for the 'Committee to Defend America by Aiding the Allies', the brainchild of the well-known author and Kansas newspaper editor William Allen White, which soon had branches across the country. The Committee's declared aim was not to bring the United States into the war, something for which opinion was still unprepared, but to give those whom Germany threatened the weapons they needed to defend themselves. Many, however, suspected that its real aims extended further. In response, an 'America First' movement was launched to warn the public that unless the government were restrained the country would find itself once again sucked into a conflict that was essentially none of its business. Thanks to the broad Atlantic, it was claimed, the United States was quite capable of defending itself. The movement's figurehead was the aviator Charles Lindbergh, whose visits to Germany had persuaded him of the *Luftwaffe*'s invincibility. The rank and file of the movement was made up of right-wing Republicans, pacifists, Anglophobic Irish, and supporters of the US

Communist Party, Russia at that time being Germany's principal ally. It was particularly active in the Midwest. Among its more prominent supporters were Henry Ford and the historian Charles A. Beard.

But opinion was shifting. Unlike the anaemic utterances of Chamberlain, Churchill's defiant oratory struck a note that appealed to Americans' fighting spirit. Such statements as 'we shall defend our island, whatever the cost may be, we shall fight on the beaches, we shall fight on the landing grounds, we shall fight in the fields and in the streets, we shall fight in the hills, we shall never surrender', showed that Britain at last had a leader who was prepared to lead. Americans were shocked, too, by the London Blitz. Thanks to the time difference, they could listen in the evenings to the live radio commentaries of Edward R. Murrow and other US reporters on the nightly bombings, punctuated by the wailing of sirens and the crump of bombs in the background. Whatever the American Firsters might say, there was no disguising the fact that here was a people much like themselves who were suffering the consequences of standing up to a bullying dictator of whose ultimate ambitions it was impossible to form any clear estimate.

Even before assuming office, Churchill had concluded that the only way of defeating Germany was to bring the United States into the war. As First Lord of the Admiralty he had conducted a genial correspondence with the President on naval matters. On becoming Prime Minister he lost no time in informing him of Britain's dire predicament.

> We expect to be attacked here ourselves, both from the air and by parachute and by air borne troops in the near future and are getting ready for them. If necessary we shall continue the war alone and we are not afraid of that. But I trust you realize, Mr. President, that the voice and force of the United States may count for nothing if they are withheld too long. You may have a completely subjugated and Nazified Europe established with astonishing swiftness, and the weight may be more than we can bear. All I ask now is that you should proclaim nonbelligerency, which means that you would help us with everything short of actually engaging armed forces.[2]

Churchill went on to list Britain's needs. These included the loan of 50 old destroyers left over from the Great War, the release of several hundred US planes, to be replaced by those already ordered by Britain and in process of construction, anti-aircraft guns and ammunition, and various raw materials of which Britain found itself in short supply. Roosevelt's reply was noncommittal, pointing out that the release of the destroyers would require Congressional approval, which it would be unwise to ask for at that time. Other materials could only be released after consideration had been given to the United States' own defence needs.

Roosevelt had to be cautious in view of the forthcoming November election. To have shown his hand too soon would have been a gift to his Republican opponents. In editorials and cartoons the Republican press was already drawing parallels between his pledges and Woodrow Wilson's. There was also the suspicion, fostered by the US Ambassador in London, Joseph Kennedy, that Britain was on the point of collapse, in which case American aid would be wasted. In an attempt to force the President's hand, Churchill raised the 'nightmare' possibility of his being replaced by a ministry anxious to sue for peace and prepared to use the British fleet as a bargaining counter. Joined with the fleets of Germany, Italy, France and Japan this would create a naval force which not even the United States could withstand.[3] Roosevelt agreed to release half a million rifles as 'surplus to America's requirements'. Releasing the destroyers, he explained, would be more difficult.

After the fall of France, Roosevelt had doubted Britain's capacity to survive, but over the summer more optimistic reports arrived, helping offset Ambassador Kennedy's increasingly pessimistic assessments. News that the Royal Navy had destroyed the greater part of the French fleet stationed in North Africa to prevent it coming under German control proved that Churchill was in earnest when he said that Britain would use every means available to ensure its survival. Given adequate supplies, there were now grounds for supposing that it might actually be able to repel a German invasion. Encouraged by these reports, Roosevelt felt sufficiently emboldened to offer Churchill the destroyers he wanted, providing Britain would agree, in return, to let the US have 99-year leases on naval and air bases in Newfoundland, Bermuda and the Caribbean. This would allow him to present the deal to Congress as essential for America's defence, the bases being far more valuable in the long run than the destroyers. He also asked for Churchill's assurance that in the event of Britain's falling into German hands the British fleet would be neither surrendered nor destroyed, but would sail to ports in America or the Empire.

Reports of fighter command's successes against the *Luftwaffe* helped further to convince Americans of Britain's willingness to fight on. Apart from the destroyers, however, there was not much they could do to help Britain out of its immediate predicament. Arthur Purvis, a Canadian businessman, headed Britain's purchasing commission in Washington. He agreed to take on the orders previously placed by the French at a cost of nearly £650 million. Being bound by the cash-and-carry legislation, however, money was already a problem. The situation was like that of World War I all over again. By the spring of 1941 Britain was as short of dollars as it had been in the spring of 1917. Already the goods on order were well in excess of its capacity to pay, but like Lloyd George on that earlier occasion, Churchill could see no alternative but to struggle on, hoping, Micawber-like, that something would turn up. Meanwhile, little in the way of war matériel was actually arriving, American industry not yet being fully geared to war production. So far, most of what Britain had paid had gone on building factories and setting up machinery rather than turning out weapons. As in the Great War, the United States was profiting, not only financially but in terms of its own readiness, at Britain's expense.

Having promised that on no account would American boys be sent to die in foreign lands, Roosevelt beat his Republican opponent, Wendell Willkie, by a comfortable margin in the November election. That difficulty out of the way, Churchill renewed his efforts to enlist the President's assistance by painting a dire picture of Britain's position. Ships were being sunk at an alarming rate, making the need for additional merchant vessels a high priority. Combat aircraft, preferably heavy bombers, were needed too, if possible at a rate of 2000 a month. Small arms, artillery and tanks were similarly required. Britain's needs, Churchill admitted, far exceeded its capacity to pay. He hoped the President would understand the sacrifice Britain was making in terms of lives and material assets, and would agree to supply the weapons needed without stripping the nation of every last vestige of the overseas investment capital it had built up over the years. This, he explained, was a struggle in which America's future was also at stake. His letter was not a plea for help but rather 'a statement of the minimum action necessary to the achievement of our common purpose'.[4]

Roosevelt responded by calling for 'all-out aid' for Britain, and for the United States to become 'the great arsenal of democracy'. If a neighbour's house were on fire, he declared, you would not quarrel over the cost of your hose. You would let him put the fire out and get the hose back afterwards. The United States should therefore give Britain the ships and guns it needed. The Bill he submitted to Congress would allow him to lend or lease military equipment to 'the government of any country whose defense the President deems vital for the defense of the United States'. Lend-lease, in effect, put America's industrial capacity at the disposal of Germany's opponents, leaving the question of payment to be negotiated at a later date. Although the inference was that the goods were simply being loaned, the reality was that they were being written off in return for the recipients' military efforts. If anything were left at the end it would be a wonder. Isolationists were naturally incandescent. Senator Burton K. Wheeler described it as a measure designed to 'plow under every fourth American boy'. Congress, nevertheless, approved it by an overwhelming majority, agreeing an initial appropriation of $7 billion. By the end of the war $47.9 billion in lend-lease aid had been extended to 38 different countries, some $27 billion of it going to Britain, mostly in the form of military supplies but including machine tools, foodstuffs and raw materials. On an equivalent basis, Britain supplied the United States with materials it needed in the form of reverse lend-lease.

Churchill called lend-lease 'an inspiring act of faith' and 'a monument of generous and far-reaching statesmanship'. But there was not much point in proclaiming the United States the arsenal of democracy unless the weapons reached their intended recipients. Germany's response to lend-lease was to proclaim an Atlantic battle zone extending eastward from Greenland within which vessels would be sunk without warning. The United States, in turn, began convoying British cargoes halfway across the Atlantic, well into the area designated by Germany. By the summer of 1941 the United States and Germany were already engaged in an undeclared shooting war.

Meanwhile, important events had been occurring elsewhere. In September 1940 Japan signed a Tripartite Pact with Germany and Italy, thereby sending out a warning that the war might well spread to the Pacific. The United States responded by cutting off Japan's supplies of scrap metal and aviation fuel. Then, on 30 June, came the news that Germany had attacked the Soviet Union, sending 100 divisions rolling eastward on a front extending from the Baltic to the Black Sea.

To consider the implications of these events, Roosevelt and Churchill held a secret meeting in Argentia Bay off Newfoundland. Neither expected that the Russians would be able to hold out for long. Remembering Russia's collapse in the First World War and Stalin's purges of the military, the possibility that the Soviet army would be able to resist Hitler's Panzer divisions seemed remote. The most that could be counted on was that Germany's turning eastward allowed a breathing space in which Britain could prepare its defences. Churchill's hope was that he could persuade Roosevelt to find a way of getting the United States to enter the war. In this he was disappointed. Nevertheless, the meetings led to a close personal friendship being established between the two leaders.

After several days visiting back and forth on their respective flagships they issued a joint statement setting forth their shared hopes for a better world once Germany had been defeated. The so-called Atlantic Charter was not a treaty. Strictly speaking, it was simply a press release. But as an indication of the understanding that existed between the two nations it was a document of key importance, later incorporated into the Declaration of the United Nations of 1 January 1942, setting forth the war aims of the anti-Axis powers. Although originally drafted by the British, it struck a high moral tone reminiscent of Wilson's Fourteen Points in a manner designed to appeal to American sensibilities. Among the points listed were the renunciation of territorial aggrandisement, opposition to territorial changes not approved by those affected, and the right of peoples to select their own forms of government. Taken at face value, these principles could be interpreted as an undertaking to dissolve the British Empire. Churchill later told the House of Commons that 'At the Atlantic meeting we had in mind the restoration of the sovereignty of . . . states . . . now under the Nazi yoke . . . quite a separate problem from the progressive evolution of self-governing institutions in the regions and peoples that owe allegiance to the British Crown.'[5] This was not quite how Americans interpreted the document. But with Britain's very survival at stake it was hardly a time for quibbling over the exact meaning of a press release. At least it could be said that the Charter showed that Britain and the United States were on the side of freedom, and for the time being that was all that mattered. On 24 September it was announced that 15 anti-Axis nations had endorsed the Charter. What private reservations the leaders of the Soviet Union had in mind as they added their signatures can only be guessed.[6]

Still, for Churchill and Roosevelt to have met and issued such a statement indicated a common purpose of sorts. Isolationists were naturally moved to fury. Lindbergh linked the British, the Roosevelt administration and the Jews, claiming that they were the three principal agencies driving America into war, a statement that did his reputation no good. But by the autumn of 1941 the isolationists were a diminishing band. Seeing one unoffending nation after another overwhelmed by Germany, Americans now had good cause to fear for their own safety. In August, after an encounter between a German U-boat and a US destroyer, Roosevelt instructed the navy to 'shoot on sight' any Axis ships in a newly-proclaimed US security zone encompassing the western Atlantic. (Something the American people were not told was that the destroyer had been tracking the submarine while a British plane dropped depth charges.) Other incidents followed, including the torpedoing of the US destroyer *Reuben James* off Iceland with the loss of 96 lives. In November Congress even went so far as to repeal the essential clauses in the 1939 Neutrality Act, thereby allowing American merchant ships to carry goods of all kinds, including arms and ammunition, directly to Britain. The isolationists were being proved right in at least one respect: the United States was rapidly moving from a position of non-belligerency to one of belligerency.[7]

The United States Enters the War

The attack on Pearl Harbor took both Britons and Americans by surprise. Largely unobserved by the public, the events leading towards war in the West had been paralleled by developments in the East, where Japan was seeking to interdict American efforts to supply the beleaguered Chinese. At their Argentia Bay meeting, Churchill and Roosevelt had agreed to send identical messages to Japan warning that if it persisted in its actions they would be 'compelled to take counter measures even though these might lead to war'. Effectively this meant that an attack on either Britain's colonies or the Philippines would bring both countries into the conflict. The Japanese were thus left with the choice of either reining in their forces, already heavily committed to the war in China, or widening the struggle. Observing Germany's successes in the West, and driven on by the need to find alternative sources of oil and metal to compensate for those denied it by the US embargo, it seemed there would never be a better time for establishing their so-called 'New Order in Greater East Asia'.[8]

Thus forced into a corner, they struck at both countries simultaneously, attacking Hong Kong, Malaya and Thailand as well as the Philippines, Guam, Wake Island and other US possessions in the Western Pacific. Churchill later recalled that when Roosevelt telephoned to tell him of the Pearl Harbor attack, he said 'We are all in the same boat now', to which Churchill replied, 'This certainly simplifies things. God be with you.'[9] Both countries declared war on Japan the following day. For a brief interval it was unclear what Hitler would do, but doubts were resolved on 11 December when Germany and Italy declared war on the United States. This was a great relief to Churchill, who feared that Americans would concentrate their efforts on defeating Japan at the expense of the struggle in Europe. It also spared Roosevelt the task of persuading Congress to fight a war on two fronts at a time when American anger was principally directed towards the Japanese. Quite why Hitler behaved so obligingly remains a mystery. Perhaps, like Ludendorff and Hindenburg in 1917, he simply underestimated America's fighting capability. Alternatively, he may have supposed that the US could not do much more than it was already doing to help the Allies in the West, and would concentrate its efforts on the war in the Pacific.

This last was a possibility that continued to worry Churchill. Earlier in the year, as a result of staff talks between British and US military personnel, it had been agreed that in the event of the two countries being drawn into a war against both Germany and Japan, priority would be given to defeating Germany as the more formidable of the two adversaries. German armies were already in the suburbs of Moscow. With the Soviets defeated, Hitler could turn his attention to invading Britain. A Nazi empire encompassing the entire European continent would pose a much greater threat to American interests than having Japan run rampant in the Pacific. With Britain occupied, Europe would be virtually impregnable. On the other hand, with Germany out of the way, coping with Japan should involve no insuperable difficulties.

The day after Germany's declaration, Churchill and his military Chiefs of Staff boarded the battleship HMS *Duke of York* for the ten-day voyage to the United States. At Roosevelt's invitation he and his immediate personal staff stayed at the White House and the rest of the British delegation at the nearby Mayflower Hotel. To Churchill's relief it turned out that the Pearl Harbor attack had not changed America's plans. Europe would remain the first priority. He and the President spent much time ensconced together discussing overall strategy while their military advisers studied the logistics. The personal rapport the two leaders had established at their earlier meeting blossomed, helped by the fact that Roosevelt now knew that he had the support of the American people behind him. The result was a merging of war effort unlike any other in modern history. It was quite unlike the arm's-length association insisted on by Wilson in the Great War. When issues that might have led to friction arose, they were resolved in an easy and casual way by the two leaders. This dispensed with much of the committee work that would otherwise have been required and had the additional advantage of keeping other interested parties out of the discussions. Western strategy thus became an Anglo-American affair: once Churchill and Roosevelt had agreed on something, there was not much that the French or the Poles could do about it.[10]

One development for which the British were not prepared was the proposal of General George C. Marshall, the US Army's Chief of Staff, that there should be a unified military command structure. This meant that in each theatre of operations the army, navy and air forces of both nations would be commanded by a single officer. The British were at first inclined to oppose this arrangement, but relented when the Americans nominated a British officer, General Archibald Wavell, for the post of supreme commander in south-east Asia. Thus, in the case of the Normandy landings, America's General Dwight D. Eisenhower acted as supreme commander, with Britain's Air Marshall Arthur Tedder as his deputy. On that occasion, as it happened, the three service commanders – land, sea and air – were all British. As theatre commanders were not answerable to their own governments, as had always been the case in the past, a joint body known as the Combined Chiefs of Staff (CCS) was given global responsibility. In theory, the CCS consisted of the general staff committees of the two nations meeting in joint session. Having Britain's senior commanders based in Washington, however, was obviously impractical. Britain was therefore represented by Field Marshal Sir John Dill, accompanied by nominees of the three services. Under this arrangement, commanders of national armies were prevented from appealing over the heads of their superiors to their own governments, as had frequently been done in the Great War. In spite of initial doubts, particularly regarding the ability of British and American officers to work together when it came to large-scale amphibious landings, the high-command structure showed itself operationally successful. Here, too, personal friendships played an important part in shaping policy, most notably that between Dill and Marshall.[11]

Other combined committees took care of aircraft production, munitions, shipping and a hundred and one other activities. Before the war, the official British presence in Washington had consisted of a handful of Foreign Office employees. By 1943 it had swelled to some 9000. Practically every branch of the British government had a task force there, including, of course, the intelligence agencies.

Earlier in their careers, as respectively First Lord of the Admiralty and Assistant Secretary of the Navy, Churchill and Roosevelt had learned the importance of secret intelligence. Back in 1909, Churchill had even been a member of the Cabinet that established the forerunners of today's MI5 and MI6. Because intelligence gathering was a function in which Britain had more experience, Americans looked to it for leadership. It was, in fact, largely British initiative that led Roosevelt in 1942 to set up the Office of Strategic Service (OSS, forerunner of the CIA), with William J. ('Wild Bill') Donovan as its head. British intelligence, however, had made its presence felt in the US well before Pearl Harbor. At that time its principal aim was to bring the United States into the war. This was an endeavour fraught with danger. Among the tactics used by William Stephenson, the newly appointed head of MI6 in New York, was feeding the US government bogus stories and forged documents relating to supposed German conspiracies in Latin America. He scored a number of successes, one of which led to Roosevelt's denouncing Hitler's designs on the Americas in one of his 'fireside chats'. Following America's entry into the war, however, Stephenson overplayed his hand by employing an agent to 'get the dirt' on Assistant Secretary of State Adolf A. Berle, who had had the temerity to advise Roosevelt against allowing British agents carte blanche to employ undercover agents in the US. When the FBI and the State Department learned of Stephenson's activities there were demands for his recall. He survived, but only by the skin of his teeth, and was later rewarded for his efforts with a Knighthood and the US Medal for Merit, America's highest civilian decoration. Fortunately for Anglo-American wartime relations, his more dubious activities were concealed from the press.[12]

One area in which America lagged far behind Britain was with regard to signals intelligence. As early as May 1940 British code-breakers at Bletchley Park had begun decrypting German Enigma messages. Churchill was initially reluctant to pass on this information, partly for security reasons but also because it might lead Americans to suspect that Britain was also decrypting their own diplomatic cables (as, in fact, it had been doing for 30 years). Well before Pearl Harbor, however, the British Admiralty was regularly supplying the US Navy with advice on the routing of convoys based on German U-boat decrypts. By December 1943, the Bletchley Park team had created the world's first electronic digital computer, Colossus, containing 1500 valves and capable of running through the millions of possible settings on German code machines. In due course there were 10 Colossus computers in operation, feeding Allied leaders and their military commanders information on Germany's intentions, often before the messages concerned had reached their intended recipients.[13]

Pearl Harbor and the American entry into the war eventually led to the BRUSA agreement under which the two countries agreed to share 'all information concerning the detection, identification and interception of signals from, and the solution of ciphers and codes used by, the Military and Airforces of the Axis powers, including secret services'. For two allies to collaborate to this extent, not merely passing on information but the details of how it was obtained, was unprecedented. As with co-operation at the political and military level, it was an association in which transatlantic friendships played an important part. Curiously, such problems as there were in the sharing of information arose, not out of Anglo-American jealousies but out of long-standing rivalries between branches of the US military.[14]

Work on the making of the atom bomb also involved close co-operation. At the outbreak of war, many British physicists were drafted into working on radar. Because this was regarded as highly secret, refugee German physicists were left to work on the potentialities of nuclear fission in uranium 235, a recent discovery not thought to have military implications. In 1940, Otto Frisch and Rudolf Peierls, colleagues at the University of Birmingham, compiled a report showing the practicability of creating an atomic weapon. Having obtained the permission of the Birmingham police, they took their report to Whitehall where it was scrutinised by a committee of government scientists. In September 1941, on the committee's recommendation, Churchill ordered work to proceed with urgency. Roosevelt, to whom the committee's findings were communicated, suggested setting up a joint project, but as the United States was still neutral and there was a reluctance on the British side to share information in a field in which they saw themselves as being more advanced, it was decided that the two countries should proceed independently.

Up to that time, American work in the area had been desultory. Within a year, however, the situation was reversed, the United States having set to work with characteristic energy. Now it was Churchill who called for a merging of efforts and the Americans who demurred. Rather plaintively Churchill observed that since Britain had provided the initial boost by releasing the contents of the Frisch–Peierls Memorandum to the US government, it should reciprocate by keeping Britain up to date on what it was doing. Vannevar Bush, Roosevelt's chief scientific adviser, suspected that Britain's principal interest was in using America's secrets in order to garner the post-war economic benefits of atomic energy. Not until August 1943, when the two leaders met at the Quebec Conference, was the way finally cleared for the two programmes to merge.[15]

Anglo-American global strategy depended first and foremost on control of the seas. The war in the Pacific, fought mainly by the United States, was from the outset primarily a naval conflict. But success in the struggle against Germany also depended on the Allies' ability to shift men and supplies by sea to where they were needed. Most immediately, it meant defeating the U-boats in the Battle of the Atlantic. Churchill, who took a particular interest in the matter, set up a Cabinet Committee, chaired by himself as Minister of Defence, to oversee shipping capacity, losses and the allocation of resources relative to civilian and military needs. This last was a fraught issue as America's first priority was getting troops, landing craft and other supplies to England in preparation for the Normandy landings. Military requirements, however, had to compete for shipping space with the foodstuffs needed to feed Britain's own population. This led to some tension, not least because losses due to U-boat action meant that Britain had to rely increasingly on the American merchant marine for the purpose.

Until the spring of 1943 it seemed as though U-boats were destined to win the Battle of the Atlantic. Before America's entry into the war the Axis had succeeded in sinking 2,162 ships, totalling 7 751 000 tons, for the loss of a mere 68 submarines and 5 surface vessels. Within a month of Pearl Harbor, U-boat packs were operating almost with impunity, or so it seemed, in American waters. The US Tenth Fleet responded by bringing all anti-submarine activities under a single command and introducing a well-disciplined convoy system. Together with improved radar, better air surveillance, and the successes of the Bletchley Park code-breakers, this enabled the U-boat menace to be gradually overcome. Between March and July 1943, monthly shipping losses dropped from 477 000 to 123 000 tons, and continued to decline thereafter. By the end of the war, 781 U-boats had been destroyed as against the loss of 2775 Allied vessels.[16]

The principal difference between British and American strategic thinking hinged on the relative priority to be accorded to the Mediterranean campaign, which Britain had begun before American entry into the war, as opposed to the planned cross-channel invasion. Being a continental power with a population of 120 million, and with almost half the world's manufacturing capacity at its disposal, the obvious policy for the United States to pursue, so its military leaders supposed, was to strike directly at Germany's main fighting force. That meant establishing a continental beachhead at the earliest possible opportunity, defeating the *Wehrmacht*, and moving on to occupy the German homeland. It was essentially the policy that Grant had adopted in the American Civil War when he advanced on Richmond, and that Pershing and the Allies had used in the autumn of 1918 in the Meuse–Argonne offensive that ended the war. From an American point of view, effort spent on peripheral campaigns was essentially effort wasted. Right from the start, therefore, the US Chiefs of Staff and most of Roosevelt's advisers took it for granted that the most effective way of defeating Germany was by means of a full frontal assault.

The United States, of course, had not had Britain's experience of four years of bloody trench warfare on the Western Front in 1914–18, nor had its forces been steamrollered by German Panzers in 1940. These experiences had badly shaken British self-confidence. Moreover, the idea of virtually closing down operations in areas where there had been some successes seemed wasteful. From the time of Elizabeth I onwards, Britain had never possessed the kind of overwhelming material superiority in confronting its continental foes that Americans took for granted. How could the British forget that only a short time before their sodden and defeated army had struggled home, its weapons abandoned, owing its very survival more to luck than good management? For a further year they had lived in the expectation of an imminent German invasion. Now they were being asked to gamble everything on a single, large-scale, amphibious landing on a well-defended shore in the face of opposition from a formidable and hitherto undefeated foe.

So eager were the Americans to press ahead with their intention of engaging Germany's main forces that Marshall was even prepared to contemplate a landing in 1942 with a view to establishing a beachhead in preparation for a major assault the following year. Britain's military leaders argued – very rightly, as the ill-considered 1942 Dieppe raid showed – that such an undertaking was highly risky and would require far more resources than were currently available. However large or small the beachhead, it would become the focus of Germany's entire military effort in the West and would soon prove untenable without first having established total air superiority. They even expressed doubts, given the amount of preparation needed, as to whether anything of the sort could be attempted in 1943. Far better to delay than run the risk of failure and seeing the Channel, as Churchill vividly put it, transformed into 'a river of blood'. This was at a time (the spring of 1942) when Britain's forces were receiving a drubbing from Rommel in the Western Desert and there were imminent fears of Egypt and the Suez Canal coming under German control.

Because it affected the principal sea route to India, the situation in the eastern Mediterranean naturally concerned Britain more than it did the United States. Both Churchill and Roosevelt, however, were eager that some American forces be committed to action in 1942 rather than be left kicking their heels until such time as a landing on the French coast became feasible. There had already been trouble with the Canadians shipped over to defend Britain in 1940. Churchill's proposal, therefore, was to have American forces land in Morocco and Algeria to attack Rommel's forces from the rear, thereby establishing control of the whole of North Africa. In spite of American objections, the plan was set in motion by the CCS, and in November more than 100 000 American and British troops under the command of General Dwight D. Eisenhower established beachheads along the French North African coast. Their arrival coincided with the British 8th Army's victory at El Alamein. Caught between Field Marshal Montgomery's and Eisenhower's advancing forces, Rommel's troops were driven back to Tunisia, where, in May 1943, disregarding Hitler's command that they should fight to the death, over a quarter of a million surrendered.

That German armies were not invincible was also becoming evident on the Eastern Front. At Stalingrad and Kursk the Soviets had won resounding victories against forces far larger than anything the Western Allies had – or, indeed, ever would – encounter. Since Pearl Harbor, Stalin had been pleading for a second front to take the pressure off his own hard-pressed forces. The North African campaign, being relatively small in scale, hardly served the purpose. Satisfying though its outcome was, its effect, as the Americans saw it, was simply to delay the planned invasion of France by a further year. Churchill, however, continued to argue in favour of an opportunistic approach, striking northward through Sicily and Italy at what he took to calling 'the soft underbelly' of Europe and pressing home the advantage wherever the enemy showed signs of weakness. This did not mean that he was against OVERLORD (the invasion of France), merely that while the vast build-up of forces in Britain continued they should do what they could to harry and weaken the German war machine, exploiting opportunities as they arose, meanwhile bombing Germany itself to smithereens.

Tempting though this approach was, it was hardly cost-effective.[17] Bomber losses were high. Also, many more Allied troops were occupied in pressing home the northward advance from the Mediterranean than were employed by Germany in opposing them. Italy left the war in September 1943 when its Prime Minister, Marshal Pietro Badoglio, met with Eisenhower and agreed to an armistice. Yet by the end of the year the Italian front was locked fast in a bloody stalemate. Even had the Allies succeeded in breaking through into northern Italy, they would still have had the encircling wall of the Alps with which to contend. Keeping Anglo-American forces in the Mediterranean tied up shipping that, in the American view, could have been put to better use, either in the Pacific or in preparation for the Normandy landings.

At the Tehran Conference of November 1943, Churchill continued to advocate expanding the Mediterranean campaign, possibly by means of a northward advance through the Aegean in conjunction with operation OVERLORD. This impressed the Russians even less than it did the Americans. Did he and his military staff, Stalin wanted to know, *believe* in OVERLORD? The same question was put to Field Marshal Sir Alan Brooke, Churchill's principal strategic adviser, by Marshal Voroshilov. Both replied in the affirmative, but doubts lingered as to whether they gave it quite the same priority as the Russians and the Americans. As testimony to Britain's diminishing role relative to that of the two great continental powers, Roosevelt held a number of preliminary discussions with Stalin, while refusing one to Churchill. Even after the Normandy landings, Churchill continued to dream of finding a way of marching his forces into Austria through northern Yugoslavia and getting to Vienna before the Russians.[18]

When it came to strategic planning, Churchill had a notorious penchant for maverick schemes. His support for extending Allied activities in the Mediterranean stirred memories of policies he had advocated in the First World War, among them his advocacy of the ill-fated Gallipoli landings. Some wondered if he might be seeking to prove a second time around that he had been right the first time. More worrying was the way he awakened the suspicion, always lurking in the back of Americans' minds, that the British were more concerned with preserving their Empire than with defeating Germany.

This was, of course, untrue. All the same, there was no overlooking the fact that British and American visions of the world that would emerge from the war were very different. Americans wanted to bring the blessings of democracy, capitalism and freedom to everyone. That was what the Atlantic Charter said. The whole world, in their view, would benefit from becoming more like the United States. This was hardly reconcilable with the continued existence of the British Empire in its present form, or perhaps in any form at all. Earlier in his career Roosevelt had been deeply shocked by what he had seen of British rule in Africa – the material poverty, the lack of education, the manifest need for a New Deal approach to problems. This, it seemed, was something the British, whose principal concern appeared to him to be milking their colonies of their resources, were incapable of providing. Looking ahead, Roosevelt regarded British imperialism and the system of imperial preference as potentially greater obstacles to international progress and understanding than Soviet communism.[19]

It was natural, therefore, for Americans to regard Britain's preoccupation with keeping the Suez Canal secure and maintaining its position in the Middle East as directed more towards the pursuit of its traditional imperial policies than the defeat the common foe. That they were prepared to support Britain to the extent they did was largely a reflection of the fact that when they entered the war the only way of engaging enemy directly, apart from assisting with the bombing of Germany, was to send troops to where British troops were already fighting.

The situation in South East Asia and the Pacific was, of course, different. There the United States was very much the dominant partner. With the sinking of the battleships *Prince of Wales* and *Repulse* off the coast of Malaya within days of Pearl Harbor, Britain effectively ceased to have a naval presence in that part of the world. Even had the two vessels survived, it is questionable how much use they would have been, since the great battles of the Pacific were essentially air wars fought between rival carrier fleets. Thus, the task of containing Japan's island-hopping advance southward towards Australia fell to the US Navy, whose carriers had fortunately escaped the Pearl Harbor attack, rather than the Royal Navy.

By the summer of 1942, Hong Kong, Malaya, Singapore, the Philippines and most of the Netherlands East Indies had fallen, putting Burma and India in the Allied front line. Here British, Commonwealth and colonial troops bore most of the burden. Once again, however, a fundamental divide on strategy opened up, the British favouring a southwest thrust through Burma and Thailand towards its lost colonies of Malaya and Singapore, the United States arguing for increased aid to China, whose friendship Roosevelt was eager to cultivate on the grounds that it was potentially a great power and the key to post-war stability in the region. The relationship between Lord Louis Mountbatten, the Supreme Allied Commander in South East Asia, and his American deputy, 'Vinegar Joe' Stillwell, verged on the poisonous.

Britain's treatment of India was another issue. Quite why the Indians should fight for Britain was not clear, least of all to the leaders of the Indian Congress, who wanted immediate self-government and full control over their country's defence policy. It was not clear to Americans either. India's leaders, resentful of the fact that they had not even been consulted when the British Viceroy had declared war on their behalf, proceeded to organise a campaign of civil disobedience aimed at disrupting the war effort. Thus Britain found itself in the paradoxical position of defending India at great cost in terms of manpower and resources without the support of India's elected political leaders. Like many Americans, Roosevelt viewed the situation as preposterous. Britain's relationship with India resembled America's with the Philippines, but in 1934 the US Congress had undertaken to grant the islands full independence by 1946. When Harry Hopkins, acting on Roosevelt's behalf, proposed that Britain make an equivalent pledge to India, Churchill exploded. India was an issue close to Churchill's heart. His political isolation during the 1930s had begun with his resignation from the Conservative Shadow Cabinet over its willingness to conciliate Indian nationalists, and he was not about to change his views on the matter under pressure from the United States. The question was not raised again.[20]

The Friendly Invasion

In the First World War rather more than a million American servicemen passed through Britain. For most it was a brief encounter, a matter of landing in Liverpool, travelling south by train, and departing from Dover or Folkestone three or four days later. Apart from medical and administrative personnel, and those shipped back for hospital treatment or recuperation, few had more than a fleeting opportunity to see the country or meet its people.

World War II was different. Between 1942 and 1945 some two million young Americans, most of whom had never been abroad before, lived in Britain for a matter of months or even years. Among the earliest arrivals were the personnel of the 8th US Army Air Force, most of whom were stationed in East Anglia. They were preceded by vast earth-moving machinery that tore up hedgerows and bulldozed flat swathes of countryside to make way for runways. By April 1943 there were some 3,500 aircraft operating out of 122 airfields in an area extending from the Wash to just north of London. Their crews lived on bases adjoining the airfields, each accommodating around 3500 personnel, a significant addition to the population in this sparsely populated region. At night, the streets of Norwich, Cambridge and Colchester were thronged with free-spending US servicemen eager for a good time. Out in the countryside it was a common sight to see groups of them cycling along country lanes on their way to local pubs and dance halls.

So too was the early-morning spectacle of the B-17 Flying Fortresses and B-24 Liberators taking off on their daytime raids, circling as they gained height, hundreds or even a thousand at a time, rising until, in tight V formations, they broke away and headed east over the North Sea.

Inhabitants of the nearby villages watched these impressive displays, counting the number leaving their local base and comparing it with the number coming back in the evening. Often they would see planes returning trailing black smoke or with parts shot away. Afterwards ambulances might be heard rushing injured crewmen to hospital. The average lifespan of air crew was 21 missions, which meant that those who completed their assigned tour of 25 missions were, statistically speaking, already dead.

Local people struck up friendships with the new arrivals and invited them home for meals. In return, they received gifts of sliced ham, tinned salmon, chocolates, and similar luxuries from the base store. Many had never met an American before and were fascinated to hear tales of life in places they might have heard of in the cinema or in popular songs. To add to the novelty were occasional glimpses of figures they had actually seen in the movies. James Stewart, identifiable even in the distance by being head and shoulders taller than any other flier, spent a year and a half in Norfolk, piloting B-24s belonging to the 445th Bomb Group out of its base at Tibenham. Clark Gable, also an officer in the USAAF although not involved in operational duties, could be seen riding his motorcycle around Oundle, where he was making training films. Other Hollywood figures, among them Bing Crosby, Bob Hope and James Cagney, toured the country as entertainers. Those who met them were disarmed by their easy manner. Americans seemed less rank-conscious than their British counterparts. Instead of having drivers, as British officers did, American officers drove themselves around in Jeeps. To many British people, children and young women especially, something of the glamour associated with the stars of the silver screen attached to all Americans.[21]

The British were impressed, too, by the quality of the Americans' equipment. Unlike their own army with its battered old Bedford lorries, Americans travelled in modernistic four-wheel-drive juggernauts hung about with towing cables, spades, fire extinguishers and deep-tread spare tyres. In place of the Lee-Enfield rifles of the British, unchanged since the First World War, Americans carried Garand self-loading rifles, Winchester carbines and Thompson sub-machine-guns. As men and equipment flooded into the country, the roads leading through English villages were choked with convoys of tanks and lorries. Along England's south coast, encampments grew to such proportions that Eisenhower later joked that 'Only the great number of barrage balloons floating constantly in British skies kept the islands from sinking under the seas.'[22]

The presence of so many Americans inevitably gave rise to friction. Off-duty GIs wore well-tailored dress uniforms, unlike British Tommies who had to make do with their heavy all-purpose battledress (surely the ugliest and most uncomfortable outfit ever invented). American troops were also paid a great deal more. This was as much a reflection of the US Government's fear of what an occupying army might get up to if its material needs were not met as of America's greater abundance. To have exposed incoming American servicemen to the kind of privations routinely endured by British Tommies would have been a recipe for trouble.[23] Nevertheless, such favoured treatment caused resentment, not least because it gave Americans an unfair advantage where women were concerned. 'Rich' and 'American' were two words that seemed to go naturally together (like 'damn' and 'Yankee' in the post-bellum South). Cartoons showed GIs toting cameras, smoking Churchill-sized cigars and generally throwing their money around. Actually, having grown up in the Great Depression, many of the servicemen who came to Britain came from backgrounds that were far from opulent. Still, by the Spartan standards of wartime Britain and of Britain's other allies, they appeared to lead privileged lives. Early in 1943 a store was opened in South Audley Street, off Grosvenor Square, from which Americans could be seen emerging laden with all manner of goods unobtainable by native Londoners. Grosvenor Square, where the US Embassy was located, and where much of the adjoining area had been taken over by those responsible for administering lend-lease, was one of the two principal centres of American activity in London, the other being Piccadilly Circus, where GIs on furlough tended to congregate. A favourite hangout for GIs was Rainbow Corner, the former Café Monaco, which stayed open all night, and offered hamburgers and American sandwiches. It also had a dance floor capable of accommodating 300 couples, where Americans could show British girls how to jitterbug, a practice forbidden in many of Britain's more traditional dance halls.[24]

Britons and Americans would later look back on the war years as a time of remarkable sexual promiscuity. Given the dislocation of ordinary family life and the imminence of death, this was hardly surprising. Around Piccadilly and its equivalent in other English towns there was no shortage of young women ready to entertain Americans. The British joked about Americans as being 'overpaid, over-sexed, and over here', the American riposte being that the British were 'underpaid, under-sexed, and under Eisenhower'. For the most part this was simply friendly banter. Entertaining GIs was regarded as a patriotic duty, and since what

GIs most craved was female companionship, it was made easier by the absence of so many of Britain's own men in distant theatres of war. The American influx was thus a boon to Britain's young women, who responded readily to Americans' easy charm and free-spending ways, as shown by the fact that some 70 000 of them eventually became GI brides and went to live in the United States. Never again would the Anglo-American relationship be quite so intimate.[25]

The Allied Victory

Then, even more suddenly than they had arrived, the troops and vehicles that had filled the lanes and fields of southern Britain were gone. Initially the British and Canadian troops in Normandy outnumbered the Americans, but within six weeks the balance shifted decisively in the Americans' favour. Thereafter the US Army became increasingly the major partner, until by VE-day the United States had three million GIs on the Continent.

Having stood alone against the Axis powers and borne the brunt of the fighting against Germany up to the launching of the D-day landings, in the later stages of the war Britain found its role diminished. In terms of men and matériel, the United States and the Soviet Union were now the major combatants. Churchill was made aware of the altering balance within the alliance at the Teheran Conference in November 1943, when Roosevelt and Stalin engaged in preliminary discussions to which he was not invited. Having come to believe not only in Britain's special relationship with the United States, but in his own special relationship with Roosevelt, he found this personally hurtful. Roosevelt, however, being a consummate politician, acknowledged no special relationships – or friendships for that matter – only particular interests affecting the United States.

Paramount among these, Roosevelt believed, was America's need to secure the friendship and co-operation of the Soviet Union, which, regardless of what he or anyone else might wish, would soon control most of Eastern Europe. The only course open to the United States, therefore, was to try to win Stalin's trust by allaying his suspicion that the United States and Britain were arrayed against him. At Teheran Roosevelt set out to woo Stalin in much the same way as Churchill had sought to woo him in 1940.

As events would later show, Roosevelt's efforts were much of a piece with Chamberlain's efforts to appease Hitler, Stalin and Hitler inhabiting different ideological universes from those with which Western statesmen were familiar. In Stalin's case this meant starting from the basic premise that offers of friendly co-operation were merely tactical manoeuvres in a long-running struggle that was destined to end eventually in the triumph of socialism.[26] Thus, unlike Churchill, who had been quite bowled over by Roosevelt's charm, the Russians remained as stony-faced as ever. But, as Churchill told the House of Commons in December 1944, there was no alternative.

> Another great war, especially an ideological war, fought as it would be not only on frontiers but in the heart of every land with weapons far more destructive than men have yet wielded will spell doom perhaps for many centuries of such civilisation as we have been able to erect since history began to be written. It is that peril which . . . we have laboured and are striving sincerely and faithfully to ward off . . . .[27]

This was a question on which, therefore, he and Roosevelt saw roughly eye to eye. Meeting for the last time at Yalta in February 1945, their main concern was nevertheless to get the war over as soon as possible. That meant encouraging Stalin to press ahead against Hitler and, more importantly, obtaining his promise that the Soviet Union would enter the war against Japan within three months of the ending of the struggle in Europe. In comparison with the Soviets, however, Britain now had little to offer. Although its forces had begun pushing the Japanese back in Burma, the war in the Pacific was essentially an American affair. Even in Europe Britain's contribution was now overshadowed by that of its two great allies. Marshall and the CCS had ruled in favour of Eisenhower's strategy of advancing on a broad front rather than a British plan to race ahead and capture Berlin before the Soviets got there. Even had they succeeded, the West would still have had no option but to depend on Stalin's goodwill concerning the fate of the rest of Eastern Europe.

Meeting at Yalta in February 1945, Stalin appeared remarkably accommodating. He agreed to a Declaration of Liberated Europe that pledged the Big Three to support post-war governments in the liberated states based on free elections. He further undertook to broaden the Moscow-organised provisional government of Poland to include democratically elected representatives from Poland itself and the London-based Polish government in exile. The joint announcement of the results of Yalta stated that the Allies had agreed on plans for the final defeat, military occupation and denazification of Germany, and the setting up of the

United Nations. What the world was not told was that the Western Allies had also agreed to the forced repatriation of Soviet nationals in return for the Soviet's agreement to enter the war against Japan. Nevertheless, the Western delegates left Yalta in high spirits, feeling that they had established a working relationship that would stand them in good stead in the future. But Stalin's pledges, as soon became clear, were not to be taken literally. This was first revealed in the case of Poland, where Stalin insisted that the former Moscow exiles control the new administration. According to Stalin, the Poles regarded Britain as 'unfriendly', and even objected to British observers being allowed into the country, which seemed implausible, not least because it was on their behalf that Britain had gone to war. A complicating factor was the London Poles' awareness of the Soviets' responsibility for the Katyn Forest massacre of some 10 000 Polish officers – virtually the entire Polish officer corps – in 1940 during the period of the German-Soviet alliance and their subsequent failure to support the Warsaw uprising.[28] Fearing that Stalin's rebuff might lead Churchill to make an intemperate statement to the House of Commons, Roosevelt pleaded with him to be patient. As in all alliances there were bound to be difficulties, and it was essential to avoid a situation dominated by 'mutual mistrust'. As he cabled Churchill only an hour before his death on 12 April 1945, 'I would minimise the general Soviet problem as much as possible, because these problems, in one form or other, seem to arise every day and most of them straighten out . . . . We must be firm, however, and our course thus far is correct.'[29] It is revealing in more ways than one that, on learning of Roosevelt's death, Stalin sent a cable to the State Department requesting that an autopsy be performed to determine whether he had been poisoned.[30]

8 Britain, America and the Cold War

Post-War Readjustments

The Second World War ended sooner than anticipated. When the Western Allies celebrated VE-day on 8 May 1945 it still looked as though the subjugation of Japan would take at least another year. Since May 1942, Japanese forces had been gradually driven back from the areas they had overrun in the first six months of the war, but it was proving a slow process. The battles for Guadalcanal, Iwo Jima and Okinawa were seen as a gruesome preview of what was to be expected when it came to invading the Japanese homeland. In preparation for such an assault, British and Commonwealth forces in the Pacific area were put under American orders. For many Americans this had all along been the war that really mattered. As the United States would be contributing the lion's share of the forces, Americans increasingly took matters into their own hands. Henceforward it was the American Joint Chiefs of Staff rather than the Anglo-American Combined Chiefs who determined strategy. There was little the British could do but acquiesce. Their diminishing role was reflected in the handling of the decision to drop atom bombs on Hiroshima and Nagasaki. At Ottawa in August 1943 the two powers had agreed that atomic weapons would not be used without British consent. In the event, Britain was consulted only perfunctorily, more or less as an afterthought. There was no longer any doubt, at least in the minds of Americans, that they were now the senior partners.

So long as the war with Japan continued, however, Britain enjoyed the benefit of lend-lease. Japan surrendered on 2 September 1945; eight days later, on Truman's instructions, the programme was abruptly terminated. The result, according to a Treasury memorandum penned by Lord Keynes, was to leave Britain 'virtually bankrupt'. In consequence, he went on to warn, 'a greater degree of austerity would be necessary than we have experienced at any time during the war'.[1] The possibility of such an outcome had been foreseen by Churchill as early as December 1940 when he had pleaded with Roosevelt *that it would be wrong in principle and mutually disadvantageous in effect if,* at the height of this struggle, *Great Britain were to be divested of all saleable assets,* so that after victory was won with our blood, civilisation saved and time gained for the United States to be fully armed against all eventualities, we should be stripped to the bone.[2]

Such an outcome, Churchill added, would be in the interests of neither country. The people of Britain would suffer 'cruel privations', and American exporters would find the demand for their products correspondingly reduced. Very possibly the United States would suffer widespread unemployment. America not even being in the war at that time, Roosevelt could give no guarantee that this would not happen. Nevertheless, Churchill clung to the hope that thanks to his own rapport with Roosevelt, the cultural affinities linking the English-speaking peoples, and what he termed 'the natural Anglo-American special relationship', the United States would again come to Britain's rescue, or at the very least not to take advantage of the one ally who had fought right through the war. But, when the war ended, neither Roosevelt nor Churchill was in office, Roosevelt having died in April 1945 and Churchill having been replaced as Prime Minister in July by his former deputy, the Labour Party leader, Clement Attlee. Even had they been still in power it is doubtful whether the result would have been much different. Generous though it had seemed at the time, particularly in comparison with the arrangements under which aid was provided in World War I, lend-lease was a two-edged sword. It had enabled the British to survive, but only on condition of having their finances closely audited to show that the materials requested could not be supplied from domestic resources. Unlike the aid given to the Soviets, who would never have agreed to open their books in the way Britain did, the aid the British received had to be used strictly for war purposes, which is to say that none of it could be used in ways considered detrimental to American interests – as, for example, by building up industries capable of competing with US businesses once the war was over.[3]

Roosevelt's successor, Harry Truman, was no Anglophile. Coming from the Midwest, he shared the suspicion of many in that section regarding Britain and its Empire. His principal concern was bringing the boys home, and getting the nation back on a peacetime footing. Like Attlee, he struggled to emerge from the looming shadow of his predecessor. The two were also alike in other respects, being personally modest, good party leaders, and simple and direct in their dealings. There might have been the makings of a close friendship, but during their years in office they met only three times: once at Potsdam in July 1945, and twice when Attlee made short visits to Washington to sort out misunderstandings. After the intimate relationship of the war years, the two nations were drifting apart.

So far as the economy of United States was concerned, Churchill's foreboding proved unfounded. The US emerged from the war not only richer than it had been before, but richer than any nation had ever been in the whole of history. Unlike the other combatants – victors and van-quished alike – it had managed to bear the cost of the war and at the same time to increase the supply of consumer goods to its own population. It was a dizzying achievement. Plants that had been idle or under-utilised through the Depression years sprang into full operation. Women found employment in jobs previously reserved for men. High wages set the nation's cash registers ringing. What rationing there was amounted to lit-tle more than token gestures. Unlike the British, Americans did not have to choose between guns and butter. They could have both – along with nylon stockings, lipstick, and all manner of other luxuries they had previ-ously been unable to afford. At war's end, with only 6 per cent of the world's population, the US possessed 50 per cent of its industrial capacity and an even larger proportion of its consumer goods in the form of cars, telephones and household appliances. By initiating a massive exercise in deficit spending the war had succeeded in doing what the New Deal had failed to do, namely revive the economy. Like Britain in 1815, the United States in 1945 was in a position that set it apart from the other belli-gerents.

During the war there had been a fear that the ending of hostilities would bring a return of the Depression, but these proved unfounded. Wartime savings, combined with a flood of new products – among them television sets, air-conditioners and dishwashers – ensured a smooth tran-sition to peacetime production. Returning servicemen found jobs waiting for them, and although these were not always the jobs they might have wished, there were generally prospects for advancement. If there was one thing on which Americans could rely it was on the capacity of the US economy to go on turning out that cascade of commodities that made them the envy of everyone else. It was what made New York the world's financial capital, the dollar the currency against which other currencies measured their value, and Detroit the city where real cars were made. It had provided them with the weapons they needed to defeat the Axis powers, and now it filled their homes with goods, stood surety for their debts, and bore testimony to the virtues of free enterprise, democracy, individualism, and all the other things they cherished. While the war was still being fought, Henry Luce, the publisher of *Time*, *Life* and *Fortune*, had proclaimed the twentieth century 'the American century'. Whatever doubts there may have been about that at the time, they were soon dispelled. In terms of economic strength, and in many other ways too, the United States was now in a class all of its own.

In the case of Britain, however, Churchill's worries proved all too well founded. Five years of conflict had stretched the country's resources to their limit. The Labour government that assumed power in July 1945, elected with the help of the votes of returning servicemen, had committed itself to creating a welfare state and to nationalising coal, steel, the railways, and other major industries. Yet the resources needed to carry through these ambitious programmes were meagre. Many of Britain's cities were in ruins. For five years the nation had concentrated its energies on war production to the virtual exclusion of all else, with the result that exports in the immediate post-war years were less than half what they had been previously. It had also been obliged to divest itself of many of its overseas investments, so 'invisible' earnings fell from £248 million in 1938 to £128 million in 1946. The German submarine gauntlet had reduced the country's merchant fleet by 70 per cent. Coal and textiles, languishing even before the war, were in a worse state than ever and desperately needed capital investment. Yet to concentrate what few resources there were on bolstering exports was politically unacceptable. What people looked to the government for were improvements in their living conditions. At the very least, after the years of privation, they expected new clothes and homes in which to raise their families. Those who took literally the promises of the newly elected Government anticipated much more.

Where the resources for all this were to come from was far from clear. The problem was exacerbated by the new commitments Britain had been obliged to take on as a result of the war. Among these was the cost of maintaining its occupation force in Germany. Unlike most wars, in which the victors obtain spoils from the vanquished, the result of World War II was quite the opposite, the victorious Allies finding themselves lumbered not only with the expense of keeping troops on the ground but having to feed and clothe the conquered population. Altogether, it was calculated, Britain would be spending £750 000 a year more on its overseas commitments than it was capable of earning.

Yet, in spite of its imperial overstretch, Britain was still indubitably one of the Big Three. Its empire remained intact, and by the late summer of

1945 all of it was back under British control. Its armies and air bases straddled Europe, North Africa and Asia. Hard-pressed though it undoubtedly was to maintain its position, it was still the world's third largest military power. Economically it was in far better shape than France or any of the former Axis countries. In spite of the bombing, the damage it had received was relatively slight compared to the wholesale destruction they had suffered. Moreover, World War II, unlike its predecessor, had created a basis for the development of new industries based on oil and electricity rather than coal and steam. Bad as things were, Britain emerged from the war in a far better condition than its continental neighbours.

This was not an unalloyed blessing. Being one of the victors made it psychologically difficult for the incoming Labour administration to adjust to the realities of the situation it confronted. Militarily, of course, Britain was overshadowed by its two former allies. The Soviet Union had borne the brunt of the land war against Germany. According to Soviet statistics, it had destroyed no less than 506 Axis divisions. Of the 13.6 million Axis troops killed or taken prisoner during the war, 10 million were lost on the Eastern Front. Even after demobilisation, the Red Army remained by far the largest military force in the world, with 175 divisions, 25 000 front line tanks, and 19 000 aircraft. Although it controlled fewer land forces, the military capabilities of the US were no less imposing. The US Navy, with a fleet of 1500 major warships, including dozens of carriers, was second to none, as was the US Air Force with its long-range bombers, capable now of unleashing the kind of devastation it had wrought in Hiroshima and Nagasaki anywhere in the world.[4]

But the war was over and there was plainly no point in Britain, a small island, trying to match the strategic capabilities of these two great continental powers. What the people wanted, and the Labour government had promised, was social reform and an end to wartime austerity. Even so, the country's new leaders had no intention of relinquishing Britain's role in world affairs. They would seek to maintain their Empire, honour their overseas commitments, nationalise the country's major industries, provide a free medical service, support the value of sterling, and embark on a wide-ranging programme of social reform all at the same time. For a country impoverished by five years of war this was a formidable agenda.

To obtain the funds required, it dispatched Lord Keynes to Washington. On arrival he was told in no uncertain terms that an outright gift was out of the question. Having supported Britain throughout the war, American taxpayers felt under no obligation to support it now.

Why provide Britain with the wherewithal to maintain an empire of which they disapproved? More to the point, why should capitalist America underwrite the expensive schemes of Britain's new socialist rulers? If that was the road the British had chosen, with all the resources of their vast Empire to draw on, surely there was surely no need to keep coming back to the United States for handouts.

In spite of these objections, the terms eventually agreed were surprisingly generous. After three months of negotiation the US undertook to tide Britain over with a loan of $3.75 billion at 2 per cent interest, repayable over 50 years, beginning in 1951. It further agreed to write off Britain's outstanding lend-lease debt of approximately $15 billion in return for a payment of $650 million. This was not, Deputy Secretary of State Dean Acheson explained, a reward for an ally. 'It is not a pension, gift, or handout of any description. It is an investment in the future.'[5] Britain's future was important because, according to Sam Rayburn, Speaker of the House of Representatives, unless Britain was helped it would be tempted go yet further down the road to socialism. Britain was 'a great natural ally' and America could not afford to 'take a position that will drive our ally into arms into which we do not want her to be folded' (i.e. those of the Soviet Union).[6] But having become accustomed to American generosity and the easy credit arrangements of the war years, the fact of having to pay interest charges came as a shock to many Britons. Not for the first time, nor for the last, they recalled that the United States had grown rich while they had paid a disproportionate price in terms of lives lost and capital expended.

Whether or not such grumbling was justified, there was no ignoring the fact that the world's financial centre had moved from London to New York, or that the United States alone was capable of supplying the capital needed to restore shattered economies and revive world trade. This had been foreseen by the representatives of the 44 countries who met at the UN Monetary and Financial Conference at Bretton Woods in New Hampshire in 1944. They had used the occasion to set up the International Monetary Fund and the International Bank for Reconstruction and Development, the largest share of the capital in both cases coming from the US Treasury. In return, Americans made plain that they expected other countries to open their markets to US trade and investment and to make their currencies freely convertible into dollars.[7]

To the financially hard-pressed British these conditions were hard to accept. Ever since the 1930s, when the international economy had split into competing blocs geared to particular currencies – pounds, dollars, francs, or whatever – Britain had sought to organise its trading arrangements within its so-called sterling area. During the war it had tightened these measures in order to earn additional dollars. This meant that colonies capable of earning dollars through their exports, like Malaya (rubber) and Nigeria (palm oil), had to convert them into sterling and lodge the unused capital in Britain in the form of low-interest loans. For this policy to operate effectively Britain had to impose strict financial controls on its colonies, meanwhile advancing its interests by setting the prices it paid for its own imports at well below the world market level. Such restrictions might be excused as wartime measures, but maintaining them once the war was over naturally caused resentment. Not only were Britain's colonists being denied a fair payment for their produce, but Americans had cause to resent the fact that those from whom they were purchasing goods were being denied the wherewithal to buy American products in return.[8]

Nevertheless, when the United States insisted that Britain make sterling freely convertible as a condition of granting a loan, there were loud protests. Conservatives, Churchill among them, claimed that this would effectively mean the end of the British Empire. Backbench Labour members claimed that capitalist America was now imposing its will on socialist Britain – as, of course, it was. Behind America's seeming benevolence there had always lurked an element of raw power. But, as the British had demonstrated in their heyday, the exercise of power is seldom disinterested. All the same, it was galling for a nation that had just emerged victorious from a long-drawn-out struggle to have its wings thus clipped. The government gained Parliament's acceptance of the loan on the terms demanded, but only at the expense of alienating much of its left-wing support.

It soon transpired, however, that even the $3.75 billion was nowhere near enough to shore up Britain's ailing fortunes. Simply keeping the population fed, as Keynes had foreseen, was becoming increasingly difficult. New austerity measures were therefore introduced. To add to Britain's woes, the winter of 1946–47 proved exceptionally severe. Freezing conditions and heavy snowfalls closed roads and railways, reduced manufacturing output and hampered fuel distribution. Businesses closed; cattle and sheep died in the fields; a million workers found themselves suddenly without jobs. As they huddled around their fireplaces, it was becoming clear to the British that, far from getting better, things were actually getting worse. Bread was now rationed, something they had not experienced even at the height of the submarine blockade. Elsewhere in Europe people were literally starving.

Meanwhile, Britain's overseas obligations continued to mount. Besides its own population, Britain was having to pay some $48 million a year feeding the Germans in its zone of occupation. In Greece, 40 000 British troops were fighting on the side of Royalist forces against communist insurgents at a total cost of some $60 million a year. In Palestine, where Britain had in the past made contradictory pledges to both Arabs and Jews, it now found itself, in fulfilment of a United Nations mandate, having to spend some $160 million a year trying to maintain the peace. In spite of the deployment of 100 000 British troops in an area smaller than Wales, it was becoming increasingly evident that this was a doomed enterprise. It also made the British highly unpopular, especially with American Jews. The world had been deeply moved by the pictures of Belsen, Auschwitz and other German extermination camps. When Britain turned back immigrant ships containing Jewish survivors, there were angry demonstrations outside the British consulate in New York.[9] India, too, was proving an economic liability. As a concession at the beginning of the war, the British government had promised to meet any exceptional costs involved in putting the Indian Army on a wartime footing. The Indian Congress had meanwhile begun levying duties on British imports. The combined result of these measures was that the traditional relationship between metropolis and colony had been reversed, Britain now finding itself in the position of owing money to India. If only for financial reasons, things could not be allowed to go on as they were.[10]

More alarming than any of these developments, however, was the growing evidence of Soviet intransigence. In spite of the promises made at Yalta regarding free elections in Poland, Romania and Bulgaria, pro-Soviet regimes were being forcibly installed with the backing of the Red Army. The Soviets were also putting pressure on Turkey to allow their fleet use of the Dardanelles and refusing to withdraw their occupying forces from northern Persia.

Whether Soviet intentions were defensive or aggressive was not immediately clear. They seemed not to alarm the United States, which by the summer of 1947 had reduced its ground forces in Europe from 3.5 million to a mere 200 000. Nevertheless, the evidence was sufficiently worrying to persuade the British Cabinet of the need to build up the country's military strength. Despite strong Treasury objections, Parliament resolved to retain conscription, the first time in history that Britain had maintained a conscript army in peacetime. The period of service was initially set at one year, but was subsequently extended to eighteen months, and eventually to two years. More significantly, Britain undertook to build its own atomic bomb, the Cabinet view being that for want of any assurance of American support, and being well within Russian bomber range, the country could not allow itself to be subject to Soviet blackmail. If America had the bomb, it was only a matter of time before Russia had it too.

Meanwhile, the American loan was running out. Plainly something would have to be done. As a first step towards cutting its losses, Labour resolved to honour its wartime pledge and grant independence to India. This was in spite of the growing evidence that withdrawal would lead to a bloodbath. Staying on, however, promised no better prospect, as it was plain that the leaders of the Hindu Congress and the Muslim League were unprepared to resolve their differences peacefully. It was also clear that Britain would have to abandon Palestine. So far as the United States was concerned, both were welcome developments. Neither required any immediate action on its part other than extending recognition to the new states. In the case of Israel, responding to the urgings of the Jewish lobby, it was the first nation to do so. Of more moment was Britain's request that the United States assume the burden of providing financial and military aid to Greece and Turkey.

Forging the Cold War Alliance

Although the Cold War is commonly represented in terms of bipolar rivalry – the US v. the USSR, capitalism v. communism – it was the socialist British who were most immediately aware of the dangers of Soviet expansionism. Russia was an old rival. Throughout the nineteenth century it had been seen as a threat to British interests in the Middle East and India. The worry in Whitehall was that, as after World War I, the United States would retreat into isolationism, leaving Western Europe virtually at Russia's mercy. Already there was evidence of growing Soviet influence in France and Italy, both of which had strong communist parties. As a former General Secretary of the National Transport and General Workers' Union, the new British Foreign Secretary, Ernest Bevin, had learned about communist intrigue the hard way. Much of his career had been spent fending off attempts to take over the British union movement. Stalin's promises, he believed, were as worthless as Hitler's, as revealed by events in Poland and elsewhere in Eastern Europe. Meeting in Moscow in December 1945 he warned Secretary of State James Byrnes, his American counterpart, that the USSR was bent on its old game of putting pressure on Turkey so as to gain control of the

Dardanelles preparatory to undermining Britain's position in the Middle East.

Warnings were also received by both nations from their representatives in Moscow. Writing to their respective governments, George Kennan and Frank Roberts, old friends from wartime days, outlined what they saw as the nature of the Soviet threat. Russia's rulers, they argued, were impervious to Western blandishments and prepared to use any means at their disposal, including making and breaking agreements, to further their interests. It was futile to try and inveigle them into the normal give and take of international relations. They were not like Western statesmen. They viewed the world through ideological glasses. What others would regard as gestures of goodwill they would interpret as signs of weakness. Their goal was world domination. On the other hand, they were not like Hitler, the man on a bicycle who had to keep going for fear of falling off. On the contrary, believing that the capitalism would eventually collapse as a result of its internal contradictions, they were in no hurry to move. There was no fixed timetable. They would take advantage of opportunities as they arose, advancing when circumstances allowed and withdrawing when the stakes became too high. From this it followed that the only way of containing them was by the steady application of countervailing force.[11] At Roberts's suggestion, the Foreign Office set up a special committee to monitor Soviet conduct. Its findings, outlined in successive reports, left no room for doubt that the Soviets were intent on exploiting Europe's current misfortunes to extend their power.

This was also the message conveyed to Americans by Churchill in his famous Iron Curtain speech, of 5 March 1946, delivered in Truman's home town of Fulton, Missouri. The world's English-speaking peoples, according to Churchill, needed to unite in lifting that curtain and countering Soviet threats, using, if required, the atomic bomb, which 'God had willed' to the American people. Admired as Churchill was by Americans, the response to his statement was one of shock. There had been no priming of public expectations in preparation for such a message, or even sense that, with one world menace lately removed, another was already looming. Some suspected that Britain was simply up to its old tricks, mobilising American support in defence of its imperial interests. So hostile was the public reaction that Truman was impelled to issue a personal statement dissociating himself from what Churchill had said.

In fact, Churchill was merely giving public expression to what Truman, who had seen and approved his text, had for some time believed. A year earlier, on his assuming office, Truman had been briefed by Averell Harriman, then US Ambassador in Moscow, on what Harriman had described as the Soviets' 'barbarian invasion of Europe'. Subsequent meetings with Stalin and Molotov persuaded him that Harriman had not exaggerated. Like Roberts's message to the Foreign Office, Kennan's 'Long Telegram' from Moscow profoundly influenced official thinking. So impressed was Truman's Secretary of State, George Marshall, that he had Kennan recalled to Washington and put in charge of a specially created committee responsible for advising on overall US foreign policy.

Truman's problem, like Roosevelt's before him, was getting the message across to the American people. Britain's announcement of its inability to continue supporting Greece and Turkey, therefore, provided the opportunity needed. Simply telling Americans that they should rally to the support of the King of Greece, however, would hardly impress them, still less the Republicans, many of them neo-isolationists, who now controlled both houses of Congress. The issue would need to be couched in moralistic terms and related to America's own defence interests. As Arthur Vandenberg, the Chairman of the Senate Foreign Relations Committee, told him, the only really effective way of getting the message across was to 'scare the hell out of the country'.[12] Addressing a joint session of Congress on 12 March 1947, Truman accordingly described the current world situation as a contest between good and evil, a Manichaean struggle between those who believed in a way of life based on free institutions and the will of the people and one that relied on 'terror and oppression, a controlled press and radio, fixed elections, and the suppression of personal freedoms'. The policy of the United States, he declared, must be 'to support free peoples who are resisting attempted subjugation by armed minorities or by outside countries'.[13] Specifically, he asked Congress for $400 million to provide loans, military equipment and personnel to help fight the communist guerrillas already operating in the country and to stiffen Turkey's resistance to Soviet pressure on its borders.

The Truman Doctrine, as it became known, set the tone for American foreign policy for the next 50 years. Effectively it put an end to any hope of establishing amicable US–Soviet relations. Some insiders, George Kennan among them, thought Truman had gone too far. Critics would later argue that by arousing public alarm in the way he did he opened the way for his Republican opponents to mount an anti-Communist crusade aimed at undermining support for his party and rooting out left-wing sympathisers – a category into which many former New Dealers readily fitted – from government. But, at least in the short run, the tactic had the intended effect of persuading Congress to make the financial appropriations required.

It also created a new basis for Anglo-American co-operation. Britain ceased to be viewed as a perpetual supplicant and became once again a valued partner. The British Empire was similarly transformed from being an embarrassing appendage into a useful bulwark against communism. In the Middle East, a continued British presence was deemed essential, both as a means of keeping the Soviets out and of safeguarding the West's oil resources. As always, there were those who suspected that Britain was simply unloading its problems on the US. There were worries, too, concerning the dangers of creeping socialism. Visits to the United States by Harold Laski, Chairman of the Labour Party, and Dr Hewlett Johnson, the 'Red Dean' of Canterbury, whose highly coloured accounts of the horrors of American capitalism found their way into the American press, helped give credence to the belief that Labour was intent on establishing, in the words of the officials at the Washington Embassy, 'a Communistic anti-American slave economy in Great Britain'.[14] Except in the case of Republican diehards, however, the concern had less to do with fear of socialism spreading to the United States than with the belief that it was jeopardising Britain's post-war recovery.[15]

Suspicion that the Truman Doctrine was merely a device for getting Britain's chestnuts out of the fire was effectively countered three months later by the announcement of the Marshall Plan for economic aid to Europe. Addressing a graduation class at Harvard University on 5 June 1947, Secretary of State George Marshall declared that the plan was directed 'not against any country or doctrine but against hunger, poverty, desperation, and chaos'.[16] Nevertheless, these were seen as the conditions in which Communism flourished and Congress was left in no doubt as to what the administration feared would happen if matters were allowed to drift. In purely financial terms the $400 million aid promised to Greece and Turkey had been of little consequence, but providing assistance on the scale needed to restore Europe to economic health involved disbursements of a quite different order. Often described as a 'New Deal for Europe', the Plan kept Congress occupied for the better part of a year. For a Democrat President to carry a measure labelled 'New Deal' through a Republican-dominated Congress (the first for 14 years) was no easy matter, and required playing on Americans' growing alarm over the rising tide of world communism. Either Americans accepted the administration's advice, they were told, or they would find themselves standing alone in a hostile world.

A year earlier the British Embassy in Washington had expressed concern over the apathy of the American public; now it reported a growing sense of popular hysteria. Playing the anti-Communist card worked like magic. What Marshall proposed was precisely what Bevin had been urging. He later described it as 'like a life-line to sinking men'.[17] The previous year's loan was almost exhausted and defending the value of sterling now that it was convertible was proving all but impossible. He lost no time in contacting his continental opposite numbers with proposals for drawing up a submission. Marshall had given no indication of the kind of sums he had in mind. In September a consortium of 16 nations, led by Britain and France, forwarded a request for $29 billion to Washington. Truman reduced the total to $17 billion and Congress subsequently pared it down to $12 billion, payable over four years. Yet, in spite of the cuts, the effect on Europe was dramatic. Between 1948 and 1952 the gross national product of the countries involved rose by 25 per cent. By the latter date it was 15 per cent above the pre-war level.

Because the Soviet Union and its satellites refused to participate, the programme's adoption effectively completed the process of dividing Europe into hostile camps. The onset of the Cold War also reminded Americans that, in spite of being overstretched, Britain was still a power to be reckoned with. It had 1.5 million men under arms, bases all around the world, and a navy second only to that of the United States. Its annual per capita income ($723), although only half that of the United States ($1453), was well above that of France ($482), West Germany ($320), Italy ($235) and Japan ($100). Otherwise, except for Canadians ($870) and Swedes ($780), the British were the richest people in the world.[18] They also took their world responsibilities seriously. Hard-pressed though they were, on a per capita basis they were spending as much on defence as Americans and a great deal more than any other Western power At $3.4 billion, Britain's 1948 defence budget was almost four times France's ($900 million) and eight times Italy's ($400 million).[19] If the United States intended to be firm with Russia, supporting Britain was a first priority.

Events now moved rapidly. In response to the Marshall Plan, the Soviets announced a Molotov Plan for their satellites. In Hungary, they organised a rigged election and purged the government of non-Communists. In February 1948 came the Communist coup in Czechoslovakia and the assassination of Jan Masaryk, its greatly admired Foreign Minister. Not only did these developments show that Britain and the United States were incapable of doing anything to defend the Hungarians and Czechs, they also raised doubts as to whether, in their current disarray, the Western powers could do much if something similar were to occur in Western Europe. Following the Czech coup, General Lucius Clay, the American commander in Germany, sent a telegram to Washington expressing his concern over the possibility of war. In March, Britain, France, Belgium, Holland and Luxembourg signed a defence treaty in Brussels, pledging mutual support in the event of any one of them being attacked. Alarmed by these developments, Truman authorised the newly created CIA to engage in covert operations against the Soviet Union.

What finally brought home to both Britain and the United States the peril of their situation, however, was the Berlin crisis of 1948–49. The two governments were already discussing ways of creating an alliance capable of standing up to the Soviets. Russia's closing of the land routes into Berlin and the Anglo-American airlift organised in response helped hurry these discussions along. Faced with such a challenge, it became difficult even for socialist members of parliament and isolationist senators not to support the plans of the two governments.

By the summer of 1948 there were B-29 bombers, equipped to carry atomic weapons, on British airfields. Whether they were actually carrying atomic weapons was not revealed. For political as well as strategic reasons the precise nature of their mission was kept vague. For a foreign government in peacetime to maintain an armed force on British soil over which the British Government had no control was unprecedented. It was all the more extraordinary in that shortly before the planes' arrival, out of deference to American wishes, Britain agreed to surrender its veto over the use of the bomb. As might be expected, not everyone was happy with this arrangement. Graffiti reading 'Yanks Go Home' began appearing in public places, presumably put there by the same people who a few years before had been writing 'Second Front Now'. On the political right, High Tories fumed over the affront to Britain's dignity and what they regarded as Churchill's supine attitude towards the United States. Nevertheless, most people regarded the American presence as reassuring, not least the fact that the US had the bomb and, if the worst came to the worst, would be prepared to use it.

The atom bomb, however, hardly afforded an effective defence against all eventualities. There needed to be a ground force capable of dealing with minor emergencies and of stemming, at least for a time, any major assault. To be effective, such a force would require full American involvement. During the latter months of 1948 work began on drafting a treaty linking the US and the signatories to the Brussels Treaty – Britain, the

Benelux countries, Canada, France, Italy, Denmark, Iceland and Portugal – together in a mutual defence pact on the understanding that an attack on any one of them would be considered as an attack on all. The North Atlantic Treaty was signed by the foreign ministers of the nations involved on 4 April 1949 and ratified by the Senate on 21 July.

The creation of NATO marked a watershed in American history. Since its birth as a nation, the US had abided by the advice given by Washington in his Farewell Address to 'steer clear of permanent alliances with any part of the foreign world', relying instead on 'temporary alliances for extraordinary emergencies'.[20] Yet here was NATO, a permanent alliance, made with the very nations whose 'frequent controversies' Washington had specified as being 'essentially foreign to [America's] concerns'. Soon it would have similar alliances with dozens of other nations, forces stationed in more than 100 countries, and world-wide commitments far in excess of anything envisaged even by the nineteenth-century British.

The Cold War Turns Global

Even so, Americans responded angrily to the suggestion that they were intent on establishing an 'empire'. Empires, in the American view, were old-fashioned affairs in which imperial power was exercised through viceroys or governors with troops at their command and who controlled the apparatus of state. They involved an exercise of authority over indigenous and often recalcitrant populations, possibly by men in cocked hats riding around in emblazoned coaches. But although that was how Hollywood frequently represented the British Empire, it was far from being an accurate description of how the British Empire had actually worked in practice. Plainly it did not apply to the white dominions, which were now self-governing (even though, on formal occasions, high commissioners did sometimes appear in coaches and wearing cocked hats). Nor did it make allowance for the extent to which, in the case of the non-white colonies, the British preferred co-opting the services of whatever indigenous hierarchies were on hand rather than ruling directly. Indeed, throughout the nineteenth century, informal empire had been the chosen option, the notion being that it was more economical, and through indirect rule colonists would progress towards objectives deemed appropriate for them at a speed that would avoid social disruption.

Thus, in more ways than they perhaps realised, Americans found themselves behaving much like the British before them. Just as in the princely states of nineteenth-century India the British 'resident' had been the effective power behind the titular ruler, so now, in countries around the world, a similar function was performed by the resident US ambassador. First in war-torn Europe and Japan, but soon in South-east Asia and Africa too, Americans found themselves behaving like latter-day proconsuls. On occasion the maintenance of their interests might involve military intervention, as in Indochina, Lebanon, the Dominican Republic, Grenada, Central America and the Persian Gulf. At other times they arranged for the removal of the ruler in question, as with Mohammed Mossadegh in Iran and Patrice Lumumba in the Congo. Generally speaking, however, personal persuasion and economic inducement sufficed.

So whether America's hegemony is viewed as an 'empire', or, as most Americans preferred to call it, a 'protective presence', is immaterial. The fact is that the United States dominated the world to an extent never previously attained by any nation, even nineteenth-century Britain. And as with the British, no single motive fully explains this projection of American power. Plainly defence considerations had much to do with it, but so, too, did business interests, and even, on occasion, altruism. Sometimes US policies conflicted, as in its supporting Israel while seeking to ingratiate itself with the Arab states on whose oil supplies it was increasingly dependent. In other words, it behaved much like other great powers in the past, not least in its wish to impose its own values on others, these taking the form of democratic government, due process, the right to own private property, religious tolerance, access to education, and all the other rights listed in the US Bill of Rights and the UN's 1948 Universal Declaration of Human Rights, along with, of course, the virtues of capitalism, and America's right of access to the world's markets and natural resources.

During the war, and in the immediate post-war years, Americans had pinned their hope of achieving these goals on a so-called 'one world' policy. This would have allowed them to reshape the world in ways more to their liking largely through the exertion of economic pressure – as when they used their financial muscle to force the British into abandoning imperial preference in return for the famous 1946 loan. The Soviet Union, however, proved far more recalcitrant, with the result that they found themselves obliged to settle for something less than they had originally hoped, which is to say for a policy based on the concept of their championing the 'free world'. Not that everyone in the 'free world' was free by American standards, but at least they were anti-Communist, which was what really mattered so far as the overall struggle was concerned.

That the Cold War had spread beyond Europe was dramatically demonstrated in June 1950 when North Korea invaded South Korea. Like Germany, Korea had been divided into separate Soviet and Western occupation zones at the end of the war. The invasion was thus seen – inaccurately as we now know – as evidence of Soviet adventurism and a test of the West's capacity to resist. Truman responded by calling on the UN Security Council, from which the Soviet Union had temporarily withdrawn, for military intervention on behalf of the South Koreans. In spite of being already militarily overstretched, Britain agreed to send troops, as did Australia, Turkey and a dozen other countries, theoretically as part of a United Nations contingent but in practice operating under American command. The original UN intention was simply to repel the invading forces. When, however, the tide of war turned following the daring American landing at Inchon, the prospect of uniting the two Koreas proved too hard to resist. Although the impetuous American commander, General Douglas MacArthur, is commonly held responsible for the northward advance to the Yalu river that brought the Chinese into the war, it was, in fact, the British who organised the UN resolution endorsing the advance into North Korea.[21] At one point, alarmed by an incautious statement of Truman's which seemed to suggest that the US might be prepared to use the atomic bomb, Attlee was obliged to rush to Washington to reassure his cabinet colleagues that this was not the case. In fact, as he soon learned, Truman was as concerned as he was to avoid all-out war with China, and official statements were accordingly toned down. This, however, failed to inhibit MacArthur, whose bellicose statements became an increasing embarrassment and eventually led to his dismissal, an act which reassured America's allies even though it angered much of the American public.

There were, nevertheless, a number of key issues on which Britain and the United States plainly did not see eye to eye. One was European integration (about which more will be said in the next chapter). Another was over recognition of what the US persisted in calling 'Red China'. Sensitive to the precariousness of their position in Hong Kong, and following their traditional practice of recognising de facto governments, however objectionable, the British could see no point in cutting off contacts with what was plainly an emerging world power. Although they agreed to support the United States in setting up the South East Asia Treaty Organisation in 1954, they strongly advised against becoming involved in Vietnam, where the French were receiving a drubbing at the hands of Ho Chi Minh's Viet Ming. The French, eager for US support, were only too happy to characterise their opponents as agents of world communism rather than nationalists. The British, being principally concerned with strengthening NATO, were more sceptical. But, as Americans had to keep on reminding them, Congress would not accept a policy of containment in Europe and laissez faire in Asia.

The Suez Fiasco

So, by the mid-1950s, in spite of these differences, Britain and the United States were once again aligned in a global struggle against a powerful and ruthless enemy. It was, the British liked to think, a 'special relationship', even though, as tends to be the case with such relationships, its specialness was principally celebrated by the lesser of the two parties. Still, it was the kind of relationship that made it easy to assume that each could take the other's support for granted. With Eisenhower in the White House and Eden at 10 Downing Street, and with many others in subordinate positions still cherishing happy memories of the wartime alliance, any major policy disagreement seemed unlikely.

The story of Eden's Suez folly has been told too often to need recounting here. As always, many factors, personal and impersonal, were involved. The American Secretary of State, John Foster Dulles, by offering and then abruptly withdrawing American financial support for building Egypt's High Aswan Dam, was no less responsible than Eden for the way things turned out. When this reversal of policy led the Egyptian President, Colonel Gamal Abdel Nasser, to nationalise the Suez Canal, Americans failed to recognise the symbolic importance of the Canal to Britain. For almost a century it had been the gateway to the Indian Ocean, enshrined in folklore and literature. Generations of Britons had passed through it on their way to the Far East. It was still the route by which Britain obtained most of its oil supplies. Dulles was also at fault in failing to alert Eden and the Foreign Office as to Eisenhower's likely reaction to any unilateral action on their part. Had the Panamanians seized the Panama Canal, Americans would no doubt have behaved in an equally high-handed way. (In fact the US did send troops to Panama in 1989 when they arrested and subsequently imprisoned its de facto ruler, General Manuel Noriega, on charges of drug trafficking.) But anti-colonialist sentiment was powerful, and with Britain and France being under intense pressure to grant independence to their former possessions, attacking Egypt appeared a regressive move. More important, perhaps, was the fact that they lacked the means to mount the sort of quick and successful amphibious operation that was required.

This was embarrassingly revealed when, having announced their intention of invading, it transpired that there were insufficient transports on hand to carry the required force to Egypt. When vessels were eventually found, it was still a matter of weeks before the invasion occurred. Quite apart from the morality of the enterprise – not helped by the transparent falsity of their claim that they were intervening to separate the Egyptians and Israelis – it showed that Britain and France were no longer military powers of the first rank. Not only were they ill-equipped militarily, they lacked the financial muscle required, as became embarrassingly clear when there was a run on sterling and they called whole operation off at the very moment that the first troops were landing. That the British, the heroic defenders of freedom in two world wars, had been upstaged by an Egyptian colonel was bad enough, but being roundly condemned by the United Nations General Assembly made it even worse. To cap it all, the Anglo-French action diverted attention from Russia's brutal crushing of the Hungarian uprising. The lesson drawn was that Britain should never again attempt a major foreign policy initiative without first consulting the United States.

Waging the Cultural Cold War

Even more than after the First World War, America's post-war affluence contrasted with the privations of people elsewhere. But it was Americans' buoyancy and optimism that as much as anything set them apart from the peoples of war-torn Europe. Rodger's and Hammerstein's musical *Oklahoma!*, which opened in London in 1948, showed a world in which there were people who got up in the morning feeling that everything was going their way. Bouncy American musicals, of course, were nothing new. Jazz had begun to catch on in the 1920s. Most of the popular songs of the inter-war years had been American, as were most of the films seen by British audiences. It was the sound of the Big Band music of Benny Goodman and Glen Miller that the GIs had brought with them in the war. Now there were new developments, like bebop and rock 'n' roll, that were soon topping British music charts. In contrast to the nineteenth century, when Americans had looked to Britain for their culture, the flow of traffic had latterly been largely the other way. Every week, millions of Britons flocked to see Hollywood's latest confections.

In the post-war years there was also a growing realisation that Americans had contributions of a more intellectually demanding kind to make. Their achievements in science and technology, symbolised by their building of the atomic bomb, could hardly be ignored. Many of Europe's top scientists had been compelled to flee to America on account of Hitler's purges. As the award of Nobel prizes showed, American scholars and scientists were at the forefront of new developments. Where big science was concerned they had the advantage of being able to command the resources required. Long gone were the days when British academics could speak patronisingly about the work being done across the Atlantic. Moreover, the United States was still in a position to attract top talent from wherever it chose by offering higher salaries and superior facilities. In Britain there was alarm at the way the so-called 'brain drain' was leading to the loss of many of the nation's best scientists, engineers and doctors. A famous cartoon of the period showed a dockside with well-dressed Britons queuing to embark and ragged West Indians arriving.

Meanwhile, British universities were waking up to the fact that the study of American history, literature and political science had for too long been neglected. This was partly the response of a new generation of academics to their wartime encounters with Americans, partly a belated realisation that there was more to America than Hollywood movies and slick salesmanship. The US was not just a country of the present and future. The old quip, 'But does America really *have* a history?' was plainly out of date. A country that wielded the power that the United States now did needed explaining, and so obviously must have a history worthy of serious attention. Even so, conditions in post-war Europe were such that the growth of scholarly interest in the United States would hardly have developed in the way it did without generous US funding. One useful source of support was that provided by the sale of surplus US war equipment. Through the Fulbright Act of 1946 and the Fulbright–Hays Act of 1961, endowments were established allowing thousands of young European graduates on exchange visas to study in the United States and equivalent cohorts of young Americans to study in Europe. For high-flying young Britons, a period of study in the United States came to be regarded almost as a normal rite of passage, much like the European grand tours of former times. Most went on to become journalists, lawyers, politicians, doctors, or whatever had been their original choice of career. A few found niches for themselves in the newly established American Studies programmes springing up in British universities. Others, having waited out the two years their exchange visas required, returned to the US to take up permanent employment.

Many other bodies besides the Fulbright Commission contributed to these developments, among them the American Council of Learned Societies, the Ford Foundation and the Harkness Fund. To what extent this outpouring of American generosity arose out of Cold War considerations it is impossible to say. Visitors were not subjected to propaganda, but they did not have to be brainwashed to see that the United States was on history's escalator. One glimpse was enough. America was the land of king-sized portions, gigantic automobiles, interstate highways, doors that opened as one approached them. The contrast with austere post-war Britain was startling. The writer Malcolm Bradbury, arriving in 1955 aboard the *Queen Mary*, found New York a 'paradise of consumer splendours'. Staying with a family in the Bronx, he recalls,

> I wandered into that place of unbelievable excitements, the kitchen, with its bulbous refrigerator, its split-level cooker, its mixer. In the middle of the sink, there was a marvel: a grinder that disposed of kitchen refuse. My amazement conveyed itself to my host's father. From the bulbous refrigerator, he took a whole chicken and thrust it down the Dispose-All. I stared at the gurgling hole as it slowly ate the entire chicken and flushed it away; and then I knew that I had seen America, and it worked.[22]

Among the things that most impressed post-war British visitors to the United States was Americans' extraordinary generosity. This applied to government as much as to private bodies and individuals. The Uncle Shylock of the inter-war years had become the Santa Claus of the post-war era. It was, to be sure, a generosity not unconnected with the fact that much of the world's gold was lodged in Fort Knox, Kentucky. Nevertheless, it would be naïve to assume that Congress would have dispensed the nation's reserves in quite the way it did had it not been persuaded that national interests were involved.[23] Similar considerations presumably applied to major foundations like Ford, Rockefeller, Carnegie and the American Council of Learned Societies, whose administrators were continually shuttling between private and government service. Their boards, as we now know, were closely attuned to government thinking and served on occasion as conduits for CIA funding. Exactly where the money they received came from was not a matter that much concerned those receiving it, so long as it came with no embarrassing strings attached. This, however, did not prevent there being a public furore in 1967 when it was revealed that *Encounter*, the leading British intellectual journal of the period, was CIA- financed.[24]

Britain was only one of the many recipients of American largesse, and the CIA presumably only a minor provider as compared with the Fulbright Commission, the US Information Agency (USIA) and the big private foundations. Until the 1960s, the USIA maintained libraries in London, Manchester, and other provincial towns. Its functions, which included sponsoring lecture tours by leading American intellectual figures, were much like those of the British Council, albeit better funded. The notion that such visits might have a political purpose was never mentioned, the assumption being that to give audiences a sense of America's scientific and scholarly achievement was advertisement enough of what the United States had to offer. From a Cold War point of view, however, waging an American *Kulturkampf* in Britain was generally seen as being less important than winning the hearts and minds of people in countries whose loyalty was less assured and where the local Amerika-Hauser competed for custom with their Cominform equivalents. By the late 1960s the changing character of the Cold War combined with financial troubles arising out of the Vietnam War led to America's cultural efforts being increasingly directed towards Asia, Africa and the Middle East.

From Blue Streak to Trident

Following the Suez debacle, friendly relations between the two countries were soon restored. Eden, seriously ill from a botched gall bladder operation, resigned on 9 January 1957. His successor, Harold Macmillan, had known Eisenhower in French North Africa in the war. He was happy, therefore, to receive an invitation to meet in March. In order to avoid any suggestion that he had been summoned for a dressing down, they agreed that the meeting be held in Bermuda, a British territory, rather than in Washington.

Macmillan's main concern was defence policy. Despite America's commitment to NATO, the British government regarded it as essential that Britain have an independent nuclear capability, both to add to the credibility to the American nuclear shield and to justify Britain's status as a world power with a seat on the UN Security Council. Britain had successfully exploded an atomic device in 1952, and was shortly scheduled to test its newly developed hydrogen bomb. It had also built a V-bomber force capable of carrying nuclear weapons, which, however, was already obsolescent due to the development of Soviet missile defences. The hope was that its capability could be maintained thanks to the development of Blue Streak, an Anglo-American missile system capable of reaching Soviet targets east of the Urals. The problem was that Blue Streak would not be ready for several years.

There were other difficulties. The cost of meeting the country's defence commitments was proving more than its economy could bear. At 8.2 per cent of GNP, Britain was spending proportionately far more than its principal economic rivals. Its defence costs were twice those of Germany (4.1 per cent), and over four times as much as Japan's (1.8 per cent). Prior to Macmillan's departure for Bermuda the Cabinet had agreed on stringent cuts. National service would be phased out, reducing the manpower of the armed services from 690 000 to 375 000. Mass armies, it was argued, were a thing of the past. In future Britain would depend on nuclear deterrence and a professional army suited to peace-keeping operations and fighting limited wars.

In Bermuda it was agreed that as an interim measure the United States would base 60 medium-range Thor missiles in Britain until such time as Blue Streak became available. They would be under dual control, American personnel being in charge of the nuclear warheads and the British of the firing mechanisms. In the course of the discussions Eisenhower also expressed his personal regret over the way Britain, having helped the United States in the wartime development of the atomic bomb, had been debarred by the McMahon Act of 1946 from receiving information about subsequent nuclear research. This paved the way for an agreement in October 1957, following Russia's launching of Sputnik, to restore full nuclear co-operation.

Even so, there was no disguising the fact that Britain remained very much the poor relation. By 1960, US defence spending was roughly the equivalent of Britain's entire GNP, or, to put it another way, to the combined government expenditures of Britain, France and West Germany.[25] Blue Streak, in spite of containing British-made components, depended on American technology for its rocketry and guidance systems. It also had the disadvantage of being liquid fuelled, which meant that preparing it for launch would take longer than the time required for a Soviet-fired rocket to reach Britain. So it was a relief to learn that the United States was developing Skybolt, which would serve admirably as an alternative. Skybolt relied on solid fuel and had the additional advantage of being air-craft launched, which meant that if Americans could be inveigled into supplying it, Britain would be able to prolong the life of its V-bomber force. In March 1960, on a trip to Washington, Macmillan prevailed on Eisenhower to let Britain have Skybolt when it became available. Quite why the British set such store on having an independent deterrent puzzled many Americans, suggesting that the British doubted their dependability. Others worried that any preference shown towards Britain would offend France and Germany. But since the principal object was to impress the Russians, and Britain's having a nuclear capability might add just possibly help in that respect, there seemed little point in refusing Macmillan's request. After all, Britain was a valued ally, and although it always seemed embarrassingly strapped for funds, its contribution to containment beyond the European sphere of operations far exceeded that of any of America's other NATO partners. The US, therefore, undertook to waive development expenses and supply the missiles at cost. In return, Macmillan undertook to let the US Navy have a base at Holy Loch on the west coast of Scotland for its Polaris-armed nuclear submarines – a feature of the agreement not made public until the following October.

Needless to say, not everyone welcomed this arrangement. Scottish nationalists complained that Scotland was being made a prime target for a Soviet missile attack. Questions were raised concerning the need for nuclear deterrence. If such weapons existed, surely they would be used. The Campaign for Nuclear Disarmament (CND) was inaugurated at a meeting in Central Hall, Westminster in February 1958, with speeches by Michael Foot, Tony Benn and other prominent figures. Marches to Aldermaston, the nuclear weapons development complex in Berkshire, followed. At meetings around the country, distinguished clergymen and academics issued doomsday warnings. The scenarios of films like *Fail Safe* (US, 1963), in which an American bomber is accidentally sent to destroy Moscow, and *Dr Strangelove* (UK, 1963), in which a mad USAF general launches a nuclear attack, impressed British audiences as all too plausible.

As was to be expected, CND had a distinctly anti-American tone. Many of its supporters were drawn from the nation's left-wing intelligentsia, who saw the United States as representing capitalist imperialism. Seeing it now brandishing nuclear weapons confirmed their suspicion that it was a nation out of control. There was talk of 'annihilation without representation' and of Britain's having become an American satellite much like the Soviet satellites of Eastern Europe. In moral terms, some claimed, there was little to choose between the two superpowers. Since the 1956 invasion of Hungary few were prepared to defend the actions of the Soviet Union, but there were aspects of American behaviour, like its treatment of minorities, that some found scarcely less repellent. Britain's destiny, it was argued, lay in finding a middle way between the extremes of state-controlled communism and American-style laissez-faire capitalism.

This was a belief shared by many who did not belong to CND, but who also found aspects of American life disquieting. One of America's less attractive traits was its obsession with issues of loyalty. Britain had had more than its share of spies, but the task of hunting them out was seen as a matter for the security services rather than of political buffoons like Joseph McCarthy. The British press gleefully reported the 'investigation' of USIA libraries by his two minions, Roy Cohn and David Schine. During their three-week tour of Europe Cohn and Schine announced to clamorous press conferences their discovery of works by such subversive writers as Henry Thoreau, Thomas Paine, Dashiell Hammett and Sigmund Freud. Among the 30 000 books they had removed were works burned by the Nazis. They even went so far as to call the liberal Catholic weekly *Commonweal* a 'Communist Catholic magazine'.[26] Such shenanigans were a source of hilarity rather than alarm. Nevertheless, they raised serious questions about America's claim to be a force for freedom. Teachers were losing their jobs, writers and actors were being blacklisted, civil servants sacked. How many Britons measured up to such standards of ideological purity? This was more than a theoretical matter for intending visitors to the United States, who were routinely questioned about their political affiliations and sexual predilections. It was common knowledge that prominent British figures, among them Graham Greene and John Gielgud, had been denied entry. It was hard to think that they constituted a threat to the Great Republic. The same applied to the American writers and actors routinely paraded before the House Un-American Activities Committee and asked to name names. Plainly the hysteria remarked by British Embassy staff in the wake of the Truman Doctrine had got out of hand.

The British were sufficiently familiar with their native communists (the CPGB, commonly known as the seepy-jeebys) to be much worried about the 'enemy within'. Dealing with 'the enemy without' was a more formidable proposition. There had been no need to 'scare the hell' out of the British to persuade them of the need to resist Soviet imperialism. Containing Russia was a familiar game. It had been a major British concern throughout the nineteenth century. (For a time Russophobes had been known as 'Jingoes', the term being derived from a music-hall song of 1878 about not letting the Russians have Constantinople, the opening lines being: 'We don't want to fight, but by Jingo if we do, / We've got the ships, we've got the men, and got the money too'.[27]) The willingness of the United States to bear the major part of this burden, however, in no way diminished the conviction of British leaders that Britain's claim to having a seat at the world's top table depended on its also having a Cold War role to play. Colonies could be (and were) dispensed with, overseas commitments reduced, but not to have an independent nuclear deter-rent, even if it was only an off-the-shelf version, meant accepting second-class status. It would mean going the way of the great powers of the past. In short, it would be an irrevocable step that no British government, whatever its ideological complexion, was prepared to take. As Ernest Bevin, Attlee's Foreign Secretary, had said in October 1946 when Britain was first contemplating entering the nuclear race, 'We have got to have this thing over here whatever it costs. . . . We've got to have the bloody Union Jack flying on top of it.'[28]

There was thus consternation in Whitehall when, late in 1962, it was learned that the United States was thinking of cancelling Skybolt. Kennedy's Secretary of Defence, Robert McNamara, a former President of Ford, had been appointed on the basis of his reputation as a business whizz-kid, with instructions to end cost overruns. McNamara according-ly set about applying the same cost-cutting principles to defence matters that had won him his reputation at Ford. Skybolt impressed him as a prime candidate for cancellation, its development being behind schedule and its test performance below expectations. There was, to be sure, Eisenhower's promise to Macmillan, but now the Democrats were in office, and in any case, as McNamara saw it, nuclear deterrence was best left to the superpowers. Participation by others was wasteful and dangerous.

Not surprisingly, Macmillan found the prospect of Britain's claim to world power status being axed as part of a Pentagon cost-cutting exercise mortifying. Labour opponents taunted him with the claim that Britain's independent deterrent was neither independent nor a deterrent. What was the point of the Tories' great-power posturing when the United States had dealt with the Cuban missile crisis all on its own? They were living in a world of illusion. For a time Macmillan's personal position appeared in jeopardy. Meanwhile, the Kennedy administration, with Cuba and Berlin to worry about, remained oblivious to the embarrass-ment it had caused. Kennedy himself, according to Theodore Sorenson, 'saw no point to a small independent British deterrent'.[29] Only belatedly, while Kennedy was on his way to a prearranged Anglo-American summit at Nassau in December 1962, did the British Ambassador, David Ormsby-Gore, succeed in persuading him of the hurt that had been done to British *amour propre*. Once apprised, however, Kennedy was disposed to be generous. He offered Macmillan a number of choices, including the option of taking over the development of Skybolt. But the one Macmillan opted for was the submarine-launched Polaris system. Being less vulnerable to enemy attack than Blue Streak and less prone to obsolescence than Skybolt, it was plainly an altogether superior weapon. The financial terms offered were attractive too: Britain would pay only a 5 per cent contribution towards the expense of the missile's development plus the actual cost of manufacture.[30]

In other respects, however, the price was high. The shift from V-bombers to submarines involved huge expenditure. The deal also meant that Britain would henceforth be dependent on the United States for its major weapon system. This was confirmed in the 1980s and 1990s when Polaris was replaced by the more powerful Trident. But in defence, as in much else, the British failed to see why they should go to the expense and effort of developing weapons of their own when what they needed could be purchased from across the Atlantic. They watched American movies, bought American detergents, listened to American popular music, filled their TV schedules with American soap operas, so why not buy American weaponry? After all, Britain and the United States were Atlantic powers, shared a common language, pursued similar goals, and were bound by treaty obligations. America invested more on the development of armaments than all the other countries of the world put together. Therefore, as in other fields, why not accept what America had to offer?

The French took a different view. The Nassau agreement impressed de Gaulle as yet another illustration of the cosiness of the Anglo-American partnership. During the war he had been excluded from the inner circles of the Atlantic alliance by Roosevelt and Churchill. He had been angered by America's behaviour over Suez. When, therefore, largely as an afterthought, Kennedy offered him Polaris, he rejected it out of hand. Unlike Britain, France had gone to the trouble of developing a genuinely independent nuclear deterrent. He had no intention of compromising its independence by entering into a deal with the United States. He had long suspected that Washington's aim was to dominate Europe politically, economically and culturally, and that Britain's role was to be America's Trojan horse within Europe's walls. France was a European rather than an Atlantic power. Its interests lay in promoting European integration, not least as a bulwark against American encroachment. Britain had a quite different set of interests, as it had made plain by its repeated attempts to divert, dilute, delay or otherwise wreck these efforts.

Britain's behaviour also angered Germany's Chancellor, Konrad Adenauer. What most impressed both de Gaulle and Adenauer about Nassau was Macmillan's sheer effrontery. It was part of a persistent pattern. In March 1957, when the nations of Europe had gathered to sign the Treaty of Rome, Macmillan had been away in Bermuda persuading Eisenhower to supply Britain with Thor missiles. Now, having condescended to apply for membership of the European Economic Community, he was off across the Atlantic again, this time to the Bahamas, begging Kennedy to let him have Polaris. On 14 January 1963, two weeks after he had returned in triumph to London, de Gaulle vetoed Britain's application. It was not, of course, Macmillan's lack of tact that led to de Gaulle's action so much as what it revealed about the British attitude towards Europe. Britain, as de Gaulle saw it, was essentially an oceanic power. Its ties were with the United States and the English-speaking Commonwealth. The EEC would be 'drowned in the Atlantic' if Britain were allowed to join.[31] There was no way that the British, along with all their dependencies, could be absorbed into an essentially continental organisation without altering its whole character. This raised the question of where, if Britain did not belong in Europe, did it belong? The answer was far from clear, least of all to the British themselves.[32]

9 Between America and the European Union

Speaking at West Point Military Academy in 1962, Truman's former Secretary of State, Dean Acheson, described what he saw as Britain's predicament:

> Great Britain has lost an Empire and has not yet found a role. The attempt to play a separate power role – that is, a role apart from Europe, a role based on a 'Special Relationship' with the United States, a role based on being the head of a 'Commonwealth' which has no political structure, or unity, or strength and enjoys a fragile and precarious economic relationship – that role is about to be played out.[1]

The British had hitherto regarded Acheson as a friend. He was the original instigator of the Marshall Plan and had worked closely with Bevin in setting up NATO. With his Ivy League background, clipped moustache, old school ties and double-breasted suits he might well have been taken for an Englishman. Yet here he was saying that Britain had been wrong in cleaving too closely to the United States, thereby distancing itself from its European neighbours.

Many were outraged. Macmillan noted in his diary that Acheson always had been a 'conceited ass'. Acheson's words were insulting. What really hurt, however, was not that they were insulting, but that they were true. Coming as they did on the heels of McNamara's announcement that the Pentagon was considering cancelling Skybolt, some in Whitehall suspected that they had been inspired by Washington. A State Department brief, rushed out on Kennedy's instructions, sought to distance the White House. Although 'special' might not be the most appropriate word to use, Anglo-American relations were based on long association and common purpose, and were undoubtedly close. But no amount of official soft-soaping could conceal the fact that Acheson had touched a raw nerve. If nothing else, he had revealed how even well-disposed Americans viewed Britain's habit of coasting along in America's slipstream.

Unlike the United States, whose main concern had been what to do with its new-found power, Britain's principal post-war preoccupation had been handling decline, which, at least in the eyes of Whitehall, effectively ruled out the notion of its striking out in bold new directions. With the wartime alliance in mind, Britain's rulers had accordingly sought to maintain close links with the United States in the hope of thereby being able to go on playing a leading role in the world's affairs. For a time it had worked. Up until about 1950, United States officials had cause to be grateful for their advice and contacts. Thereafter, however, no amount of hands-across-the-sea rhetoric could make up for the asymmetry of power, quite apart from their different views on such key questions as China, Vietnam and Israel. In such circumstances, partnership was out of the question. Emollient statements could not disguise the fact that the United States was far more important to Britain than Britain was to the United States. That was the message of Suez, Blue Streak, Skybolt and the Cuban missile crisis.

By the early 1960s, the Anglo-American relationship was thus no longer what it had been at the height of World War II, or even in the early years of the Cold War. The United States still needed allies, and Britain's support was valued. When it was denied, as over Vietnam, the fact was resented. But to harp on, as the British did, about there being a 'special relationship', as if in the expectation of being granted favours, came to be regarded by Americans as something of a joke. This remained the case in spite of the two countries' continuing close co-operation in signals intelligence, weapons development and other military-related fields. Raymond Seitz, US Ambassador in London in the 1990s, illustrates the point by recalling an incident that occurred soon after Bill Clinton became president. John Major, following British prime-ministerial tradition, had flown to Washington to pay his respects. As the President waited for his visitor to arrive, one of his aides observed: 'Don't forget to say "special relationship" when the press comes in.' 'Oh yes, the special relationship,' Clinton said. 'How could I forget?' Then he threw back his head and laughed.[2]

The point was that the United States now had many allies. What with NATO, SEATO, CENTO, ANZUS[3] and various bilateral agreements it was tied by treaty to practically every state in the non-Communist world. Having once breached the Founding Fathers' principles with regard to entangling alliances, it had gone to the other extreme. By no means all of the aid provided was used for the purpose intended (as when India and Pakistan used US weaponry against one another). But having once decided that the only thing the Soviets would respond to was superior force, there seemed no alternative but to proceed on the basis of a worst-case scenario. That was the assumption of NSC 68, the secret 1950 National Security Council plan drawn up by Paul Nitze, George Kennan's successor on the State Department's Policy Planning Committee, that effectively militarised containment and served as the blueprint for global victory over Soviet communism for the next 30 years.[4] Containment also required cultivating the support of temperamental political leaders, some of whose countries were anything but free. In short, maintaining a worldwide network of alliances ruled out public acknowledgement of the notion that some relationships were more privileged than others. Every one of America's relationships was in some way 'special'.

After the intimacy of the wartime alliance it was hard for the British to think of themselves as being simply one ally among many. For one thing, it failed to take into account the ties of language, literature, history and family which were arguably what *really* made the relationship special. Ties of that sort, however, do not necessarily affect policy. They had existed long before there had been any thought of political co-operation and had arguably been at their strongest in the post-Revolutionary years, when Britain had filled a place in America's political bestiary not unlike that occupied latterly by the Soviet Union. But in politics interest usually outweighs sentiment. Hard though it was to accept, there was no disguising the fact that as its power in the world had declined, so had Britain's usefulness to America's policy makers.

Britain and Europe

It had, of course, been foreseen that with the return to peacetime conditions Britain's influence would diminish. Nevertheless, in the 1940s the United Kingdom, besides offering advice, could still claim to be a major imperial power and one of the two undisputed leaders of the West. There was hardly an issue anywhere that did not in some way impinge on its interests. By the 1960s, all that had changed: the Empire had gone, the garrisons had been disbanded, the troops summoned home, the mercenary armies paid off, the far-flung bases either abandoned or handed over to the United States. It had all happened with extraordinary speed. Quite suddenly Britain had gone from having world-wide responsibilities to being a medium-sized power much on a par with France and West Germany.

It was, to be sure, only a *relative* decline. In *absolute* terms, once the economic effects of the war had been overcome, Britain prospered as never before. In the late 1950s, Harold Macmillan was able to boast that the British had 'never had it so good'. But the same applied to the whole of Western Europe. The French and Germans, admittedly starting from a lower base, had experienced an even more dramatic rise in living standards. Between 1950 and 1960 the gross domestic product of West Germany had grown on average three times faster than Britain's. France, with roughly the same population as Britain but a land area twice as great, had the advantage of being able to draw on its large agricultural workforce for industrial expansion, much as Britain had done in the nineteenth century.[5] So, as the effects of the war receded, things were returning to normal, which in Britain's case unfortunately meant resuming the long-term process of relative decline which had begun back in the mid-nineteenth century.

Acheson, however, had not been referring to long-term trends of this sort, but rather to the fact that the British had deliberately chosen a role 'apart from Europe'. In fact, what Acheson was saying was not new at all. It was essentially what he and others had been saying in the 1940s and ought therefore to have come as no surprise to British policy makers. All that was different was that he was now speaking in public in a way that required the press to pay attention. In common with most Americans, he found the British view of themselves as separate from and superior to their continental neighbours puzzling. Like the British class system, it was based on distinctions more readily perceived by the British themselves than by outsiders. Naturally the British had their peculiarities, but so too did the French, the Germans, the Italians and everyone else. That was what gave Europe its character. Geographically speaking, Britain plainly *was* part of Europe. Viewed from across the broad waters of the Atlantic, the narrow straits separating England from France appeared almost inconsequential. London was as close to Paris as Washington was to New York. By American standards, Britain's land area – roughly the size of Oregon or Wyoming – was tiny. Geographically speaking, Britain was one of a group of islands off the European archipelago, itself a westward extension of the great Eurasian land mass. The whole of Western Europe, with its many languages and lilliputian political divisions, could be fitted into the United States several times over. The post-war United States was a global power with global responsibilities. Where nineteenth-century British strategists had thought of the world in terms of its seaways, their twentieth-century American successors viewed it from the air. To the generals of Strategic Air Command in their headquarters in Omaha, and their B52 air crews cruising the periphery of Soviet airspace, the world looked very different from the way it appeared to the denizens of Whitehall and Leamington Spa.

In politics, however, it is not the reality so much as the perception of reality that counts. If maintaining a partnership with the United States of the kind Churchill had envisaged was no longer feasible, what choices remained? As Acheson indicated, the Commonwealth option, that nineteenth-century dream which for a time had assumed a measure of reality in the form of imperial preference and the sterling area, was no longer a viable proposition. It had proved its worth in 1914 and 1939 when the Commonwealth and Empire had risen to Britain's defence. But those days were gone. Imperial preference had been abandoned and the Commonwealth no longer looked to Britain for protection. This was demonstrated in 1951 when Australia and New Zealand concluded a defence pact with the United States, from which Britain was excluded on the grounds that Truman did not want to give Congress the impression that the US was committing itself to defending British colonies. The Pacific Security Pact, however, was merely a formal acknowledgement of a shift in the political orientation of the white Commonwealth countries that, in Canada's case, had begun well before the war. As for Britain's non-white colonies, with nationalist movements stirring, attempts to cling on to them would merely be a further drain on the nation's resources, as shown by the French experience in Vietnam and Algeria. Compared to others, Britain had cause to congratulate itself on the manner of its withdrawal from its colonial commitments.

A second option was to revert to something like the 'splendid isolation' of Victorian times. Isolation, of course, was still possible, but with the Empire gone, splendour was not. Isolation for a country in Britain's reduced circumstances was rather something to be feared, although for those on the right wing of the Tory Party and others of a nostalgic disposition a return to something resembling former grandeur remained an enduring dream. The third possibility was Europe. The fourth was to stumble on, uncertain which of the other options to choose.

When nations of the first rank are reduced to second-rank status it is usually as a result of defeat in war. That, however, had not been Britain's experience. Britain's decline had been gradual. Its forces, it is true, had suffered catastrophic defeats in 1940–42, first in France and then in the Far East. Yet, in spite of that, thanks to its mighty allies, it had contrived to emerge victorious from World War II. It was a source of national pride that Britain never had suffered defeat in war, at least not a defeat of the kind that had been the common experience of its continental neighbours.

At Yalta, Potsdam and the early post-war conferences it had been accorded the respect befitting it as one of the Big Three. And being very much at the centre of things, the fact that its position had undergone a fundamental change since 1815 and 1919, when its representatives had last participated in drawing up post-war settlements, was not immediately apparent.

The war had also contributed to Britain's sense of superiority to its continental neighbours, most of whom had either been enemies or suffered the humiliation of defeat and occupation. It was the British and Americans (the Soviets, who had borne the heaviest burden, were commonly ignored in this regard) who had saved the continent from Nazi domination. From this it was tempting to take the additional step of supposing that the United States was Britain's 'natural' ally, and that Britain's continental neighbours, besides being 'foreigners', were not altogether trustworthy. In spite of the passage of time since the ending of the war such ideas have lingered on. According John Redwood, a former Tory minister and one-time contender for the Party's leadership, writing in 2001: 'Britain has a very different history from the continental countries. Britain is at peace with its past in a way that many continental countries can never be. . . . British people are happy that their country has fought on the side of right and liberty in many wars and has often been victorious.'[6] An even greater contrast, Redwood goes on to argue, is to be found between the attitudes of 'the Anglo-Saxon world' – by which he means Britain, the United States and the white Commonwealth countries – with its 'love of liberty, private property, free speech and limited government', and the European world with its 'belief in bureaucratic solutions, in powerful central government from behind closed doors, managed consensus and banning [of] difficult or "extreme" views'.[7]

Such notions have not been confined to any one party or political persuasion. In 1999 a MORI poll carried out for *The Economist* revealed that when asked 'In a crisis, which of these – Europe, the Commonwealth or America – do you think would be Britain's most reliable ally?' 59 per cent of Britons chose America over Europe (16 per cent) and the Commonwealth (15 per cent).[8] Likewise, respondents believed that they could learn more about the workings of government and democracy from America than from any of their European neighbours. Euroscepticism, Europhobia and xenophobia are deeply embedded in the British psyche, and are periodically exploited by politicians and the press. In the 1970s they were identified most closely with the Labour Left, but latterly, as the Redwood statement indicates, they have become one of the principal defining features of the Tory Right.

British versus American Attitudes to European Integration

During the war there had been talk of schemes for European unification among those involved in the various resistance movements. The French statesman and economist Jean Monnet, regarded by many as the father of European integration, had begun formulating his ideas while in exile in the United States. There had been speculation along the same lines in England too. In 1940, Churchill had gone so far as to conceive of some sort of union based on the Franco-British alliance. This, to be sure, had been intended principally as a way of keeping France in the war. Still, he continued to speak favourably of the idea of a Council of Europe, and in 1946, in a famous speech in Zurich, went so far as to call for a 'United States of Europe'. That same year, he and other leading European statesmen, with US encouragement, agreed to lend their support to the newly-formed European Union of Federalists, and two years later to its successor, the European Movement, an umbrella organisation aimed at co-ordinating the efforts of the various bodies working for European unity that had lately sprung up.[9] These developments spurred on Europeanists to further efforts, with the result that schemes to promote political and economic integration proliferated. Some saw these as a means of checking Communist influence; others of finding ways of containing a resurgent Germany. But a key question for both groups was whether Britain would provide the required leadership. Britain's reputation was high, partly because of its war record but also because Europeans looked to it as, economically and militarily, the strongest state in Western Europe. Although weakened, its production of coal and steel equalled that of all the other Western European nations combined. The United States might offer encouragement, but it could not, by its very nature, be a European power. Also, its intentions were suspect, as, of course, were those of the Soviet Union. In these circumstances there seemed little choice but to turn to Britain.

Those favouring integration had been disappointed when Churchill, on whose support they had counted, lost the 1945 election. Labour, as soon became clear, was more concerned with building its New Jerusalem than with promoting utopian schemes abroad. However, Churchill continued to offer encouragement, and in 1948 lent his authority to the launching of a so-called Congress of Europe. As he told its opening session, political unity must 'inevitably' accompany military and economic collaboration. 'It is said with truth that this involves some sacrifice or merger of national sovereignty [but] it is also possible and not less agreeable to regard it as the gradual assumption, by all nations concerned, of that larger sovereignty which can also protect their diverse and distinctive customs and characteristics, and their national traditions.'[10] But Churchill's support, it turned out, was not quite what it had seemed, as it belatedly dawned on the Congress's members that it never had been his intention to have Britain absorbed into the kind of Pan-European organisation he had been advocating. In fact, he did not even regard Britain as part of Europe. Like the United States, it could provide advice and assistance, but it could never give up its status as a sovereign power. European integration was for Europeans. Britain was an oceanic power; its destiny lay elsewhere.[11] 'Britain cannot be thought of as a single state in isolation', he declared on 28 November 1949 at a meeting supposedly to advance the cause of European Union. 'She is the founder and the centre of a world-wide Empire and Commonwealth. We shall never do anything to weaken the ties of blood, of sentiment, of tradition and common interest which unite us with the other members of the British family of nations.'[12]

Still, there was no question of the British disengaging from Europe. Their troops in Germany had to be kept supplied and their occupation zone governed. In the immediate post-war years German resurgence was regarded as a potent threat. Partly to help assuage French fears on that score, Britain concluded the Treaty of Dunkirk in 1947, guaranteeing them the sort of support they had craved between the wars. Even at that early stage, however, there were signs of the differences that were to bedevil Anglo-European relations in the years ahead. One was the eagerness of the continentals for a greater degree of economic integration than the British were prepared to contemplate, another was the anti-Americanism of the French and the talk of creating a 'third force' independent of both superpowers. Although it was easy to see why such ideas might appeal to continentals, it was hard to see how they would advance British interests.

So far as European integration was concerned, however, British thinking was as much at odds with that of the United States as with that of its European neighbours. To Americans, the notion of a United States of Europe made sense. It appealed to US aid officials because it offered a way of getting over the difficulties they were encountering in their efforts to rebuild Europe's economy. It appealed to the Truman and Eisenhower administrations, because a unified Europe offered a way of reincorporating Germany into the European community and of containing Russian expansionism. The US Congress was so taken with the notion that it went so far as to require that rapid progress towards integration be made a pre-requisite of Marshall Plan assistance. To Americans in general it offered the prospect of ending, once and for all, the bitter rivalries that had led to their being drawn into two world wars.[13]

The idea of a United States of Europe appealed to Americans also because it resembled their own national experience. America, they liked to think, was as the world ought to be. More specifically, it was as Europe would need to be if it hoped to attain American levels of prosperity. The parallels were striking. In agreeing to sink their differences and establish a federal union, Europeans would be following in the footsteps of America's Founding Fathers. The Anti-Federalists of the 1780s had taken much the same line as that taken by Britain's post-war governments. They had argued that federalism was impractical, that it challenged Americans' hard-won liberties, and that it took power away from where it rightly belonged – namely in the hands of the sovereign people of each individual state. Above all, it placed too much power in the hands of a super-state over whose affairs they would have little control. Having freed themselves from one tyranny, the Anti-Federalists claimed, Americans were about to saddle themselves with another. Yet, in spite of these objections, Americans had gone ahead and adopted their Constitution, thereby creating a nation that was now the envy of the rest of the world. This, of course, is to overlook the Civil War, the cauldron out of which the modern United States emerged. Still, that aside, the parallels and advantages to be gained were sufficiently evident to exert a powerful influence on American attitudes.[14]

Thus, from the end of World War II, and more positively with the onset of the Cold War, European integration became one of the principal aims of US foreign policy. It was an issue, however, that required tactful handling. If too much overt pressure were exerted suspicions would be aroused, there would be talk of American imperialism, and the policy would backfire. The impulse would have to come from within Europe.

This was already happening. It was as clear to Europe's leaders as it was to Americans that for the European economy to become fully functioning a new international framework was needed. From an economic point of view, there was no sense in each country attempting to support a full range of industries. Consolidation was needed, and as the principal providers of post-war credit Americans were in a position to ensure that it occurred. To reproduce the factors responsible for American prosperity – a large domestic market, free competition, an efficient transportation network, economies of scale – there had to be co-operation on a continent-wide basis.

Reluctant though the British were to involve themselves in supranational initiatives, it was the Americans who called the tune. The Marshall Plan of 1947, officially known as the European Recovery Program, required that European countries act collectively. Britain and France took the lead in drawing up the required submissions, establishing a Committee on European Economic Co-operation, later transformed into the Organisation for European Economic Co-operation (OEEC). From the first, the British insisted that the OEEC and other bodies involved were merely intergovernmental committees, in spite of the fact that in practice they behaved far more like supranational authorities. Under pressure from its continental associates, Britain also reluctantly agreed to the setting up of the Council of Europe and the European Assembly, both of which, operating out of their headquarters in Strasbourg, were destined to play important parts in the process of European integration in the years ahead.

Reluctant agreement to continental initiatives became the hallmark of British policy towards Europe. This did not, of course apply to NATO which, being American-led, in many ways resembled the old wartime alliance. When, in recognition of America's superior contribution, the United States insisted in appointing an American admiral head of NATO's Atlantic forces there were anguished cries at the ending of centuries of British naval supremacy. The cries would have been much more anguished, however, had the admiral been French or Belgian.[15]

Thus, as early as 1948, a consistent pattern of behaviour was established. To supporters of European integration, the Council of Europe represented a major step forward. The British, true to form, sternly refused to admit that it was anything more than yet another intergovernmental body. Ernest Bevin spoke contemptuously of 'this talking shop in Strasbourg'.[16] Not surprisingly, having conceded so much ground in the process of allaying British fears, Europeanists, caught in a vicious circle in which they lacked Britain's support yet felt too weak to go ahead without it, grew increasingly disillusioned. Nevertheless, the Council survived as a symbol of European unity, and as a forum for discussing matters of common interest. It also set about creating other bodies that were later to play an important role in the integration process, most notably the European Convention for the Protection of Human Rights and the European Court of Justice.[17]

The Marshall Plan proved a remarkable success. It was clear to the supporters of European integration, however, that the OEEC, under which the aid was being distributed, was not a body adequately equipped to serve their purposes. France's Foreign Minister, Robert Schuman, accordingly took the initiative by proposing that the states of Western Europe agree to pool their coal and steel resources and eliminate all tariffs affecting heavy industry, thereby creating what was in effect an embryo common market in manufactured products. The establishment of the European Coal and Steel Community (ECSC) in 1952 represented the first significant step towards what eventually became the European Union. At the time, however, its far-reaching consequences were far from clear. Only six OEEC nations – France, West Germany, Italy, Belgium, the Netherlands and Luxembourg – voted to become members. Britain and the Scandinavian countries, although invited, chose not to become involved.

Europeans were not alone in being disillusioned by Britain's attitude. Americans, too, were becoming impatient. In 1948, to speed up the integration process and as an 'unofficial counterpart' to the Marshall Plan, leading figures in the US intelligence community set up an American Committee on United Europe (ACUE) with offices at 537 Fifth Avenue, New York. ACUE's Chairman was General William J. Donovan, former head of the wartime Office of Strategic Services, and its Vice-Chairman Allen Dulles, Director of the Central Intelligence Agency (CIA). Although supposedly a private organisation, by far the largest proportion of the sums it dispensed on behalf of European unity came from the CIA, a fact unbeknown to its private donors and most of their recipients.

In March 1949, Churchill travelled to New York to plead for ACUE's assistance on behalf of the European Movement. In spite of having the support of many leading European figures, the Movement was desperately short of funds. ACUE thus became the European Movement's paymaster, and over the next ten years passed on some three to four million dollars – which is to say rather more than half of its entire operating budget. Initially the money was sent to Duncan Sandys, who, largely on the basis of being Churchill's son-in-law and confidant, had been elected Chairman of the European Movement's international executive. At Sandys's insistence the Movement's supporters were not told of the arrangement on the grounds that it would make it appear as though the drive for greater integration was an American rather than a European initiative. However, foreseeing the embarrassment that would arise should the truth leak out, ACUE stipulated that, at the very least, the organisation's leaders be informed of the true situation.[18]

What Churchill and Sandys had not fully anticipated was the enthusiasm of their continental colleagues or the scale of their ambitions. Sandys's attempts to rein them in divided the Movement into warring factions. The British Labour government had hitherto been seen as the principal obstacle to progress; it now transpired that the Tories were no different. Furious over Sandys's intransigence, ACUE suspended funding, and in collaboration with the Movement's continental members, engineered his resignation and replacement by the former Belgian premier, Paul-Henry Spaak. Control now passed the Movement's federalist element, in acknowledgement of which its international offices were moved from London to Brussels.

When ACUE was 'deactivated' in 1960, Spaak, Jean Monnet and other key figures involved in the European 'project' spoke warmly of its contribution, even claiming that without its help they could never have achieved as much as they had. The impulse behind the post-war drive for integration was, of course, primarily European, American assistance merely helping the process along. The fact that American policy makers regarded the United Kingdom as a major stumbling block, however, did not prevent the British from basking in the belief that they enjoyed special American favour. Not surprisingly, this provoked Americans to fury. Averell Harriman, in charge of distributing Marshall aid, urged strong action on the grounds that 'the US should no longer tolerate interference and sabotage of Western European integration by the United Kingdom'.[19] The head of the State Department's policy planning staff, George Kennan, took a more moderate line, noting that Britain was proving a valuable ally in other respects and it would be counter-productive to attempt to press it further than it was prepared to go. In the early 1950s, the hope of those in administration circles was that due course Britain could be eased into divesting itself of its Empire and merging with its continental neighbours as part of a new federal Europe.[20]

Despite Britain's foot-dragging, the six ECSC powers, led by France, had meanwhile pressed ahead with their arrangements. In March 1956 they agreed in principle to establish a full customs union, and the following year signed the Treaty of Rome setting up the European Economic Community (EEC). Not wishing to be involved in this venture, but feeling obliged to come up with some sort of an alternative, the British responded by forming the European Free Trade Association (EFTA), a consortium of seven nations committed to easing trade in industrial products.

This represented an advance on anything they had previously been prepared to contemplate. Its virtue from Britain's point of view was that, being a customs union pure and simple, it constituted no threat to national sovereignty.

Other things being equal, American policy makers would have preferred having a firm ally like Britain rather than France at the heart of the EEC. France had already withdrawn its Mediterranean fleet from NATO, and was showing signs of wanting to quit NATO altogether, as shortly afterwards it did. American support for European integration was predicated on the belief that the new Europe would be pro-American. Britain could mostly be relied on in that respect; France, under de Gaulle, was a less certain quantity. It was partly in response to gentle American urging that in 1961 Macmillan applied for EEC membership. De Gaulle's veto was a humiliating slap in the face for both countries.[21]

Up to that time Labour had been resolutely opposed to EEC membership. Its leader, Hugh Gaitskell, had even gone so far as to claim that entry would mean 'the end of Britain as an independent nation; we [would] become no more than Texas or California in the United States of Europe. It means the end of a thousand years of history.'[22] When, however, it emerged that the rate of economic growth of the EEC member states was higher than Britain's, the fear of those on the Labour Left that competition from low-paid European workers would lead to a loss of jobs evaporated. Wages in many parts of the EEC, it transpired, were higher than in Britain. A groundswell of popular opinion favouring membership developed, along with a growing sense that Britain was in danger of being left behind. In 1967, with Labour back in power and Harold Wilson Prime Minister, Britain submitted a second application for EEC membership, but to no better effect. By way of rubbing salt into the wound, de Gaulle volunteered that one reason for denying Britain membership was its poor economic performance.

Britain finally gained admission in 1973, de Gaulle having meanwhile fallen from power. Its application was strengthened by the fact that the Conservative Prime Minister, Edward Heath, was a committed European. Heath was unique among British post-war statesmen in that he shared with his continental counterparts a belief in the EEC's future role as a major player on the world stage. The United States, as he saw it, was simply too large and too bound up in its own affairs to serve as an appropriate vehicle for the promotion of British interests. On visits to Washington Heath avoided referring to 'the special relationship', the wartime alliance, or anything else suggesting he was angling for special favours.

America he saw as a whale among minnows. Europe, on the other hand, was an entity whose affairs Britain could influence from the inside far more effectively than it could ever hope to influence the United States from the outside. In terms of population and gross national product Britain was roughly on a level with France, Italy and West Germany. Europe thus offered the prospect of a partnership of equals. In any case, most of Britain's customers were now in Europe, well over two-thirds of them members of the EEC. Between 1950 and 1975 its trade with Europe had practically doubled, now accounting for approximately 50 per cent of all imports and exports, whereas trade with North America had remained roughly constant at something under 15 per cent.[23] Whether the British liked it or not, their destiny was ineluctably linked to that of their continental neighbours. Language, sentiment and culture might incline them towards the United States, but geography, trade and self-interest required that they carve out a role for themselves in Europe.

British Views of America, American Views of Britain

John Locke once famously remarked that 'In the beginning all the world was America.'[24] By the late twentieth century many were beginning to suspect that in the end the same might also be the case. American culture seeped into every nook and cranny of British life. In the 1950s and 1960s the term commonly used to describe this process was 'Coca-Colonisation'; by the latter part of the century McDonald's had replaced Coca-Cola as the most pervasive symbol of America's influence. Attempts were made to stem the tide. The Iron Curtain countries put up a stalwart defence, but with limited success. The harder they strove, the greater became the kudos of owning an American sweatshirt or pop record. When eventually the Iron Curtain came down McDonald's opened branches in Moscow, Prague and Budapest and crowds duly lined up for their burgers, fries and shakes. Elsewhere the story was much the same. The French have been particularly active in trying to keep the beast at bay; however, they are as fond of fast food and Hollywood extravaganzas as everyone else, the result being that there is now a McDonald's on the Champs Elysées – and a Planet Hollywood too. The British, as usual, have shown less resistance, although a campaign by London's intelligentsia did succeed in delaying by nine years the opening of a McDonald's on Hampstead High Street.[25]

Preserving national cultures in a world awash with American products is no easy matter. This applies to language as much as consumer items.

What are Europeans to call rock 'n' roll except rock 'n' roll? It is hardly surprising that, having pioneered the commercial development of most modern consumer products, Americans have largely determined the terminology used to describe them. It is, of course, possible to subsidise native products and impose restrictions, as the British did in the early days of cinema, but if American products are what people aspire to, in a consumer-driven world there is effectively no way of preventing them from getting what they want.

Thanks to a common language, the British have been more exposed to American influence than most. Some have welcomed it, others have seen its effects as wholly deleterious. Writing in the letter columns of *The Independent* on 12 December 2000, a correspondent produced a typical list of gripes:

> Dumbing down, the rise in street violence, the decline of public services, the contrast between haves and have-nots: most defining aspects of American society today have been reflected here, and virtually everywhere else in the world. There are more goods in the shops and a significant number of people have a bit more money to spend for as long as they have a job, which is more and more uncertain. Otherwise, I don't think that the American Way has made people here any happier than they were 30 years ago. Rather than being concerned whether Gore or Bush wins, we should be more concerned about how to look after ourselves now that the calibre of American politicians matches the quality of their TV.

The list could be extended to include drug abuse, excessive energy consumption, environmental degradation and all the other ills modern societies are heir to. One thing that is worth remarking, however, is the degree to which popular stereotypes of America and Americans have changed over the years. Long gone are the days when the United States was seen as exemplifying simple values such as hard work and political virtue. Gone, too, is the need to warn Americans of the corrupting effects of European life, the vices of the city, the inequalities stemming from industrial development, and the danger of being tempted down the primrose path to perdition by transatlantic sophisticates. It is hard to think what temptations Europe might have to offer that are not already available in the United States. Today it is rather the United States that is seen as the new Babylon, the society that in most generous measure exhibits the features, good and bad, of Western capitalism.

Comparisons between Britain and the United States in terms of the temptations they offer have provided fertile material for novelists. Kingsley Amis's *One Fat Englishman* (1963) and Malcolm Bradbury's *Stepping Westward* (1965) follow the picaresque adventures of British visitors. In similar vein, but going one better, David Lodge's *Changing Places* (1975) contrasts the vicissitudes of life in California and Birmingham as experienced by two professors, Philip Swallow, an English innocent, and Morris Zapp, a thrusting American academic careerist, who exchange jobs, offices, apartments, and eventually wives. Although their lifestyles, environments and expectations are very different, the moral dangers they encounter turn out to have much in common.

No one, of course, is better at revealing America's shortcomings than Americans themselves. Hollywood thrives on exposing the nation's vices. Anyone wanting to compile a list of what is wrong with America need look no further than its own its media for evidence, although sometimes the message conveyed is not quite that officially intended. In the film *Wall Street*, for example, what was apt to impress British audiences was not so much the greed of the inside traders as the jet-set lifestyles of New York's upper echelons. In earlier days, the British could not but be struck by the fact that even America's poor were shown as owning cars and telephones.

According to its detractors, however, the United States is a nation of crass, obese, diet-obsessed, energy-consuming, Bible-quoting, gun-crazy fanatics, given to suing one another at the drop of a hat. It is a culture of ignorance that rejects evolution but embraces notions of alien abduction. All this, it can be claimed, would be of no concern to anyone but themselves were it not that their Disneyfied culture floods the world's TV screens in the form of sitcoms, soap operas, violent films and interview freak shows run by lamé-suited hosts. Driven on by a combination of heartless corporate greed and lower-class bad taste, it is polluting people's cultures with the same thoughtless exuberance as it is contributing to global warming .

Were Americans so minded, they could compile a complementary list of Britain's shortcomings. It would represent the British as being toffee-nosed, class-obsessed, backward-looking, unable to come to terms with the fact of their national loss of status, more concerned with being something than doing something, running their lives according to their own pettifogging rules. Their industry has been strike-prone because they have yet to emancipate themselves from the class antagonisms left over from former times. Their lower orders are either comic or subservient, their ruling class arrogant, living by a code forged in the years of Empire, war, class-consciousness and deference. Generations of British actors have profited from Hollywood's exploitation of these characteristics. Even America's cartoon villains – Shere Kahn in *The Jungle Book*, Scar in *The Lion King*, Cruella DeVil in *A Hundred and One Dalmatians*, the Devil in *The Devil and Bob* – speak with English accents. If Hollywood's choice of accents is anything to go by, mad scientists, Roman Emperors, Nazi sadists, sexual perverts and international terrorists were all upper-class Englishmen.

Anglophobia, however, is largely a thing of the past, Americans having latterly acquired other enemies by which to affirm their identity and goodness.[26] Disparaging views of Britain, therefore, have tended to come, not from Americans, but from Britons unhappy about their own society – a remarkable number of them from newspaper correspondents lately returned from a sojourn across the Atlantic. Typical of this sub-genre is Robert Chesshyre's *Return of the Native Reporter* (1987). Back in London after four years as the *Observer*'s correspondent in Washington, Chesshyre describes his sense of disillusion at 'coming from a capital city where events of real significance to the world took place, to one that had lost its power, but not all its delusions'.[27] Viewed from Washington, Britain's self-important airs appeared ridiculous, as revealed by the way the American press treated the Falklands War as if it were something out of Gilbert and Sullivan. As for Britain itself, the drive from the airport was enough to persuade him that he was returning to 'an overcrowded, dirty, sluggish corner of Europe'.[28] What Chesshyre found he missed more than anything was 'the optimism, the classlessness' of America. Thirteen years later, another returning *Observer* correspondent, Anthony Holden, was similarly moved to reflect that 'the old country seems more than ever like some overgrown, nose-in-the-air, single-sex Pall Mall club'.[29] Jonathan Freedland, a former *Guardian* correspondent, in *Bring Home the Revolution: The Case for a British Republic* (1998), goes further, arguing that the British are still in the grip of their feudal past, a nation of subjects rather than citizens, ruled from the top down rather than from the bottom up. Americans, he claims, assume that the government is *their* government and is there to serve them – unlike the deferential British, who assume the reverse. The tragedy, as he sees it, is that the British *did* once have a democratic revolution, only they had it in America instead of in Britain. They exported their libertarian ideas across the Atlantic, since when they themselves have clung tenaciously to the traditions of secrecy and social deference from which their former colonists had had the good sense to free themselves.

Many Americans would regard Chessyre's, Holden's and Freedland's views as suspect, not least as regards their starry-eyed account of life in the United States. Most would agree that America is far from classless, as the latter-day concern over its so-called 'underclass' testifies, nor are the workings of American democracy, where voter turnout is significantly lower than in Britain, as unproblematic as Freedland and others make out. Well-informed Americans tend to take a more sober view. In *Managing Cultural Differences: Leadership Strategies for a New World of Business* (1996), Americans are told that in most respects life in Britain is much like life in the United States – or any other developed country. They should not be misled, however, into thinking that there are not important historical and cultural distinctions. 'Even though the sun is setting on the British Empire, their global influence in the past, and to some extent in the present, is staggering to conceive.'[30] This is something about which the British are both proud and sensitive. In the case study that follows, a hypothetical American executive encounters this touchiness when he announces his firm's intention of downsizing its British subsidiary. This unleashes a totally unexpected tirade of anti-American abuse from its English chief executive officer concerning the way the United States in two world wars milked Britain of its assets, and now treats it as if it were a mere branch factory. In Scotland he has a similar encounter. There, the man in charge is strongly pro-American but is unhappy that the firm concentrates all its research and development activities in the United States, despite the fact that its Scottish workforce has employees well qualified to work in R&D. American executives are accordingly advised to inform and consult their British colleagues and to make full use of their talents. They should regard Britain as a thoroughly modern country with a well-educated workforce.

Tourists, in contrast, are told to think of Britain as a land of tradition, sophistication and gracious living. Travel advertisements in the *New Yorker* tend to feature Beefeaters, Welsh castles and log-burning fireplaces. This is also the view encouraged by Hollywood and by British television dramas such as *Upstairs, Downstairs, Pride and Prejudice* and *Brideshead Revisited*, which attract large audiences on American television. It is, therefore, the Britain of the past that Americans mostly tend to admire, and that brings some three million of them to Britain annually. It is also what takes them to such places as Bath, Stratford-upon-Avon, Oxford and Edinburgh – following the trails mapped out by Washington Irving almost two centuries ago. When they are in London their itineraries are apt to take them to Buckingham Palace, St Paul's Cathedral,

Westminster Abbey and the Tower of London rather than Canary Wharf. British travellers to the United States, by contrast, trend to be attracted more by the super-modern: Las Vegas, Disney World and Cape Canaveral.

One important difference between American attitudes towards Britain and British attitudes towards America is that Americans spend relatively little time thinking about Britain – the opposite of the situation in the nineteenth century, when British news was world news. Americans are interested in the royal family and gossip about figures in the world of entertainment, but British politics concern them scarcely at all. American politics, on the other hand, are of great concern to the British, who follow American elections almost as avidly they do their own. This is because whoever America chooses as President automatically becomes leader of the Western world. In this, as in other respects, it is America's power that fascinates and accounts for the popularity of television programmes like *The West Wing*. During the Cold War's more anxious moments it was the actions of the current incumbent of 1600 Pennsylvania Avenue rather than of 10 Downing Street that really mattered.

The same applies to economic matters. It is the Chairman of the US Federal Reserve rather than the Chairman of the Bank of England or the Chairman of the European Central Bank who occupies the key position on the world economic scene. His power was demonstrated in 1987 when Wall Street plunged 22 per cent in one day, carrying London's FTSE 100 down with it. Over the next few weeks London shares continued to fall, reaching their lowest point in November, having dropped 36.6 per cent since the previous July. In the end it was the Chairman of the Federal Reserve, Alan Greenspan, who intervened to stop the slide by ensuring that central banks around the world released enough money to cover the enormous losses, thereby setting a floor under stock prices and allowing financial markets to return to normal. London stock traders keep a weather eye on New York, so that what happens to the FTSE 100 on any particular day is apt to mirror what happens to the Dow Jones. By the late 1990s the correlation had become so close that it was reckoned that 80 per cent of the price movements on the London Stock Exchange were responses to movements on Wall Street.[31]

Social Issues

Although less immediate in their impact, similar tendencies are evident in other fields. In fact, the United States has been the source of most of the social and ideological crusades that have latterly swept the West. Not all the issues that concern Americans are readily exportable. Some, like flag-burning, prayer in schools, the death penalty and ownership of hand-guns, arise out of Americans' peculiar concern with religion, race and personal freedom.[32] Likewise abortion, which some regard as murder and others as a woman's inherent right to treat her own body as she pleases, does not have the same resonance in Britain that it does across the Atlantic, partly because the Catholic Church exerts less influence, but also because the notion of individual 'rights' is less developed. On the other hand, the British are far more used to the redistribution of wealth through taxes than is the case across the Atlantic. When British politicians discuss welfare, the issue is not whether it should exist but at what level it should be maintained. Thus many of the issues that divide Americans either have not arisen or have been laid to rest in Britain.

The civil rights movement of the early 1960s, arising as it did out of the South's peculiar race problem, was also an essentially American affair, but the great wave of student protest of the later 1960s, which shared many of the same libertarian ideals, brought chaos to European as well as US campuses. Its beginnings are commonly traced back to the Berkeley anti-Vietnam war movement of 1964, organised in opposition to the draft and the Johnson administration's decision to escalate the war. Because the United Kingdom had refused to send troops to Vietnam, the disturbances in Britain were less violent than in the US. In fact, it was not entirely clear what the British protesters hoped to achieve, apart from demonstrating their indignation at what America was doing to the Vietnamese. Opposition to the war, however, also served as a vehicle for youthful protest against corporate capitalism, bourgeois oppression, the authority of their elders and 'the system', meaning the way society was currently run. This was at a time when there were more young people in the population than ever before, many of whom took for granted a standard of living that had previously been confined to the sons and daughters of the well-off. In both the US and the UK, the post-war baby boom, growing affluence and a rapid expansion in the numbers going to university combined to create a belief that just around the corner there lay an altogether freer, more relaxed and just society – one without wars, killing, industrial corporations, or even the need for regular employment.[33]

Inspired by such thoughts, the British Vietnam Solidarity Campaign, launched in 1965, soon absorbed what remained of the old Campaign for Nuclear Disarmament, whose mostly elderly leaders were delighted by the sudden influx of so many youthful recruits. There followed 'teach-ins' at the London School of Economics, Oxford and other universities around the country. American proselytisers arrived hotfoot from across the Atlantic with exhilarating tales of what was unfolding there. The assassination of Martin Luther King and Robert Kennedy in 1968, the occupation of New York's Columbia University and the riots at the Chicago Democratic Convention persuaded some that the United States was in the throes of a genuine revolution. In Britain, too, 1968 was the high point of protest, with university registries occupied, examinations cancelled, and academic life disrupted. In London's Grosvenor Square, crowds assembled in front of the US Embassy, chanting 'Hey, hey, LBJ / How many kids did ya kill today?' Leading the assault and intent on torching the building were anarchists, Maoists, Trotskyites and other left-leaning groups. These, however, were only a small minority and none of them got beyond the Embassy steps. The great majority of those present were either spectators or young people out for a good time.[34] Compared with what was happening in the United States and across the Channel (where barricades were erected in Paris there were long-running battles between students and the police), the Grosvenor Square protests were relatively good-natured affairs. At the end of one demonstration, members of the crowd linked arms with the police and sang 'Auld Lang Syne'.[35]

Modern feminism, too, owed much to transatlantic influences. In the nineteenth century, British and American women had led the world in becoming politically active on behalf of a number of social causes, among which were the abolition of slavery, improvements in working conditions and equal access to education. Demands for women's suffrage also gained momentum in the two countries at roughly the same time, Colorado granting women the right to vote in 1893, and Idaho in 1896. Britain's unitary constitution ruled out such a piecemeal approach. Nevertheless, British women were given the vote in 1918, two years before the same privilege was granted to American women.[36]

The rise of modern feminism, however, was closely bound up with the civil rights movement. If blacks deserved equal treatment, so did women. Women had been active in the freedom rides of the early 1960s in support of black voter registration. This coincided with the advent of the contraceptive pill, the effect of which was to transform sexual attitudes. Initially women welcomed what seemed, along with the rest of youth culture, a new freedom. By the late 1960s, however, some had begun to suspect that the pill had done more to free men than it had women. This was not a uniquely American insight. Women in Britain and on the

Continent were coming to similar conclusions. Nevertheless, the hard-line anti-male feminism of the early 1970s was largely confined to America. In general, though, the British movement took its cues from across the Atlantic. When American feminists gained a public relations coup by disrupting the 1968 Miss World competition at Atlantic City, their British counterparts responded by doing the same at the 1970 competition in London's Albert Hall. Although strongly in favour of equal treatment, British women mostly rejected the accusatory, anti-male line taken by Kate Millett, Shulamith Firestone and other transatlantic radicals.[37]

Events in America also gave impetus to the British gay liberation movement. Like women's liberation, gay liberation represented an assault on what had come to be seen as the repressive character of traditional Western culture. One sign that British attitudes on the subject were changing was the publication in 1957 of the Wolfenden Report, calling for the decriminalisation of homosexual acts committed in private between consenting adults, although it was not until 1967 that a law was passed putting this into effect. It was in America, however, that gays first began to assert themselves openly, beginning with the Stonewall riot of 1969. Stonewall was a bar in Greenwich Village, New York, frequented by homosexuals and subject to frequent police raids. On this occasion, however, the clientele fought back, using tables and chairs as weapons, and went on to carry their protest against police harassment into the streets. Arising out of that event the American Gay Liberation Front was founded. The London Gay Liberation Front followed a year later. As a result of the 1967 Act, police harassment had largely ceased to be an issue in Britain, but the public's attitude towards homosexual behaviour was slow to change. From the early 1970s onwards, British organisations followed the lead of their American counterparts in demanding further alterations in the law, 'outing' closet gays, and organising 'gay pride' marches, although seldom on the scale of those across the Atlantic.

Just as the Vietnam War and the Watergate scandals helped to validate the beliefs of those who held that there was something fundamentally wrong with 'the system', so the growth of sexual promiscuity, rising rates of illegitimacy, increasing incidence of drug taking and what to many seemed like the virtual collapse of traditional ethical standards persuaded their opponents that the time had come to call a halt. It was also becoming clear, both in Britain and the United States, that stimulating the economy by increasing public spending no longer worked. The effect of continual injections of government cash was not more productivity but

'stagflation', which is to say high taxes, ballooning government expenditure and inflation. In Britain, high unemployment, growing welfare costs
and unions competing with one another to keep abreast of the spiralling
cost of living gave rise to what has become known as 'the winter of discontent', when the streets were piled high with rubbish and even the dead
remained unburied. In cities across the United States things were scarcely better. Worries about the decline of the work ethic, low industrial productivity and the mounting economic challenge of Asia raised doubts
about the continuing viability of American-style capitalism. In both
countries the liberal Left seemed to have run out of energy and ideas.

The Thatcher–Reagan Years

The rise to power of the Thatcher Conservatives in May 1979 and the
Reagan Republicans in November 1980 represented a political backlash
against what voters in both countries had come to regard as the excesses
of the preceding decades. Both Thatcher and Reagan claimed to represent traditional values. In Mrs Thatcher's case this meant extolling hard
work, self-help and the integrity of the family. It also meant reducing government expenditure, cutting back on red tape and taking the axe to anything else that she saw as standing in the way of individual ambition and
commercial enterprise. As Education Minister she had shown her determination by ending the practice of providing free milk to schoolchildren,
earning herself the title of 'Maggie Thatcher, the school milk snatcher'.
She now applied the same cost-cutting principles to the country's economy as a whole with the intention of squeezing socialism out of the system. This was much in line with President Reagan's approach, to which
was added, in his case, a belief in a largely mythical American past of
innocence and simplicity. Democrats in particular, but Republicans also,
had been too given to meddling in people's affairs. The only way to sort
out America's difficulties was to give free rein to market forces. The problem, as he was much given to pointing out, was not *with* government; the
problem *was* government.

Never before – not even in the days of Churchill and Roosevelt, or
Macmillan and Kennedy – had the two nations' leaders seen eye-to-eye
on so many issues. Their styles, however, could not have been more different. Mrs Thatcher was a workaholic, with a firm grasp on her subordinates and an appetite for detail. Reagan was easy-going, affable, happy to
indicate the general direction in which he wished his administration to go
but ready to leave the specifics to others. Had he been required to appear

at an American dispatch box to answer questions put to him by Congress in the manner of a British prime minister in the House of Commons he would not have lasted ten minutes. But that is not what is required of an American president.

Their friendship owed more than a little to political calculation, at least on Mrs Thatcher's side. She had long admired America, wishing that Britain had more of its get-up-and-go. On assuming office, however, she soon found herself out of sympathy with President Carter's well-intentioned but faltering approach to issues. The European Community impressed her even less. Its budgetary demands, cumbersome decision-making processes and left-wing leadership seemed to her the opposite of what was required. It spoke with too many voices and spent too much on spirit-sapping welfare schemes. If people wanted economic security they should be prepared to work for it. Having vowed to purge Britain of socialism, she had no intention of letting it in through the back door in the form of measures emanating from Brussels. Reagan's friendship, on the other hand, offered precisely what she wanted, and Churchill had set out to achieve, namely a chance for Britain to go on 'punching above its weight'.

Americans took to Mrs Thatcher as someone who was not afraid to speak her mind and got things done. They also welcomed her influence on their President, whose heart might be in the right place but whose grasp of issues remained rather hazy. One of Reagan's problems was allowing his thoughts to wander. Her hard-line anti-communism, sharp mind and forthright views helped compensate for his often wavering utterances. An alarming instance occurred at the 1986 Reykjavik meeting with President Mikhail Gorbachev when the President suddenly began talking about the possibility of scrapping nuclear weapons altogether. US officials were horrified. So was Mrs Thatcher, who was among those who later put him straight as to where NATO and his own Department of Defence stood on that question. Towards the end of his second term, Reagan was becoming increasingly forgetful, as shown by his confused performance before the congressional committee appointed to look into Iran–Contra affair. What he had known about his subordinates' illegal financing of the Nicaraguan Contras with funds obtained from the sale of weapons to Iran is still a mystery. Mrs Thatcher remained supportive. Nevertheless, foreign leaders increasingly turned to her rather than Reagan for advice on issues affecting the Western alliance as a whole.

Americans also credited Mrs Thatcher with having turned around her own country. By the late 1970s many Americans had come to regard

Britain as virtually ungovernable. Mrs Thatcher made plain that the days of fudge and compromise were at an end. Gone was the time when a miners' strike could overthrow the nation's elected government, or an electricians' work-to-rule put the country on a three-day week, as had happened in the case of her Conservative predecessor, Edward Heath. At last, it seemed to Americans, Britain had a leader with enough mettle to sort out the country's problems. Ironically, her approval ratings were higher in America than in Britain, where many were repelled by her imperious manner and alarmed by the effects of her monetarist policy. As she approached the end of her first Parliament, with industries collapsing and unemployment at 13 per cent, the highest level for half a century, her political survival appeared in doubt.

What saved her was the invasion of the Falklands by Argentinian troops in April 1982. On this occasion the Thatcher–Reagan friendship proved invaluable, for without the help of the United States it is unlikely that the islands could have been recaptured. For Americans, who saw Argentina as a staunch anti-Communist ally, supporting Britain's efforts to recapture one of its few remaining colonies was a difficult decision. But thanks to Reagan and his pro-British Secretary of Defence, Caspar Weinberger, the invading force was given access to US satellite information and logistical support and allowed the use of the American naval station on Ascension Island as a forward base. Mrs Thatcher revelled in her role of war leader. With the Falklands recaptured and her reputation enhanced, the Conservatives emerged from the 1983 election with an increased majority. In April 1986 Mrs Thatcher reciprocated the favour by allowing US F–111 bombers based in Britain to bomb Libya.[38]

In the 1970s, détente had lulled many in Britain into believing the Cold War at an end. Thus, Reagan's denunciation of the 'evil empire' and his massive increases in military spending set alarm bells ringing. At the news that US cruise missiles were to be sited on Greenham Common RAF base in Berkshire, the Campaign for Nuclear Disarmament, largely dormant since the 1960s, sprang once again into action. Attempts were made to stop the missiles arriving, and a band of women protesters took up semi-permanent residence in an encampment alongside the perimeter fence. Although the stationing of the missiles was in response to Soviet moves to station missiles in Eastern Europe, many suspected that it was the United States that was most to blame for stirring up trouble. These suspicions were strengthened by Reagan's 1983 announcement that he intended to press ahead with his so-called 'Star Wars' or Strategic Defence Initiative (SDI), a space-based system aimed at providing the US with the capacity to shoot down incoming missiles. Cartoonists took to representing him as a gun-slinging cowboy. Capitalising on this mounting tide of anti-Americanism, the 1983 Labour Party campaign manifesto (subsequently described as 'the longest suicide note in history') called for the scrapping of American bases in Britain and of Britain's own nuclear weapons. This naturally alarmed the US Department of Defence, which regarded a non-nuclear defence of Europe impossible. However, it alarmed the British public too, and was subsequently abandoned by the Labour Party. When, in 1997, Labour was eventually returned to office, its defence policy was virtually indistinguishable from that of its Tory predecessors.

The Reagan–Thatcher years left a contradictory legacy. The attempt to reverse the permissive tendencies stemming from the 1960s and 1970s was only partially successful. Some of their manifestations, like hippie communes, student protests, and theories about language and knowledge being instruments of bourgeois oppression, disappeared along with love-beads, bell-bottomed trousers and long hair. However, there was no return to tuneful music, patriotism, respect for the family and social discipline of the kind that, at least in theory, had characterised the 1950s. People did not become more chaste, drugs did not cease to be a problem, illegitimacy rates did not fall, gays did not return to their closets. Even government spending increased – in Britain's case largely as a result of mounting unemployment, in America's because of Reagan's ballooning defence expenditure. What was new, indeed revolutionary, was the speed of economic change resulting from the deregulation of business and the introduction of information technology. One of Mrs Thatcher's first acts on assuming office in 1979 was to remove restrictions on overseas investment, one consequence of which was that by the end of her term in office British investment in the United States exceeded American investment in Britain.

Important though the Thatcher–Reagan partnership was politically, larger forces were at work, economically and culturally, drawing the two countries together. British visitors to the United States no longer had to cope with the stringent currency restrictions imposed by their own government or the elaborate vetting procedures formerly required by the US for the granting of visas. Those who made the journey, as increasing numbers did, encouraged by the ease and falling cost of air travel, no longer experienced the sort of culture shock encountered by new arrivals in the 1940s and 1950s. Plainly the US was richer than Britain, but no longer did it appear uniquely affluent. The post-war optimism, born of the Eisenhower boom, that poverty might disappear in much the same way as the effects of the Great Depression, no longer seemed plausible. On the contrary, while the country had grown richer, signs of destitution were as apparent as ever, nowhere more so than in the nation's capital, where visitors who wandered a block or two from the Washington Mall came upon scenes of urban dereliction reminiscent of parts of bombed-out post-war London. Conversely, American visitors to the UK found that it had increasingly become a multicultural society on account of immigration from the West Indies and the Indian subcontinent, the new arrivals tending to congregate in urban ghettos much as immigrants had traditionally done in New York, Boston and other American cities. In fact, by the 1990s, Britain had a higher proportion of foreign-born residents than did the United States.[39]

As the two nations become more alike, transatlantic travellers are no longer apt to feel the same sense of moving forward or backward in time that was the common experience in the days before the British had motorways, multi-storey car parks, dishwashers, television, central heating, waste-disposal units, automatic doors and all the other modern appurtenances and gadgets that are today taken for granted in the world's developed countries. Technological change continues on a broad scale and at an ever-increasing rate, much of the impetus behind it coming from the United States. Many, although by no means all, of the multinational corporations responsible for hurrying this process along are American. Whether this is evidence of Americanisation or simply of economic progress may be debated. What is clear is that by the end of the millennium the differences between life in Britain and America had become altogether less striking than formerly.

Living in a Unipolar World

The United States entered the new millennium as arguably the greatest power in history. Not since Rome has a single nation so dominated its surroundings. Spain, France and Great Britain, even in their heyday, always had rivals. America's principal rival, the Soviet Union, had suddenly collapsed, much to the astonishment of observers, leaving the US as the only nation with a global reach. Militarily it was in a class all of its own, with over a million military personnel on active service, their weaponry a generation ahead of everyone else's. The sheer size and weight of the United States meant that others instinctively looked to it for leadership when problems arose. Whether they be wars in the former

Yugoslavia, sectarian feuds in Ireland, Israeli–Palestinian disputes, or Islamic terrorism, all the world's troubles had a way of ending up on America's doorstep.

Comparing America's twenty-first-century hegemony to that of the great powers of the past, however, is misleading in more ways than one. Most obviously the American Empire, if it can be called that, lacks the formal trappings associated with imperial status. There are, to be sure, overseas garrisons. But although at the start of the new millennium there were still some 120 000 US troops in Europe, and as many more stationed elsewhere around the world, they were there by common consent rather than by virtue of conquest. For the most part, the US exercises its power through diplomacy, trade, trustworthy money and its influence on the world's media rather than by force. The agents through whom it is exercised are not troops but armies of entrepreneurs, technicians, scientists and businessmen. In *Fortune*'s 1999 listing of the world's 500 leading companies ranked by turnover, 185 were American. Increasingly it is they, rather than governments, that make the decisions that affect people's lives. Some are enormous. Of the 100 largest economies in the world, 51 are corporations. The combined revenues of General Motors and Ford exceed the combined GDP of all of sub-Saharan Africa.[40] Nor is it a coincidence that the world's top-rated business schools are all in the United States. Above all, America's power derives from the size and dynamism of its economy, from which practically everything else follows – most notably the use of English as a world language in the fields of business, aviation, computing, film and practically every other international undertaking. Even EU press briefings are nowadays conducted in English on the grounds that not enough people understand French and German.

In the late 1980s there was talk of the United States being in relative decline. For a time it even looked as if Japan might be destined to overtake it in terms of GNP. There were worries, too, over the enormous external trade deficit that had built up during Reagan's years in office, which had transformed the US from a creditor into a debtor nation. No less alarming was the internal debt arising out of Reagan's military expenditure. Plainly America was living beyond its means. In *The Rise and Fall of the Great Powers: Economic Change and Military Conflict from 1500 to 2000* (1988), the Yale historian Paul Kennedy argued that the United States had reached the apex of its power in 1945, since when its power had steadily declined.[41]

Events quickly proved Kennedy's assessment wrong. The collapse of the Soviet Union, Japan's economic tribulations, tumbling Asian share values, and the long economic boom of the Clinton years transformed the picture. With the arrival of the new millennium came claims that the twenty-first century, like the twentieth century, would also be America's.[42] Except in tiny enclaves like Cuba and North Korea, communism had effectively been abandoned. Even China was Communist only in the sense of being ruled by a residual gerontocracy desperately clinging on to power. Throughout the West, socialism was in retreat. The British Labour Party, in power since 1997, pursued Thatcherite policies of privatisation and deregulation. Those who, only a short time before, had praised the virtues of alternative European and Asian models of capitalism fell silent. Hard though it was for those on the Left to admit, it was the low-tax, limited-welfare-provision American version that during the 1990s was most successful at providing high employment, new jobs and economic growth – as shown by the way European investment funds flooded across the Atlantic. The British might trade with Europe, but they invested in America.

This, however, did nothing to resolve their political dilemma. Politically and culturally the British felt more than ever drawn to the United States. The European Union might be very fine in theory (although some doubted that), but getting it to take action, even when trouble occurred on its own doorstep, as in the Balkans, proved well-nigh impossible. The United States could at least be dealt with as a single unit; the European Union spoke with many voices. While others quibbled and debated, British and American forces spearheaded the military campaigns in the Gulf War, Kosovo and Afghanistan. Thus the close links forged by Reagan and Thatcher were maintained. Although John Major and George Bush Senior found one another congenial company, the connection in their case owed less to personal friendship than to shared interests and the natural affinities between Conservative and Republican thinking. As the two countries have grown more alike, so, too, have their political parties. Increasingly they have looked to one another for support and inspiration – a fact embarrassingly highlighted when news leaked out that Conservative Central Office had sought to assist Bush's 1992 campaign for re-election by relaying damaging stories concerning Clinton's behaviour as a Rhodes Scholar at Oxford in the 1960s.[43]

Meanwhile, Labour had been cultivating transatlantic connections of its own. Unlike Old Labour, which tended to identify the United States with the capitalist enemy, New Labour looked to America for inspiration. In the early 1990s, both Labourites and Democrats realised that to be elected they had to rid themselves of their tax-and-spend reputations.

Clinton's famous memorandum to himself, 'It's the economy, stupid', helped remind New Labour of the need for fiscal responsibility. The emphasis in both instances was increasingly on wealth creation rather than on its redistribution. 'Clinton blazed the trail', declared Blair, standing next to the US President outside Number 10 shortly after Labour's return to office in 1997. 'We copy each other shamelessly', volunteered Clinton. Shorn of their anti-nuclear commitments and ready to embrace global capitalism, educational diversity and consumerism, Labour ministers regularly toured the United States in search of solutions to common problems. The idea of allowing the Bank of England to set interest rates came from America, as did electronic tagging, privately funded prisons, zero tolerance and the 'three strikes and you are out' response to criminal recidivism. In fact, much of the New Labour programme was taken over lock, stock and barrel from the 'new' Democrats.[44] On being elected to a second term, Labour's first priority, according to Chancellor Gordon Brown, was to create a 'truly entrepreneurial culture' to match that of the United States.[45] The Conservatives also turned to America for inspiration. Writing in the *Sunday Times* in December 2000 under the heading 'Bush shows that Conservatism can win again', the Tory leader William Hague hopefully cited George W. Bush's victory as evidence that the ideas shared by British Conservatives and American Republicans were again on the march.

These manifestations of transatlantic camaraderie contrasted sharply with British politicians' statements about Europe. In spite of Britain's having been a fully paid-up member of the European Union for a generation, acknowledgements of common endeavour were notably lacking. When Europeans discussed further moves towards integration, it always seemed to be the Eurosceptics who made the running. Margaret Thatcher was famous for her anti-European tirades, which embarrassed her colleagues and eventually contributed to their rebellion. In 1990, when John Major replaced her, he announced his intention of putting Britain 'at the heart of Europe'. Instead, he spent his years in office struggling to save his party from being torn apart by pro-and anti-European factions. Labour Members of the European Parliament belonged to the Socialist Group in the European Parliament, Liberal Democrats to the Liberal Democratic and Reform Group, but the Conservatives sat alone, having refused to join the Christian Democrats on the grounds that it would have meant endorsing a programme designed to lead to greater EU integration. Although Americophilia had become universally acceptable, Europhilia was judged an electoral liability. In 1785, Christopher Gadsden of South

Carolina declared, 'There should be no New England men, no New York men, etc., but all of us Americans.'[46] No politician of equivalent rank was willing to say in Parliament, or anywhere else, the same with regard to the British being Europeans.

Future historians may find it difficult to explain why it was that a middle class that tended to regard America as vulgar, abhorred McDonald's, spent its holidays in Tuscany or the Dordogne and professed to admire European culture found the idea of establishing political links with their neighbours across the Channel so repugnant. Yet Britain was gradually adjusting, albeit in a gingerly fashion, to being part of Europe. Distances were still measured in miles but petrol was sold in litres and groceries in kilograms. Asked which bodies would have most influence over their lives in 20 years, many more people opted for the European Parliament and European Union than the Parliament at Westminster.[47] But although they expected the EU to become dominant in their lives, the prospect failed to stir their imaginations. Above all, they found it hard to rid themselves of the feeling that there was something unnatural, if not positively perverse, about an arrangement that linked them politically to those whose languages they did not speak and with whom they felt they had fewer ties than with the English-speaking peoples of the United States and Commonwealth.[48]

Geographical Mobility and the Rise of Global Culture

It is tempting to conclude with grand generalisations – for example, concerning the enduring nature of the 'special relationship', but as has already been explained, the factors contributing to the specialness of that relationship have varied greatly over the years. Political relations were at their worst in the early nineteenth century, which was when the influence of British culture was greatest and virtually all of America's leaders were of British stock. Or, again, it could be said that the Anglo-American relationship resembles that between parent and offspring, and draws attention to the problems of adolescence and the difficulties of the old in coming to terms with the fact that they no longer wield the authority they once did. Some have likened the British to the Greeks and Americans to the Romans.[49] There is a temptation, too, to construct grand symmetries – comparing, for example, the modern *Pax Americana* to the nineteenth-century *Pax Britannica*, and both to the *Pax Romana* of ancient times.

Such comparisons are all very well so long as they are not pushed too far, which means not very far at all. What is most revealing in each case are the differences rather than the similarities. Technological change has made the modern world very different from anything that has gone before. In some ways it has rendered states more powerful, but in others it has made them weaker. It is easier for governments to keep track of people's doings but harder to keep those over whom they rule from knowing about and responding to developments occurring beyond the nation's borders. This is what is meant by globalisation. There was, to be sure, a global economy in the nineteenth century and earlier. What is different now is its scale and the speed of communication.

One result of this has been to make it increasingly difficult to distinguish what is British from what is American. In former times, when people talked about British or American industry, they meant industries owned by people living in those countries and operations that took place within their borders. That, however, is no longer necessarily the case. With the rise of multinationals, production as often as not occurs outside the countries where the parent companies are situated and is administered at its higher levels by a meritocratic elite chosen largely without regard to nationality. Ford is an American company, but the components out of which it makes even the cars sold in the US are as apt to come from Japan, Indonesia or Europe as from Detroit. Its current chief executive officer, Jacques Nasser, is an Australian of Lebanese origin; his predecessor was a Scot. Sweden's Volvo and Britain's Jaguar are also part of the Ford empire. Increasingly, governments are having to negotiate with companies as though they were states. When General Motors in 2000 decided to close its Vauxhall plant in Luton there was nothing the Blair government could do to dissuade it. Even the location of a company's headquarters is optional, as was revealed when the pharmaceutical giant Glaxo, unhappy over tax arrangements, threatened to move its headquarters to the US. If companies do not like what countries offer, they are free to take their operations elsewhere.

So rapid has been the growth in international communication and human mobility that it is easy to forget how different matters were in the past. In the nineteenth century many British people went through life without having heard an American accent. That changed with the advent of the phonograph, radio and talking pictures. Even so, it was not until World War II that those living in remoter parts of the country had the opportunity to meet a real live American, which for many was a memorable experience. Until the advent of cheap air travel, tourist trips to America were available only to the well-off, and from the 1940s to the 1970s currency controls made it difficult even for the rich to travel. So far as the impact of American culture on Britain was concerned, a big change occurred in the 1960s with the switch from radio to television. This meant not only that British people were able to see events in the United States as they occurred, but it opened up a vast cornucopia of US television programmes and old movies, the result being that viewers became as familiar with goings-on in New York, Dallas and Los Angeles as with events in Britain's own cities. The same was less true the other way around. Nevertheless, what with broadcast television, cable, satellite, video, film and the World Wide Web it is at least theoretically possible for people living in either country to immerse themselves almost entirely in the culture of the other without ever leaving home.

This, of course, is not a uniquely Anglo-American experience. The whole world is being swept by a tidal wave of Western culture, much of it emanating from America. Hollywood films are watched the world over. The tale is told of an anthropologist trekking to a remote part of Cambodia to observe the local culture and arriving only to find the villagers watching *Basic Instinct,* a rubbishy sex-and-violence film set in Los Angeles.[50] During the Gulf War it was said that the Iraqi military got their information on how things were going from CNN (Cable News Network) rather than from their own intelligence sources. In short, information flows freely across borders carrying news of political events, entertainment, advertising, commodity prices and financial transactions. Every *day* sums in excess of Britain's *annual* GNP are traded through paperless electronic data exchanges on the world's currency markets.[51]

Thus traditional boundaries between states are steadily being eroded. Even the Iranian ayatollahs are hard pressed to maintain Islamic purity in a world where anyone tuned into the World Wide Web or with a television set and satellite dish can access practically anything he or she wants. But although globalisation affects all countries, it is those like Britain and America at the centre of the process that are most affected. London and New York remain the world's principal financial markets and English the language of international communication.[52] At the risk of some exaggeration, it can even be argued that there is a sense in which Britain and the United States should be regarded not so much as separate countries as constituent parts of an all-encompassing Western economy and culture. Clearly it is no longer plausible to think of there being a British motor-car industry or a British film industry. Cars, or at all events their parts, continue to be manufactured in Britain and films depicting aspects of British life continue to be made. In fact, a disproportionate amount of the English-speaking world's acting, directing and movie-making talent is British. But nowadays movie-making is an international enterprise. Where the financial backing comes from and where the profits go are matters known only to the lawyers and money-men concerned.

Similar considerations apply to culture and what is sometimes called the 'weightless economy'. British popular music has more than held its own thanks to the Beatles, the Rolling Stones, and the musicals of Andrew Lloyd Webber. The same can be said of writing. The novels of Ian Fleming, John Fowles, John Le Carré and J. K. Rowling have been as popular in America as in Britain. So, too, have the designs of Mary Quant and Laura Ashley. But, here again, questions arise as to whether these should be celebrated as national achievements, as in one sense they are, or as contributions that happen to be made by British men and women to a common cultural pool from which consumers pick and choose at will. Some, of course, reflect the peculiar traditions of the countries or regions involved, although sometimes the label can be misleading, as in the case of English muffins, obtainable only in the United States. But just as Kentucky Fried Chicken and Country and Western music (along with Indian and Chinese cuisine) have become part of Britain's eclectic cultural mix, so too have English costume dramas and the music of the Beatles become part of America's. As far as consumers are concerned, where these products actually originate matters no more than whether the shirts they happen to be wearing were made in Taiwan or Hong Kong. What matters is that they meet the standards required to compete in the global marketplace.

So life flows on, as does the Anglo-American relationship, driven by impersonal forces largely independent of government.[53] Travel becomes cheaper, telephone calls cost less, borders become more permeable, the Atlantic ceases to be the barrier it once was, and culture becomes more eclectic. Governments, of course, will continue to do what governments do, which is to say provide for the national defence, negotiate with foreign powers, uphold the law and promote the public welfare. In Britain's case the most contentious question facing government as this work goes to press is whether or not to sign up for the euro. It is not, however, the only challenge to the notion of Britain as a unitary state that is occurring. With the devolution of power to Scotland and Wales, competing claims are increasingly heard from within Britain's own borders. In Scotland, education, health, transport and law enforcement are issues for the Edinburgh Parliament rather than London. There is no equivalent assembly for England. It may be argued, therefore, that questions of national identity – which is what the euro debate is really about – are more of an issue for the English than for the Scots or Welsh, many of whom would welcome integration into a federal Europe as a means of further reducing the power of Whitehall. Such is the nature of political ambition that, having been given a measure of autonomy, the Scots and Welsh will continue pressing for more, including control over fiscal policy. It may well be, therefore, that in the long run the principal challenge to the authority of Westminster, and thus to the notion of Britain as a unitary state, will come from Edinburgh and Cardiff rather than Brussels.[54]

It is, however, the challenge from Brussels that currently causes most alarm. Whether membership of the North American Free Trade Association or the proposed Free Trade Area of the Americas, although never touted as a serious alternative, would suit the Europhobes any better is open to question. In the post-war years it was America rather than Europe that was seen as the encroaching menace, and it is still Americanisation that is most feared at the cultural level.

Americans, for their part, have long since ceased worrying about the insidious influence of British culture. What Britain has to offer is largely admired for what are seen as its characteristically British qualities, not least its internationalism. Following the 2001 suicide attack on New York's World Trade Center, the Blair government immediately set about putting together an international coalition in support of America's 'war on terrorism', with Tony Blair delivering speeches of such messianic fervour as to lead many to wonder who was actually leading the coalition. Of the forty-odd nations supposedly enrolled, the only one that immediately and energetically provided military support was Britain. President Bush expressed his appreciation of these efforts, declaring: 'The United States has no better friend than Great Britain.' Nevertheless, America wants the British fully integrated into Europe, and for 50 years has consistently exerted its influence with that end in view. In the future US policy makers are going to need the support, vision – and on occasion perhaps the restraining hand – of democratic allies with whom it can share the burden of maintaining international stability. The world is rapidly changing. With India and China, each with a population in excess of one billion, emerging as major players, Britain on its own is too small to perform that function. Collectively, however, the states of Europe are the equal of the United States in wealth and population, although not as yet in terms of political organisation or military strength. As Americans see it, there is a logic to the idea of having political federations, committed to similar ideals, on the two sides of the Atlantic. From this it follows that the best way for Britain to relate to the United States is through its influence as a member of the European Union.[55]

British Europhobes argue that this is a great mistake and something that Americans will live to regret.[56] Yet it is hard to see that it will ever be to Britain's advantage to leave the EU altogether. The deeply ingrained Atlanticism of the British makes full integration into a continental system hard to accept. Perhaps, in the end, it does not greatly matter whether integration proceeds rapidly or slowly. As the EU expands eastward its character is bound to change, very likely becoming more of an economic and less of a political union. That would certainly be more to Britain's liking. Meanwhile, being not quite American, yet not quite European either, there are worse positions to be in than having a foot in both camps.

Notes

Introduction

1. Oliver Wendell Holmes, *The Autocrat at the Breakfast Table* (1858; Everyman edn, 1906), p. 52.
2. For this and other transatlantic misapprehensions see Charles Dickens, *Martin Chuzzlewit*, chapter 27.
3. Aristotle, *Politics* in *The Works of Aristotle* (11 vols., Oxford, 1921), 10, 1327–8; Thomas Jefferson, *Notes on the State of Virginia* (1781; Torchbook edn, 1964), pp. 56–66, 88–98.
4. Henry Adams to Charles Francis Adams, Jr, London, 27 January 1863, in H. S. Commager, ed., *Britain Through American Eyes* (London, 1974), p. 371.
5. Quoted in Margaret Armstrong, *Frances Kemble: A Passionate Victorian* (New York, 1938), p. 365.
6. Ralph Waldo Emerson, *Address Delivered in the Court House in Concord on the First of August 1884* (Concord, 1884), p. 18.

1   The Colonial Legacy

1. Bill Bryson, *Made in America* (London, 1994), chapter 2.
2. See the chapter on population and immigration in Richard Hofstadter, *America at 1750, A Social Portrait* (London, 1972).
3. On the subject of colonial liberties and imperial authority, see P. J. Marshall, 'The Case for Coercing America before the Revolution', and Elga H. Gould, 'The American in Britain's Imperial Identity', in Fred M. Leventhal and Roland Quinault, eds, *Anglo-American Attitudes: From Revolution to Partnership* (Aldershot, 2000), pp. 9–22, 23–37. For the way British liberties were admired by other nations, see Ian Buruma, *Anglomania: A European Love Affair* (London, 1999).
4. The learning process which led Americans first to question and finally to deny the legitimacy of British rule is admirably described in Edmund S. Morgan, *The Birth of the Republic, 1763–89* (Chicago, 1956). The European, and especially the British, origins of their ideas are dealt with in Bernard Bailyn, *The Ideological Origins of the American Revolution* (Cambridge, MA, 1967). The classic contemporary statement was Thomas Paine's *Common Sense* (Philadelphia, 1776).
5. *Letters from an American Farmer* (originally Paris, 1782; many subsequent editions).
6. Robert Brown, *Middle-Class Democracy and the Revolution in Massachusetts, 1691–1780* (New York, 1955); J. R. Pole, *Political Representation in England and the Origins of the American Republic* (London, 1966).

2   Troubled Times: 1783–1815

1. H. C. Allen, *Great Britain and the United States: A History of Anglo-American Relations, 1783–1952* (London, 1952), p. 250.
2. J. Stephen Watson, *The Reign of George III, 1760–1815* (Oxford, 1960), p. 517.
3. The text of the Articles of Confederation, along with those of the Declaration of Independence and the Constitution, can be most readily located in the appendices of a number of standard American history textbooks. See, for example, Paul S. Boyer et al., *The Enduring Vision: A History of the American People* (3rd edn New York, 1993).
4. William Reitzel, ed., *The Autobiography of William Cobbett* (London, 1933).
5. The above account, including the quotations, is taken from Howard Temperley, 'Frontierism, Capital and the American Loyalists in Canada', *Journal of American Studies*, 13 (April 1979), 5–27. On the subject of Loyalist claims see Wallace Brown, *The King's Friends: The Composition and Motives of the Loyalist Claimants* (Providence, RI, 1965) and *The Good Americans: The Loyalists in the American Revolution* (New York, 1969).
6. Charles S. Campbell, *From Revolution to Rapprochement, 1783–1900* (New York, 1974), pp. 3–4, 10; Charles R. Ritcheson, *Aftermath of Revolution: British Policy Toward the United States, 1783–1795* (London, 1969).
7. Jerrald A. Combs, *The Jay Treaty: Political Battleground of the Founding Fathers* (New York, 1970).
8. J. Leitch Wright, *Britain and the American Frontier, 1783–1815* (New York, 1975).
9. Watson, p. 323.
10. Samuel Flagg Bemis, *A Diplomatic History of the United States* (4th edn New York, 1955), pp. 96–8.
11. These struggles are described in the Allen, Campbell, and Bemis volumes cited above. For more detailed accounts, see Reginald Horsman, *The Causes of the War of 1812* (New York, 1962) and Bradford Perkins, *Prologue to War: England and the United States, 1805–1812* (New York, 1961).
12. Allen, pp. 281–3; Watson, pp. 372–3, 472–4.
13. Campbell, p. 15; Bemis, pp. 145–6.
14. In addition to the works already cited, these issues are comprehensively dealt with in J. C. A. Stagg, *Mr. Madison's War: Politics, Diplomacy and Warfare in the Early Republic* (New York, 1983).
15. But it was not until 1931 that Congress officially recognised it as such. The actual star-spangled banner that flew over Fort McHenry is on display in the Smithsonian Institution in Washington.

3   Political Rivalries and Cultural Affinities: 1815–1865

1. P. J. Marshall, 'Britain and the World in the Eighteenth Century: I, Reshaping the Empire', *Transactions of the Royal Historical Society*, sixth series, VIII (London, 1998); Lawrence James, *Raj: The Making and Unmaking of British India* (London, 1997), pp. 119, 131.
2. Paul Kennedy, *The Rise and Fall of the Great Powers: Economic Change and Military Conflict from 1500 to 2000* (New York, 1988), pp. 183–8.

3. This is a theme that runs right through the southern pro-slavery argument; it was most effectively exploited, however by George Fitzhugh in *Sociology for the South, or the Failure of Free Society* (Richmond, 1854) and *Cannibals All! or Slaves Without Masters* (Richmond, 1857). For a collection of southern writings on the subject see Drew Gilpin Faust, *The Ideology of Slavery: Proslavery Thought in the Antebellum South, 1830–1860* (Baton Rouge, 1981).

4. Quoted in Rowland Tappan Berthoff, *British Immigrants in Industrial America, 1790–1950* (Cambridge, MA, 1953), pp. 37–8, 49.

5. Ibid., pp. 47–9.

6. Frank Thistlethwaite, *America and the Atlantic Community: Anglo-American Aspects, 1790–1850* (New York, 1963), p. 8. Much of what is said here regarding the economic relationship is taken from this source, pp. 3–38.

7. Allen, pp. 395–8.

8. Ibid., p. 397.

9. F. W. Howay et al., *British Columbia and the United States: The Pacific North Slope from Fur Trade to Aviation* (Toronto, 1942); W. J. Trimble, *The Mining Advance into the Inland Empire* (1914, reprint New York, 1972).

10. Quoted in Matthew Macfie, *Vancouver Island and British Columbia: Their History, Resources, and Prospects* (London, 1865), p. 395.

11. Douglas to Lytton, 29 September 1858, quoted in Margaret A. Ormsby, *British Columbia: A History* (Toronto, 1958), p. 161.

12. Pierre Berton, *Klondike: The Last Great Gold Rush* (Toronto, 1972). Also revealing with regard to the law and order issue is Paul F. Sharp, *The Whoop-Up Country: The Canadian-American West, 1865–1885* (Helena, Historical Society of Montana, 1955).

13. Captain Frederick Marryat, *A Diary in America* (1839, reprint New York, 1962), pp. 472–80.

14. Frances M. Trollope, *Domestic Manners of the Americans* (London, 1832). For a more general overview of British accounts of Jacksonian America, see Allan Nevins, ed., *America Through British Eyes* (New York, 1948), pp. 79–200.

15. Jacksonian notions regarding history as class politics are described in John Ashworth, *'Agrarians' and 'Aristocrats': Party Political Ideology in the United States* (London, 1983).

16. See Alexis de Tocqueville, *Democracy in America* (1835–40).

17. Marryat, p. 480.

18. Quoted in Walter L. Arnstein, 'Queen Victoria and the United States', in Leventhal and Quinault, p. 92.

19. *The Charter*, 20 October 1839, quoted in G. D. Lillibridge, *Beacon of Freedom: The Impact of American Democracy on Great Britain, 1830–1870* (Philadelphia, 1954), p. 49.

20. *Northern Star*, 2 August 1845, quoted in James Epstein, ' "America" in the Victorian Cultural Imagination', in Leventhal and Quinault, p. 114.

21. Quoted in William Brock, 'The Image of England and American Nationalism', *Journal of American Studies*, 5 (December 1971), 239.

22. These matters are discussed in Paul Langford, 'Manners and Character in Anglo-American Perceptions, 1750–1850', in Leventhal and Quinault, pp. 76–90.

23. Cushing Strout, *The American Image of the Old World* (New York, 1963), p. 16.

24. Henry James, *Hawthorne* (1879), quoted in Malcolm Bradbury, *The Expatriate Tradition in American Literature* (British Association for American Studies Pamphlet, 1982), p. 18.
25. See R. B. Mowat, *Americans in England* (London, 1935).
26. These and other themes associated with the transatlantic literary relationship are described in Malcolm Bradbury's *Dangerous Pilgrimages: Trans-Atlantic Mythologies and the Novel* (London, 1995).
27. Quoted in Brock, p. 237.
28. Ibid., p. 238.
29. Anthony Trollope, *North America* (London, 1862), pp. 182–206.
30. Bradbury, pp. 91–2.
31. Marcus Cunliffe, *The Literature of the United States* (Harmondsworth, 1961), p. 46.
32. Quoted in Marc Pachter, ed., *Abroad in America: Visitors to the New Nation, 1776–1914* (Washington, DC, 1976), p. 89.
33. Dickens, *Martin Chuzzlewit*, chapter 34.
34. Thomas Moore, 'To the Lord Viscount Forbes, From the City of Washington', in *Poems Relating to America, Moore's Poetical Works* (London, n. d. [1870]), p. 463.
35. Terry Coleman, *Passage to America: A History of Emigrants from Great Britain to America in the Mid-Nineteenth Century* (London, 1972).
36. The Anglo-American anti-slavery relationship is described in Howard Temperley, *British Antislavery, 1833–1870* (London, 1972) and Betty Fladeland, *Friends and Brothers: Anglo-American Antislavery Cooperation* (Urbana, 1972).
37. Quoted in Arnstein, p. 95.
38. Bemis, pp. 264–5; Fladeland, pp. 329–32.
39. W. L. Mathieson, *Great Britain and the Slave Trade* (London, 1929), p. 175.
40. Hugh Thomas, *The Slave Trade: The History of the Atlantic Slave Trade, 1440–1870* (London, 1997), pp. 774–85.
41. Temperley, pp. 202–3.
42. These events are fully described in E. D. Adams, *British Interests and Activities in Texas, 1838–1846* (Baltimore, 1910).
43. Quoted in Campbell, pp. 88–9.
44. The text of the Address is in B. B. Sideman and L. Friedman, eds., *Europe Looks at the Civil War* (New York 1960), pp. 166–8; Lincoln's characteristically gracious reply is in Roy P. Basler, ed., *The Collected Works of Abraham Lincoln* (8 vols., New Brunswick, NJ, 1953–55), VI, 63–5.
45. Quoted in Allen, p. 484; see also E. D. Adams, *Great Britain and the American Civil War* (2 vols., London, 1925), II, 49.
46. For British popular responses to the Civil War, see R. J. M. Blackett, *Divided Hearts: Britain and the American Civil War* (Baton Rouge, 2001). More general accounts of Anglo-American relations during the Civil War years are given in Adams (see n. 45), and in Brian Jenkins's *Britain and the War for the Union* (2 vols., Montreal, 1980).
47. Bemis, pp. 377–9.
48. See David M. Potter, 'Civil War', in C. Vann Woodward, ed., *A Comparative Approach to American History* (Washington, DC, 1968), pp. 146–57.
49. Quoted in Roland Quinault, 'Anglo-American Attitudes to Democracy from Lincoln to Churchill', in Leventhal and Quinault, p. 127.

50. Ibid., p. 128.

4 Rapprochement: 1866–1914

1. On this subject see Daniel R. Headrick, *The Tools of Empire: Technology and European Imperialism in the Nineteenth Century* (New York, 1981).
2. L. H. Jenks, *The Migration of British Capital to 1875* (London, 1973).
3. Kennedy, *Great Powers*, pp. 191–5.
4. H. J. Habakkuk, *American and British Technology in the Nineteenth Century: The Search for Labour-Saving Inventions* (Cambridge, 1962), p. 5.
5. Bryson, p. 106. According to Bryson's sources, Emerson made no mention of a mousetrap.
6. R. C. K. Ensor, *England, 1870–1914* (Oxford, 1936), pp. 115–18, 511–12.
7. Quoted by Gary Wills in 'Storm Over Jefferson', *The New York Review of Books*, XLVII, 5 (23 March 2000), 17.
8. Berthoff, p. 60.
9. Ibid., pp. 38, 60–74, 77; William E. Van Vugt, *Britain to America: Mid-Nineteenth-Century Immigrants to the United States* (Urbana, 1999); Charlotte Erickson, *American Industry and the European Immigrant, 1850–1885* (Cambridge, MA, 1959), *Invisible Immigrants: The Adaptation of English and Scottish Immigrants in Nineteenth-Century America* (Coral Gables, FL, 1972). For a more general account of the subject, see M. A. Jones, *American Immigration* (Chicago, 1960).
10. Kennedy, p. 197.
11. 'An Interview with Dr Youmans', reprinted in Allan Nevins, ed., *America Through British Eyes* (Oxford, 1948), p. 349.
12. Habakkuk, p. 217.
13. Henry Adams, *The Education of Henry Adams* (privately printed, 1907; New York, 1917).
14. Nevins, pp. 328–32, 256.
15. 'America Revisited – Changes of a Quarter Century', 1905, reprinted in ibid., p. 384.
16. Quoted in James Morris, *Pax Britannica* (vol. I, London, 1968), p. 8.
17. *Oxford Dictionary of Quotations*. The statement first appeared in *The United States Magazine and Democratic Review* (1837).
18. Ibid.
19. The lines are, of course, from James Thompson's 'Rule Britannia'.
20. *The United States Magazine and Democratic Review* (July–August, 1845), p. 5. On the subject of America's expansionist ideology see H. W. Brands, *What America Owes the World: The Struggle for the Soul of Foreign Policy* (Cambridge, 1998).
21. Morris, II, 94–7; on the subject of social class in relation to Empire, see David Cannadine, *Ornamentalism: How the British Saw their Empire* (London, 2001).
22. Queen Victoria's journal for 11 May 1887, quoted in Leventhal and Quinault, p. 99.
23. The quotations, most of which come from Roosevelt's *African Game Trails* (New York, 1910), are from Michael McCarthy, 'Africa and the American West', *Journal of American Studies*, 11 (April 1977), pp. 187–201.

24. See Alfred Thayer Mahan, *The Influence of Sea Power upon History, 1660–1783* (London, 1890) and *The Interest of America in Sea Power, Present and Future* (London, 1898).
25. *Nostromo* (1904), p. 65.
26. See, for example, Bemis, chapter 26.
27. *From Sea to Sea*, II, 14, quoted in Allen, p. 524.
28. The text of Salisbury's statement is quoted in R. J. Bartlett, ed., *The Record of American Diplomacy* (New York, 1947), pp. 346–7.
29. Ibid., p. 351.
30. J. L. Garvin, *The Life of Joseph Chamberlain* (3 vols., London, 1937), III, 159–60.
31. Kathleen Burk, *War and Anglo-American Financial Relations in the Twentieth Century*, in Leventhal and Quinault, pp. 224–5.
32. David Dimbleby and David Reynolds, *An Ocean Apart: The Relationship Between Britain and America in the Twentieth Century* (London, 1988), p. 28.
33. Allen, pp. 609–14.
34. Lee Server, *The Golden Age of Ocean Liners* (New York, 1996).
35. These are listed in Maureen E. Montgomery, *Gilded Prostitution: Status, Money and Transatlantic Marriages, 1870–1914* (London, 1989), pp. 249–57.
36. See *The American Commonwealth* (London, 1888), especially the chapter on 'Why the Best Men do not Become President'.
37. Bradbury, chapters 5 and 6.
38. Ibid., pp. 114, 203–6.
39. Seymour Martin Lipset and Gary Marks, *It Didn't Happen Here: Why Socialism Failed In the United States* (New York, 2000).
40. Quoted in Morris, II, 7.
41. Quoted in Allen, p. 96. As regards the supposed destiny of Anglo-Saxons to rule the world, see Brands, pp. 13–21.
42. Quoted in Dimbleby and Reynolds, p. 31.

5 The Great Divide: 1914–1920

1. Paul Kennedy, *The Realities Behind Diplomacy: Background Influences on British External Policy, 1865–1980*, p. 35.
2. Dimbleby and Reynolds, pp. 34–9.
3. Correlli Barnett, *The Collapse of British Power* (London, 1972), chapter 2.
4. Dimbleby and Reynolds, p. 25.
5. Sidney Pollard, *The Development of the British Economy, 1914–1990*, (4th edn London, 1992), p. 2.
6. Paul Kennedy, *The Rise of the Anglo-German Antagonism, 1860–1914* (London, 1980), p. 470.
7. Dimbleby and Reynolds, p. 45.
8. Allen, pp. 640–1.
9. Quoted in ibid., pp. 668–9.
10. Ibid., p. 661. On the subject of neutral rights generally, see Bemis, chapter 32.
11. Quoted in Allen, p. 657.
12. Quoted in Christopher Andrew, *For the President's Eyes Only: Secret Intelligence and the American Presidency, from Washington to Bush* (London, 1995), p. 33.

13. Ibid., pp. 37–41.
14. Dimbleby and Reynolds, p. 46.
15. Quoted in Allen, p. 639.
16. Quoted in Dimbleby and Reynolds, p. 51.
17. Allen, p., 683.
18. Dimbleby and Reynolds, pp. 52–4.
19. The episode is fully discussed in Andrew, pp. 41–5.
20. Quoted in ibid., p. 45.
21. Arthur Link, ed., *Papers of Woodrow Wilson*, vol. 41, pp. 519–27. For other examples see Abraham Lincoln's 'Gettysburg Address' and Roosevelt's 'Four Freedoms'.
22. Quoted in David Reynolds, *Rich Relations: The American Occupation of Britain, 1942–45* (London, 1995), p. 6.
23. Allen, p. 706.
24. Dimbleby and Reynolds, p. 70.

6 The Inter-War Years

1. Correlli Barnett, *The Collapse of British Power* (London, 1972), p. 80.
2. The British inter-war dream of establishing an imperial commonwealth is described in ibid., pp. 123–236.
3. David Reynolds, *Britannia Overruled: British Policy and World Power in the Twentieth Century* (London, 1991), pp. 114–20.
4. Allen, p. 738.
5. For a general discussion of war debts see ibid., pp. 750–61, and Dimbleby and Reynolds, pp. 85–93.
6. The international implications of American protectionism are described in Akira Iriye, *The Cambridge History of American Foreign Relations, Volume III, The Globalising of America, 1913–1945* (Cambridge, 1993), pp. 99–100.
7. Aldous Huxley, *Harper's Magazine* (August 1927).
8. Scott Fitzgerald, *This Side of Paradise* (1920); Evelyn Waugh, *Decline and Fall* (1928), *Vile Bodies* (1930).
9. Morris, III, 38–9; see also Cannadine.
10. On the subject of Americanisation, see Dimbleby and Reynolds, chapter 6.
11. Francis W. Hirst, *The Consequences of the War to Great Britain* (London, 1934), p. 251.
12. Kennedy, *Realities*, pp. 226–30.
13. William Ashworth, *An Economic History of England, 1870–1939* (London, 1960), pp. 285–360.
14. Bradbury, p. 339.
15. Jim Potter, *The American Economy Between the Wars* (Basingstoke, 1985), p. 47.
16. The strengths and weaknesses of the US economy in the 1920s are well described in William E. Leuchtenburg, *Perils of Prosperity, 1914–32* (Chicago, 1964).
17. Quoted in Barnett, p. 490.
18. A fuller account of the role played by American interests in the British inter-war economy will be found in Dimbleby and Reynolds, chapter 6.

19. Richard B. Morris, ed., *Significant Documents in United States History, Volume II, 1898–1968* (New York, 1970), pp. 76–7.
20. H. L. Mencken, 'Calvin Coolidge', *The American Mercury*, 1933, reprinted in John Gross, ed., *The New Oxford Book of English Prose* (Oxford, 1998), p. 722.
21. Ashworth, p. 415.
22. Allen, pp. 758–61.
23. See George Kennan, 'Mr. Hippisley and the Open Door', in *American Diplomacy, 1900–1950* (Chicago, 1952), pp. 23–37.
24. Quoted in Reynolds, p. 128.
25. Allen, pp. 764–70.
26. Quoted in Reynolds, p. 131.
27. The motives of the appeasers are admirably set out in Kennedy, *Realities*, pp. 290–301.
28. Quoted in Allen, p. 778.

7 World War II and the Grand Alliance

1. A. J. P. Taylor, *English History, 1914–1945* (Oxford, 1965), pp. 390–2, 432.
2. Churchill to Roosevelt, 15 May 1940, in Warren Kimball, ed., *Churchill and Roosevelt: The Complete Correspondence*, 3 vols. (Princeton, 1984), I, 37–8.
3. Churchill to Roosevelt, 20 May, 15 June 1940, in ibid., pp. 40, 49–50.
4. Churchill to Roosevelt, 7 November 1940, in ibid., pp. 102–9.
5. Quoted in Allen, p. 825.
6. Taylor, pp. 529, 534–5.
7. Bemis, pp. 857–62.
8. Ibid., pp. 863–73.
9. Winston S. Churchill, *The Second World War* (6 vols., London, 1948–53), III, 605.
10. Taylor, pp. 536–40.
11. Dimbleby and Reynolds, pp. 138–40.
12. Andrew, pp. 100–2, 128–31. On the pro-British propaganda campaign in general, see Nicholas John Cull, *Selling War: The British Propaganda Campaign Against American 'Neutrality' in World War II* (Oxford, 1995).
13. Stephen Budiansky, *Battle of Wits: The Complete Story of Codebreaking in World War Two* (London, 2000), pp. 314–15. The story of how Colossus was created is described in more detail in *The History of Newmanry*, a 500-page report released by the Public Record Office in October 2000 and named after Max Newman, the mathematician who headed that section of Bletchley Park's operations.
14. The above account is based on Christopher Andrew's 'Anglo-American-Soviet Intellegence Relations', in Ann Lane and Howard Temperley, eds., *The Rise and Fall of the Grand Alliance, 1941–45* (London, 1995), pp. 108–35.
15. Dimbleby and Reynolds, pp. 153–5; Taylor, pp. 491; Kimball, I, 249, 279; II, 317, 351, 420–1.
16. These figures are taken from Taylor, pp. 505, 564, and Harold W. Chase et al., ed., *Dictionary of American History* (revised edn, 8 vols., New York, 1976), I, 214.
17. Correlli Barnett, *Engage the Enemy More Closely: The Royal Navy in the Second World War* (London, 1991), pp. 368–9, 516.

18. For a succinct account of Anglo-American differences over strategy, see Correlli Barnett, 'Anglo-American Strategy in Europe,' in Lane and Temperley, pp. 174–89.
19. Peter Duignan and L. H. Gann, *The United States and Africa: A History* (Cambridge, 1984), p. 284.
20. Dimbleby and Reynolds, pp. 146–8, Taylor, pp. 545–6.
21. Norman Longmate, *The GIs: The Americans in Britain, 1942–1945* (London, 1975), pp. 244–5; David Reynolds, *Rich Relations: The American Occupation of Britain, 1942–45* (London, 1995), pp. 266–7.
22. Quoted in Taylor, p. 579.
23. Reynolds, pp. xxxviii, 127–40.
24. Longmate, pp. 228, 232.
25. Dimbleby and Reynolds, pp. 151–2.
26. On the subject of Soviet ideology, see George Kennan, 'The Sources of Soviet Conduct', *Foreign Affairs*, 25 (July 1947), pp. 566–82.
27. Winston Churchill in the House of Commons, 15 December 1944, quoted in Robert Kee, *1945: The World We Fought For* (London, 1985), p. iii.
28. Kimball, II, 389–402.
29. Ibid., III, p. 630.
30. Ibid., p. 631.

8   Britain, America, and the Cold War

1. Taylor, p. 599; Hugo Young, *This Blessed Plot: Britain and Europe from Churchill to Blair* (London, 1998), p. 23.
2. Churchill to Roosevelt, 7 December 1940, in Kimball, I, 108. The italics are in the original.
3. On the subject of lend-lease, see Kathleen Burk, 'American Foreign Economic Policy and Lend Lease', and Mark Harrison, 'The Soviet Economy and Relations With the United States', in Lane and Temperley, pp. 43–68, 69–89. The case that in turning to the US for assistance Churchill had made a Faustian bargain is argued in John Charmley, *Churchill's Grand Alliance: The Anglo-American Special Relationship, 1940–57* (London,1995).
4. These figures are taken from Paul Kennedy, *Great Powers*, pp. 461, 465.
5. Allen, p. 914.
6. Ibid.
7. Post-war financial arrangements are described in Alfred E. Eckes, Jr, *A Search for Solvency: Bretton Woods and the International Monetary System, 1941–1971* (Austin, 1975).
8. Reynolds, pp. 188–9.
9. Richard Crockatt, Introduction to *British Documents on Foreign Affairs: Reports and Papers from the Foreign Office Confidential Print, Part IV, From 1946 through 1950, Series C, North America, 1947* (New York, 2001).
10. Reynolds, pp. 163–6.
11. This and other key Cold War documents are in Kenneth M. Jensen, ed., *Origins of the Cold War: The Novikov, Kennan and Roberts 'Long Telegrams' of 1946* (2nd edn Washington, DC, 1994).
12. Dimbleby and Reynolds, p. 172.

13. The text of Truman's message is in Robert A. Divine, ed., *American Foreign Policy: A Documentary History* (New York, 1960), pp. 264–5.
14. Quoted in Crockatt, p. xviii.
15. Crockatt, Introduction, *North America, 1947*.
16. Marshall's text is in Divine, pp. 266–7.
17. Dimbleby and Reynolds, p. 175.
18. The figures represent per capita income in 1949 in dollars of 1949 purchasing power. *National and Per Capita Incomes of Seventy Countries* (United Nations Statistical Papers, Series E, No. 1, 1950), in David Potter, *People of Plenty: Economic Abundance and the American Character* (Chicago, 1954), p. 82.
19. There is a table giving comparative figures on defence expenditures, 1948–70, in Kennedy, *Great Powers*, p. 495.
20. Divine, p. 37.
21. Ritchie Ovendale, *Anglo-American Relations in the Twentieth Century* (Basingstoke, 1998), p. 95.
22. Malcolm Bradbury, 'How I Invented America', *Journal of American Studies*, 14 (April 1980), p. 130.
23. Frank A. Ninkovich, *The Diplomacy of Ideas: US Foreign Policy and Cultural Relations* (Cambridge, 1981), pp. 132–9, 168, 177.
24. Frances Stonor Saunders, *Who Paid the Piper? The CIA and the Cultural Cold War* (London, 1999). Much of the book is concerned with the subsidising of *Encounter* and its putative benefactor, the CIA-financed Congress for Cultural Freedom. How much money the CIA injected into the American *Kulturkampf* through other channels is not revealed.
25. For comparative figures on defence expenditure, see H. G. Nicholas, *Britain and the United States* (London, 1963), pp. 11–27.
26. Ibid., pp. 192–4.
27. The song goes on: 'We've fought the Bear before, and while we're Britons true, / The Russians shall not have Constantinople.' *Brewer's Dictionary of Phrase and Fable* (14th edn London, 1991).
28. Bevin, as recalled by Sir Michael Perrin, quoted in Dimbleby and Reynolds, p. 169.
29. Robin Renwick, *Fighting With Allies: America and Britain in Peace and War* (London, 1996), p. 185.
30. Dimbleby and Reynolds, pp. 232–40.
31. Renwick, p. 279.
32. Reynolds, pp. 215–21; Ovendale, p. 138.

9 Between America and the European Union

1. Quoted in Renwick, p. 184.
2. Raymond Seitz, *Over Here* (London, 1998), p. 322.
3. The North Atlantic Treaty Organisation, the Southeast Asia Treaty Organisation, the Central Treaty Organisation (Turkey, Pakistan) and the Australia, New Zealand Pacific Security Pact.
4. The text of NSC 68 is reprinted in Ernest R. May, ed., *American Cold War Strategy: Interpreting NSC 68* (Boston, 1963).

5. For figures on relative growth rates, 1950–70, see Arthur Marwick, *The Sixties: Cultural Revolution in Britain, France, Italy, and the United States, c.1958–c.1974* (Oxford, 1998), p. 251.

6. John Redwood, *Stars and Strife: The Coming Conflicts between the USA and the European Union* (London, 2001), p. 2.

7. Ibid., p. 1.

8. 'Britain Survey,' *The Economist*, 6 November 1999, p. 4.

9. F. X. Rebattet, 'The European Movement, 1945–1953: A Study in National and International Organisations', D. Phil. thesis, St Anthony's College, Oxford, 1962.

10. Young, pp. 5–25.

11. Derek R. Urwin, *Western Europe Since 1945: A Political History* (4th edn Harlow, 1989), p. 93.

12. Martin Gilbert, *Winston Churchill* (8 vols., London, 1988), VIII, 496.

13. Gier Lundestad, *Empire by Integration: The United States and European Integration, 1945–1997* (Oxford, 1998), pp. 13–28.

14. The best discussion of the issues involved in securing the ratification of the US Constitution is to be found in James Madison, Alexander Hamilton and John Jay, *The Federalist Papers* (originally published in 1787–88, available in many subsequent editions). The historical background to the adoption of the Constitution is described in Edmund Morgan, *The Birth of the Republic, 1783–1789* (Chicago 1956), chapter XI.

15. Robert M. Hathaway, *Great Britain and the United States: Special Relations Since World War II* (London, 1990), p. 42.

16. Lundestad, p. 33.

17. Urwin, pp. 95–9.

18. Richard J. Aldrich, 'European Integration: An American Intelligence Connection,' in Anne Deighton, *Building Postwar Europe: National Decision Makers and European Institutions, 1948–63* (New York, 1995), pp. 159–79; 'OSS, CIA and European Unity: The American Committee on United Europe, 1947–60,' *Diplomacy and Statecraft*, 8, 1 (March 1997), 184–227.

19. Ibid., p. 201.

20. Ibid., pp. 200–1.

21. Lundestad, pp. 67–70. British attitudes towards integration are more fully described in Hugo Young and in John W. Young, *Britain and European Unity, 1945–1992* (Basingstoke, 1993) and John Dumbrell, *A Special Relationship: Anglo-American Relations in the Cold War and After* (Basingstoke, 2001), chapter 8.

22. Quoted in Jeremy Black, *Modern British History Since 1900* (Basingstoke, 2000), p. 307.

23. T. O. Lloyd, *Empire, Welfare State and Europe: English History, 1906–1992* (4th edn Oxford, 1993), addendum, table 6.

24. John Locke, *Two Treatises on Civil Government* (1690, Everyman edn, 1924), p. 140.

25. Jonathan Freedland, *Bring Home the Revolution: The Case for a British Republic* (London, 1998), pp. 1–2.

26. John E. Moser, *Twisting the Lion's Tail: Anglophobia in the United States, 1921–48* (Basingstoke, 1999), pp. 188–9.

27. (London, 1987), p. 8.

28. Ibid., pp. 13, 16, 17.
29. Anthony Holden, 'I'll Take Manhattan', *Observer*, 27 August 2000.
30. Philip R. Harris and Robert T. Moran, *Managing Cultural Differences: Leadership Strategies for a New World of Business* (4th edn Houston, 1966), pp. 304–14.
31. 'Dancing in Step', *The Economist*, 27 March 2001, p. 114.
32. On these issues, see Seymour Martin Lipset, *American Exceptionalism: A Double-Edged Sword* (New York, 1996).
33. See, for example, Charles Reich, *The Greening of America* (New York, 1970).
34. Interviews with Tariq Ali and other organisers of the demonstrations, BBC 2. 4 December 2000.
35. Marwick, pp. 10–13, 560, 632–42.
36. Ibid., chapter 13.
37. However, it was initially restricted to women over 30, and not reduced to 21 in line with the male (and US) requirement until 1928.
38. Dumbrell, pp. 102–5.
39. Bryson, p. 430.
40. Noreena Hertz, *The Silent Takeover: Global Capitalism and the Death of Democracy* (London, 2001), p. 7.
41. Kennedy, *Great Powers*, pp. 631–92.
42. See, for example, Andrew Sullivan, 'The 21st century belongs to US.com', *Sunday Times*, News Review Section, 12 December 1999.
43. Seitz, p. 321.
44. David Smith and Michael Prescott, 'Raiding America', *Sunday Times*, News Review Section, 5 March 2000.
45. 'The man who would make you rich', *The Economist*, 23 June 2001, p. 11; *Times*, 18 June 2001, p. 1.
46. Quoted in Page Smith, *A People's History of the United States* (8 vols., New York, 1984), I, 223.
47. 'Survey Britain', *The Economist*, 6 November 1999, p. 4.
48. Ibid., pp. 12–14.
49. Polly Toynbee, 'Who's Afraid of Global Culture?', in Will Hutton and Anthony Giddens, eds., *On the Edge: Living with Global Capitalism* (London, 2000), p. 191. The film in question was *Basic Instinct*.
50. These comparisons are described at more length in Dumbrell, chapter 2.
51. Manuel Castells, 'Information Technology and Global Capitalism', in Hutton and Giddens, p. 55.
52. 'English is Still on the March', *The Economist*, 24 February 2001, p. 50.
53. The nature of these forces is discussed in Eric Hobsbawm, *The New Century* (London, 1999).
54. These points are developed further in Paul Giles, ed., *Blair's Britain, England's Europe: A View from Ireland* (Dublin, 2001).
55. Seitz, pp. 333–4.
56. 'I urge US policy-makers to think again about the idea that dialling one number for Europe will make Washington's task easier.' Redwood, p. 4.

Select Bibliography

Adams, E. D., *Great Britain and the American Civil War*, 2 vols., London, 1925.

Adams, Henry, *The Education of Henry Adams*, New York, 1917.

Aldrich, Richard J., *The Hidden Hand: Britain, America and Cold War Secret Intelligence*, London, 2001.

Allen, H. C., *Great Britain and the United States: A History of Anglo-American Relations, 1783–1952*, London, 1954.

Andrew, Christopher, *For the President's Eyes Only: Secret Intelligence and the American Presidency, From Washington to Bush*, London, 1995.

Ashton, N. J., *Eisenhower, Macmillan and the Problem of Nasser: Anglo-American Relations and Arab Nationalism, 1955–59*, London, 1966.

Ashworth, William, *An Economic History of England, 1870–1939*, London, 1960.

Barnett, Correlli, *The Collapse of British Power*, London, 1972.

Bartlett, C. J., `The Special Relationship': A Political History of Anglo-American Relations since 1945*, London, 1992.

Bemis, Samuel Flagg, *A Diplomatic History of the United States*, 4th edn, New York, 1955.

Berthoff, Rowland Tappan, *British Immigrants in Industrial America: 1790–1950*, Cambridge, MA, 1953.

Black, Jeremy, *Modern British History: Since 1900*, London, 2000.

Bourne, K., *Britain and the Balance of Power in North America, 1815–1908*, London, 1967.

Bradbury, Malcolm, *Dangerous Pilgrimages: Trans-Atlantic Mythologies and the Novel*, London, 1995.

——— , *Stepping Westward*, London, 1965.

Brands, H. W., *What America Owes the World: The Struggle for the Soul of Foreign Policy*, Cambridge, 1998.

Brebner, J. B., *North Atlantic Triangle: The Interplay of Canada, the United States and Great Britain*, New Haven, 1945.

Bryce, James, *The American Commonwealth*, 2 vols., London, 1888.

Bryson, Bill, *Made in America*, London, 1994.

Burchell, R. A., ed., *The End of Anglo-America: Historical Essays in the Study of Cultural Divergence*, Manchester, 1991.

Buruma, Ian, *Anglomania: A European Love Affair*, London, 1999.

Campbell, Charles S., *From Revolution to Rapprochement: The United States and Great Britain, 1783–1900*, New York, 1974.

Cannadine, David, *Ornamentalism: How the British Saw their Empire*, London, 2001.

Charmley, John, *Churchill's Grand Alliance: The Anglo-American Special Relationship, 1940–57*, London, 1995.

Churchill, Winston S., *The Second World War*, 6 vols., London, 1948–63.

Cobbett, William, *A Year's Residence in America*, New York, 1818, reprinted London, 1922.

Coleman, Terry, *Passage to America: A History of Emigrants from Great Britain and Ireland to America in the Mid-Nineteenth Century*, London, 1972.

Commager, H. S., ed., *America in Perspective: The United States Through Foreign Eyes*, New York, 1947.

—— , *Britain Through American Eyes*, London, 1974.

Conrad, Peter, *Imagining America*, London, 1980.

Cull, Nicholas John, *Selling War: The British Propaganda Campaign against American 'Neutrality' in World War II*, Oxford, 1995.

Cunliffe, Marcus, *The Literature of the United States*, Harmondsworth, 1961.

—— , *In Search of America: Transatlantic Essays, 1951–1990*, New York, 1991.

Deighton, Anne, *Building Postwar Europe: National Decision Makers and European Institutions, 1948–63*, New York, 1995.

Dickens, Charles, *American Notes*, London, 1842.

—— , *Martin Chuzzlewit*, London, 1844.

Dimbleby, David, and Reynolds, David, *An Ocean Apart: The Relationship Between Britain and America in the Twentieth Century*, London, 1988.

Divine, Robert A., ed., *American Foreign Policy: A Documentary History*, New York, 1960.

Dobson, A. P., *Anglo-American Relations in the Twentieth Century: Of Friendship, Conflict and the Rise and Decline of Superpowers*, London, 1995.

Duignan, Peter, *The USA and the New Europe, 1945–1993*, Oxford, 1994.

Dumbrell, John, *A Special Relationship: Anglo-American Relations in the Cold War and After*, London, 2001.

Eckes, Alfred E., Jr, *A Search for Solvency: Bretton Woods and the International Monetary System*, Austin, TX, 1975.

Erickson, Charlotte, *Invisible Immigrants: The Adaptation of English and Scottish Immigrants in Nineteenth-Century America*, Coral Gables, FL, 1972.

Fladeland, Betty, *Men and Brothers: Anglo-American Antislavery Cooperation*, Urbana, IL, 1972.

Freedland, Jonathan, *Bring Home the Revolution: The Case for a British Republic*, London, 1999.

Gelber, L. M., *The Rise of Anglo-American Friendship*, Oxford, 1925.

Habakkuk, H. J., *American and British Technology in the Nineteenth Century: The Search for Labour-Saving Inventions*, Cambridge, 1962.

Hathaway, Robert M., *Great Britain and the United States: Special Relations since World War II*, London, 1990.

Hobsbawm, Eric, *The New Century: Eric Hobsbawm in Conversation with Antonio Polito*, London, 2000.

Honour, Hugh, *The New Golden Land: European Images of America from the Discoveries to the Present Time*, London, 1976.

Horsman, Reginald, *The Causes of the War of 1812*, New York, 1962.

—— , *Race and Manifest Destiny: The Origins of American Racial Anglo-Saxonism*, Cambridge, MA, 1981.

Hutton, Will, and Giddons, Anthony, eds., *On the Edge: Living With Global Capitalism*, London, 2000.

Hyam, R., *Britain's Imperial Century, 1815–1914*, London, 1975.

Iriye, Akira, *The Globalizing of America, 1913–1945*, Cambridge, 1993.

James, Henry, *Portrait of a Lady*, London and New York, 1881.

Jenks, L. J., *Migration of British Capital to 1875*, London, 1973.

Jensen, Kenneth M., *Origins of the Cold War: The Novikov, Kennan, and Roberts `Long Telegrams' of 1946*, 2nd edn, Washington, DC, 1994.

Jones, M. A., *American Immigration*, Chicago, 1960.

Kennan, George, *American Diplomacy, 1900–1950*, London, 1951.

Kennedy, P. M., *The Rise and Fall of British Naval Mastery*, London, 1976.

——, *The Rise and Fall of the Great Powers: Economic Change and Military Conflict from 1500 to 2000*, New York, 1988.

——, *Strategy and Diplomacy, 1870–1945*, London, 1983.

——, ed., *The War Plans of the Great Powers, 1880–1914*, London, 1979.

Kimball, Warren, ed., *Churchill-Roosevelt: The Complete Correspondence*, 3 vols., Princeton, NJ, 1984.

Lane, Ann, and Temperley, Howard, eds., *The Rise and Fall of the Grand Alliance, 1941–45*, London, 1995.

Leventhal, Fred M., and Quinault, Roland, *Anglo-American Attitudes: From Revolution to Partnership*, Aldershot, 2000.

Lillibridge, G. D., *Beacon of Freedom: The Impact of American Democracy upon Great Britain, 1830–1870*, New York, 1955.

Lipset, Seymour Martin, *American Exceptionalism: A Double-Edged Sword*, New York, 1996.

Lodge, David, *Changing Places*, London, 1975.

Longmate, Norman, *The GIs: The Americans in Britain, 1942–45*, London, 1975.

Louis, William Roger, *Imperialism at Bay: The United States and the Decolonization of the British Empire, 1941–1945*, London, 1978.

Louis, William Roger, and Bull, Hedley, eds., *The `Special Relationship': Anglo-American Relations since 1945*, Oxford, 1986.

Lucas, S. W., *Divided We Stand: Britain, the United States and the Suez Crisis*, London, 1991.

Lundestad, Geir, *`Empire' by Integration: The United States and European Integration, 1945–1997*, Oxford, 1998.

McDougal, Walter A., *Promised Land, Crusader State: The American Encounter with the World Since 1776*, New York, 1997.

Martineau, Harriet, *Retrospect of Western Travel*, London, 1838.

——, *Society in America*, London, 1837.

Marwick, Arthur, *The Sixties: Cultural Revolution in Britain, France, Italy, and the United States, c.1958-c.1974*, Oxford, 1999.

May, E. R., *Imperial Democracy: The Emergence of the United States as a Great Power*, New York, 1961.

Mencken, H. L., *The American Language: An Enquiry into the Development of English in the United States*, 4th edn., New York, 1995.

Montgomery, Maureen, *Gilded Prostitution: Status, Money, and Transatlantic Marriages, 1870–1914*, London, 1989.

Morgan, Edmund, *The Birth of the Republic: 1783–1789*, Chicago, 1956.

Morris, James, *Pax Britannica*, 3 vols., London, 1968–78.

Moser, J. E., *Twisting the Lion's Tail: Anglophobia in the United States, 1921–48*, Basingstoke, 1999.

Mowat, C. L., *The New Cambridge Modern History, vol. XII, The Shifting Balance of World Forces, 1898–1965*, Cambridge, 1968.

Mowat, R. B., *Americans in England*, London, 1935.

——, *The Diplomatic Relations of Great Britain and the United States*, London, 1925.

Mulvey, Christopher, *Anglo-American Landscapes: A Study of 19th Century Anglo-American Travel Literature*, Cambridge, 1983.

Murphy, B., *A History of the British Economy*, London, 1973.

Nevins, Alan, ed., *American Social History Recorded by British Travellers*, New York, 1923, subsequently reissued as *America Through British Eyes*, Oxford, 1948.

Nicholas, H. G., *Britain and the United States*, London, 1963.

Nincovich, Frank A., *The Diplomacy of Ideas: United States Foreign Policy and Cultural Relations*, Cambridge, 1981.

O'Gorman, Edmundo, *The Invention of America: An Enquiry into the Historical Nature of the New World and the Meaning of its History*, Bloomington, IN, 1961.

Orde, A., *The Eclipse of Great Britain: The United States and British Imperial Decline, 1895–1956*, London, 1996.

Ovendale, Ritchie, *Anglo-American Relations in the Twentieth Century*, Basingstoke and New York, 1998.

Paine, Thomas, *Common Sense*, Philadelphia, 1776.

Pelling, Henry, *America and the British Left: From Bright to Bevan*, London, 1956.

Pells, Richard, *Not like Us: How Europeans Have Loved, Hated, and Transformed American Culture Since World War II*, New York, 1997.

Perkins, Bradford, *The Creation of a Republican Empire, 1776–1865*, Cambridge, 1993.

——, *The First Rapprochement: England and the United States, 1795–1805*, Philadelphia, 1955.

——, *The Great Rapprochement: England and the United States, 1895–1914*, New York, 1968.

——, *Prologue to War: England and the United States, 1805–1812*, Berkeley, CA, 1961.

Pollard, Sydney, *The Development of the British Economy, 1914–1990*, 4th edn, London, 1992.

Porter, B., *Britain, Europe and the World, 1850–1982: Delusions of Grandeur*, London, 1983.

——, *The Lion's Share: A Short History of British Imperialism*, London, 1976.

Redwood, John, *Stars and Strife: The Coming Conflict Between the USA and the European Union*, London, 2001.

Renwick, Robin, *Fighting with Allies: America and Britain in Peace and War*, London, 1996.

Reynolds, David, *Britannia Overruled: British Policy and World Power in the Twentieth Century*, London, 1991.

——, *Rich Relations: The American Occupation of Britain: 1942–1945*, London, 1995.

Ritcheson, Charles R., *Aftermath of Revolution: British Policy Towards the United States, 1783–1795*, London, 1969.

Sanders, David, *Losing an Empire, Finding a Role: British Foreign Policy since 1945*, London, 1990.

Saunders, Frances Stonor, *Who Paid the Piper? The CIA and the Cultural Cold War*, London, 1999.

Seitz, Raymond, *Over Here*, London, 1998.

Strout, Cushing, *The American Image of the Old World*, New York, 1963.

Taylor, A. J. P., *English History, 1914–1945*, Oxford, 1965.

Temperley, Howard, *British Antislavery, 1833–1870*, London, 1972.

Thistlethwaite, Frank, *The Anglo-American Connection in the Early Nineteenth Century*, Philadelphia, 1959.

Trollope, Frances, *Domestic Manners of the Americans*, London, 1832.

Urwin, Derek R., *Western Europe Since 1945: A Political History*, 4th edn, Harlow, 1989.

Van Vugt, William E., *Britain to America: Mid-Nineteenth Century Immigrants to the United States*, Urbana, IL, 1999.

Watt, D. C., *Succeeding John Bull: America in Britain's Place, 1900–1975*, Cambridge, 1984.

Williams, Francis, *The American Invasion*, New York, 1962.

Woodward, C. Vann, ed., *A Comparative Approach to American History*, Washington, DC, 1968.

Wright, J. Leitch, *Britain and the American Frontier, 1783–1815*, New York, 1975.

Young, Hugo, *This Blessed Plot: Britain and Europe from Churchill to Blair*, London, 1998.

Young, J. W., *Britain and European Unity, 1945–1999*, London, 2000.

Index